ENDORSEMENTS

"It is refreshing to have an exposition of the tabernacle that avoids the allegorizing excesses that have so often been a feature of the 'Christianizing' of this important part of the Old Testament. Daniel Hyde seeks to give a sound exegesis of the text and, only then, to lead us 'to see it through New Testament eyes,' and thus to discover its testimony to Christ and its role in edifying the faithful."

—DR. GRAEME GOLDSWORTHY
Visiting lecturer in hermeneutics
Moore Theological College, Sydney, Australia
Author, *According to Plan: The Unfolding Revelation of God in the Bible*

"Saturated with sound exegesis, helpful insights, pointed application, and warm devotion, *God in Our Midst* helps us to see in the tabernacle not merely pieces of furniture or sets of curtains, but Christ Himself, in the beauty of His holiness and the peace of His pardoning grace. This book will drive pastors from the study to the pulpit, and parishioners from study to worship."

—REV. BRIAN VOS
Pastor, Trinity United Reformed Church, Caledonia, Michigan

"Danny Hyde has distinguished himself as someone who is historically and theologically grounded while consistently keeping things clear, Christ-centered, and relevant. This book on the tabernacle is no exception. Each chapter is a fine meal elegantly served up for the nourishment of the saints. I know now where I will turn first when it comes to books on the tabernacle."

—DR. GERALD M. BILKES
Professor of New Testament and biblical theology
Puritan Reformed Theological Seminary, Grand Rapids, Michigan

"This work on the tabernacle not only demonstrates how the tabernacle foreshadows Christ in its exposition of Exodus 25–40, it lays out principles to help people read the Old Testament properly. The appendix on 'Preaching the Pentateuch' is worth the price of the book. Such passionate preaching of the Old Testament is greatly needed in the church today."

—Dr. Richard P. Belcher Jr.
Professor of Old Testament
Reformed Theological Seminary, Charlotte, North Carolina
Author, *The Messiah and the Psalms*

"In *God in Our Midst*, Rev. Danny Hyde provides a true feast for the reader. He demonstrates a grasp of the Scriptures in terms of the grand storyline as well as the particular texts that flesh out the points he makes. His examination of the tabernacle—its building, sacrifices, personnel—are gateways to discuss a wide variety of theological matters and directions of rich, spiritual application. The tabernacle centers around the person and work of Jesus Christ. This book is rich in content devoted to theology and to piety. Lay members and ordained pastors will learn and relearn much in this book. Highly recommended!"

—Rev. Mark Vander Hart
Associate professor of Old Testament studies
Mid-America Reformed Seminary, Dyer, Indiana

"As children learn with concrete objects and figures, the Old Testament people were taught by God with physical symbols such as the tabernacle. With centuries in between, most Christians have missed the beauty of God's provisional dwelling place. Danny Hyde takes us back in time through the lens of the New Testament to grasp God's artistic demonstration of His awesome and redeeming presence. What pointed to Christ in His first coming will shine with much more splendor in God's definitive tabernacle in the new heaven and new earth."

—Dr. Heber Carlos de Campos Jr.
Chaplain and professor of systematic theology
Instituto Presbiteriano Mackenzie, São Paulo, Brasil

"How refreshing to have a book that unlocks the treasures of this section of God's Word so clearly and so faithfully. Daniel Hyde has handed us not only an excellent series of devotional studies on the tabernacle, he has given us an example of how to allow Scripture to interpret Scripture. So many have sought the key to unlocking these chapters in allegory, imagination, and speculation, all of which has proven to make things complex and unprofitable. Instead, we are guided to simply read the text as it was intended to be read. Daniel helps us to hear God teaching His people about the promised Savior, Jesus, and the great things He would do to redeem and transform sinners. The secret, the mystery in it all, is Jesus. It is so exciting to be able to see these things for oneself. After the first few chapters of this little book, I am sure readers will be able to see the patterns for themselves, and make connections with more familiar New Testament passages. What could be more exciting than to know in greater detail the wonder it is to experience God in our midst? This would be an excellent resource for any Bible study group or class to open up a section of Scripture that sadly continues to remain closed to so many."

—Dr. David R. Jackson
Head teacher, biblical studies
William Carey Christian School, Prestons, Australia
Author, *Crying Out for Vindication: The Gospel According to Job*

DANIEL R. HYDE

GOD *in* O D

Our

MIDST

The TABERNACLE & OUR
RELATIONSHIP *with* GOD

IR *Reformation Trust*   A DIVISION OF LIGONIER MINISTRIES, ORLANDO, FL

Library of Congress Cataloging-in-Publication Data

Hyde, Daniel R.
  God in our midst : the tabernacle and our relationship with God / Daniel R. Hyde. -- 1st ed.
    p. cm.
  Includes bibliographical references and indexes.
  ISBN 978-1-56769-281-5
  1. Tabernacle--Typology. 2. Bible. O.T. Exodus XXV-XL--Criticism, interpretation, etc.
3. Spirituality--Biblical teaching. I. Title.
  BS680.T32H94 2012
  222'.12064--dc23
                                                    2012002657

Para os pastores da Igreja Presbiteriana do Brasil e Igrejas
Reformadas do Brasil:
"O cerne da questão é este: pregar a Cristo,
por meio de Cristo, para o louvor de Cristo."

—William Perkins, *A Arte de Profetizar*

To the pastors of the Presbyterian Church of Brazil
and Reformed Churches of Brazil:
"The heart of the matter is this: preach one Christ,
by Christ, to the praise of Christ."

—William Perkins, *The Art of Prophesying*

CONTENTS

ILLUSTRATIONS

ABBREVIATIONS

BC—Belgic Confession

CD—Canons of Dort

HC—Heidelberg Catechism

WCF—Westminster Confession of Faith

WLC—Westminster Larger Catechism

WSC—Westminster Shorter Catechism

FOREWORD

Like me, you probably have been disappointed by many books on the Old Testament. The covers look great, the titles sound enticing, and the blurbs appear exciting. But one chapter in and you begin to flag. They are so boring, so academic, so impractical, and so suitable for your large pile of "read-one-chapter" books.

So, how can you improve your chances of selecting a book on the Old Testament that will bless your life? Let me tell you six things I look for when I'm choosing books on the Old Testament for my own spiritual edification.

First, I want a reverent and diligent handling of the text of Scripture. For too long the Old Testament text has been treated with less respect than a daily newspaper. It has been attacked, lampooned, and neglected, not just by those outside the church but by many within it. So, I want to be sure that the author views the Old Testament as the inspired Word of God, and then works hard to mine the maximum meaning out of each precious word.

Second, I expect any interpretation to start with the original context and park there for a while. Many books and sermons seem to regard the Old Testament as something hot off the presses and addressed directly to twenty-first-century culture. They fail to consider the original message to the original audience thousands of years ago and thousands of miles away. If you want to get on the wrong track immediately and lead others astray, that's a sure-fire way of doing it.

Third, while accounting for the slow, progressive unfolding of God's truth over many years, the book should portray that truth as having one clear and constant message. At times, some writers imply that God started with Plan A, and when that didn't work He tried Plan B, then C, then D, and so on. In other words, instead of seeing God's message of a gracious salvation for sinners through the Messiah as one seed that gradually grows from root to shoot to stem to flower to fruit, they imply that God was forever starting over; planting then uprooting, replanting then uprooting, over and over again.

Fourth, I look for a book that follows Jesus' and His disciples' example in using the New Testament to interpret the Old. I know of one Old Testament professor who refuses to allow any New Testament verse ever to be mentioned in his classes; that's kind of like studying with the lights off. Of course, we should not read into the Old Testament what was known only to those in the New, but as Christ and His Apostles make clear, there was a lot more knowledge of the gospel in Old Testament times than is usually thought.

That brings me to my fifth requirement—the book must connect Old Testament believers with the New Testament church by demonstrating that both Old and New Testament saints were united in being saved by grace alone, through faith alone, in Christ alone, to the glory of God alone. Was Old Testament faith as clear or strong? Did Old Testament believers see Christ as we see Him? Were Old Testament believers in possession of as much of the Holy Spirit as we possess? No, no, and no again. However, they did have saving faith, it was in the Messiah alone, and without the internal work of the Holy Spirit regenerating, sanctifying, and preserving them, they had no hope.

Finally, the book must apply the truth to the modern church. Too many Old Testament books are addressed only to the head. They stop far short of connecting the truth to people's hearts and lives. Worship, communion, obedience, and service are almost swear words to some writers.

Well, you're probably thinking by now, "There aren't many Old Testament books like that today, are there?" You're right, I'm afraid. But

I'm glad to announce that one has just been added to their ranks. It's this book on the tabernacle by my friend Danny Hyde, and what a rare treat it is to read!

Danny handles the text with reverent care and rigorous diligence, mining the text for all its meat and milk. He describes the original context, people, and situation so graphically that eventually you wonder if he possibly lived in tabernacle times. While respecting the varying degrees of revelation through the ages, he demonstrates the covenantal unity of God's sovereign and gracious plan in both testaments. He avoids the pitfall of imputing New Testament understanding to Old Testament believers, but also welcomes the graciously provided light of the New to understand the Old. And he gives us, at last, a modern book on the Old Testament that treats the believing Israelites as brothers and sisters in Christ rather than as slightly confused, animistic, legalistic idolaters. Of course, if you've read any of Danny's previous nine million books (a joke to brighten up the editor's day), you'll know that he has a passion to bless the church with books that minister to the head, the heart, and the hand. This book is no different. It will lead you to worship, it will prompt obedience, and perhaps above all it will inspire you to commune with the God who delights to dwell among us and in us.

This will be a great book for pastors and teachers who have been inspired by the wonderful resurgence of interest in the Old Testament, and especially of a Christ-centered understanding of the Old Testament, and yet open their Bibles at Exodus and Leviticus and wonder, "Eh, what do I do now?" Danny shows you.

But any serious Christian will also benefit from this book. It will not only open up previously undiscovered parts of the Bible, it will show you the wonderful unity of the Scriptures from start to finish. Above all, it will inspire you to seek communion with God through Jesus Christ, Immanuel, "God with us."

—Dr. David P. Murray
Professor of Old Testament and practical theology
Puritan Reformed Theological Seminary, Grand Rapids, Michigan
January 2012

ACKNOWLEDGMENTS

Since this book is the fruit of my preaching through the book of Exodus, I must acknowledge first and foremost the congregation the Lord has called me to serve. We have experienced all of the ups and downs, joys and sadnesses, as a church family these past twelve years. I am blessed to have gone through with you "a time to weep, and a time to laugh; a time to mourn, and a time to dance" (Eccl. 3:4). Through it all, we have known the comfort and correction of our gracious triune God's presence in our midst.

I thank Dr. David Murray of Puritan Reformed Theological Seminary, who is not only a colleague but a friend, for his foreword to this book and for his gracious words about life and ministry. Our discussions about the tabernacle and the need for believers today to see the riches of Jesus Christ's grace in ancient biblical institutions have spurred me on in writing this book.

Of course, Greg Bailey, director of publications for Reformation Trust, and the whole publishing ministry of Ligonier Ministries deserve my gratitude. Although you often go unnoticed, all the books that are being read across the world because of your efforts are the fruit of your God-glorifying work.

Finally, I praise my loving, gracious, and precious triune God for giving me my wife, Karajean. From the beginning of our relationship, when we would read the Word together on our college campus, until now, as we read it together as a family with our beautiful boys, we have always experienced the presence of God in our midst as a team. I pray that our family will continue to be a little camp in the wilderness of this world, facing the glorious presence of our God in Christ, even as we await the addition of yet another member into our tent at this time of writing.

INTRODUCTION

"An earnest and prayerful study of the tabernacle, and the purposes it served, cannot fail to increase our knowledge of the grand truths of redemption."[1] This is how William Brown, writing at the end of the nineteenth century, called serious students of the Word of God to read and meditate on the tabernacle narratives of the Old Testament.

Yet few Christians seem to have done this. I learned this over the first seven years of my ministry. In those years, I preached through a great portion of the New Testament: John, Acts, Romans, Colossians, Titus, Hebrews, 1 Peter, Jude, and Revelation. I did this in order to lay a foundation of solid biblical doctrine for the church I was planting. Toward the end of those years, the Holy Spirit led me to give my people a basic overview of the Old Testament so that they could read it in a Christ-centered way, as the Apostle Paul did: "For all the promises of God in him are yea, and in him Amen" (2 Cor. 1:20, KJV). I ended up preaching a series that highlighted the story line of Christ and His redemption, beginning in Genesis and going through His coming in the Gospels. Though I thought this would be just a brief survey before I returned to preaching through the New Testament, I realized that my people—like so many other Christians today—had a woefully inadequate grasp of the Old Testament.

What I experienced has been confirmed to me by many colleagues. Vast numbers of Christians and churches in our time and place do not know the Old Testament well.[2] In the words of Brown, we pastors need

1

to give our people an earnest and prayerful study of the Old Testament, including the centerpiece of its religion for four hundred years, the tabernacle. That is what I hope to provide in this book.

Of course, one challenge we face in doing this comes from the New Testament itself:

> A tent was prepared, the first section, in which were the lamp-stand and the table and the bread of the Presence. It is called the Holy Place. Behind the second curtain was a second section called the Most Holy Place, having the golden altar of incense and the ark of the covenant covered on all sides with gold, in which was a golden urn holding the manna, and Aaron's staff that budded, and the tablets of the covenant. Above it were the cherubim of glory overshadowing the mercy seat. *Of these things we cannot now speak in detail.* (Heb. 9:2–5, emphasis added)

Ever since those words were written, generations of Christians and preachers have wished that the Apostolic writer *had* spoken in detail of the tabernacle and its furnishings. But since one aspect of the doctrine of the inspiration of Scripture is not only that the authors were "carried along by the Holy Spirit" (2 Peter 1:21) in their writing, but even that they were led away from writing what they originally intended (Jude 3), the Holy Spirit did not go into detail about the furniture in the tabernacle. Because of this, the task falls to preachers to exposit and to apply the meaning of these structures and articles of furniture. Let us, then, enter behind the curtain and into the Most Holy Place.

However, before we jump in and start seeking to understand the particulars of the tabernacle, we need to grasp some general facts and principles: what the tabernacle was; how it fit into the story of Israel's wilderness wandering; how we can best read and understand the narratives about it, especially in light of the theme of God dwelling with His people; and how we ought to respond as Christians to the biblical teaching about it.

WHAT WAS THE TABERNACLE?

The tabernacle (Latin, *tabernaculum*, "tent") was the Lord's temporary dwelling place during the Israelites' forty-year wilderness wandering and their first three hundred-plus years in the land of Canaan. God revealed the instructions for building it to Moses (Ex. 25:1–31:11) and inspired him to write an account of its construction (Ex. 35:4–40:38).[3]

The tabernacle actually has several Hebrew names in the narrative of Scripture, all of which signify something about its purpose. First, it is called "the sanctuary" (Ex. 25:8, *miqdash*; Ex. 38:24, *qodesh*), as it was the place of the holy presence of God. So, it was a holy place. Second, it is called "the tent of the Lord" (Ex. 25:9, *mishkan*; Ex. 26:7, *'ohel*), as it was the place of His temporary dwelling among His people. It is also called the "tent" in the New Testament letter to the Hebrews (Heb. 8:5; 9:21, *skēnē*). Third, it is called "the tent of the testimony" (Ex. 38:21; Num. 9:15; cf. Acts 7:44, *'ohel ha-edut*), as it was the place where He testified to His covenant of grace with Israel.[4] In fact, the two tablets of the law were also called the "testimony" (*edut*). The conservative Lutheran commentator C. F. Keil (1807–1888) wrote that the law of God was described as the "testimony" because it was housed in the tent of the testimony:

> [The tablets were so called] not merely because they bore testimony to the divine will, but also and at the same time to the divine nature, because they manifested those divine attributes under which Jehovah reveals Himself, His essence and being, in and to Israel. It is not merely what Jehovah requires of His people Israel as their covenant God, but it is, at the same time, what He is and desires to be for Israel, that was embodied in the ten words written upon the tables of stone; and this testimony it was that constituted the pith and essence of the old covenant.[5]

Fourth, the tabernacle is called "the tent of meeting" (Ex. 27:21; 28:43; 30:20; 40:32; Num. 8:24, *'ohel moed*), as it was the place where the Lord met with His people, as represented by the priests. In fact, until the tabernacle was constructed, the Lord met with Moses alone, as the representative of the entire people, in another tent also known as the tent of meeting, "face to face, as a man speaks to his friend" (Ex. 33:11). That meeting and fellowship between the Lord and Moses was to occur on a larger scale in the tabernacle between the Lord and His people, although the one-on-one, personal aspect was lessened.

THE STORY LINE

We also need to be familiar with the story line of the book of Exodus and how the tabernacle fits into that story. What happened before and after the tabernacle was built? How did the tabernacle flow from and into this larger story?

Geography

The story line of the book of Exodus takes place in three geographic locations. The story opens where Genesis ends—with Israel in Egypt— and continues there in chapters 1–13 (cf. Gen. 50:22–26). After leaving Egypt in the dark of night, the Israelites proceed into the wilderness, the Sinai desert, which is the setting for chapters 14–18. Surprisingly, however, the book of the "exodus," that is, the departure from Egypt, does not spend most of its time on that dynamic event. Instead, the majority of the book takes place at a static location: Mount Sinai. The narrative in this location covers more than half of the chapters, 19–40.

There is a wonderful theological and practical reason why more than half of Exodus is set at Sinai. The Holy Spirit is teaching us that redemption occurs for the purpose of invocation, that salvation happens for the purpose of adoration. The Israelites were saved from Egypt that they might serve the Lord. Likewise, our purpose for being called out of the darkness of the world is that we might be called into the brilliant presence of God. We exist, as the memorable words of the Westminster Shorter Catechism teach us, "to glorify God, and to enjoy him for ever"

4

(Q&A 1). Meditating on the tabernacle, then, like meditating on the rest of Scripture, should help us fulfill this purpose, "that [we] may proclaim the excellencies of him who called [us] out of darkness into his marvelous light" (1 Peter 2:9b).

Literary

This last and largest section of Exodus can be divided into two parts. In chapters 19–24, the Lord enters a sacred covenant relationship with His liberated people. In chapters 25–40, He gives His covenant people the means to worship Him for that liberation in the tabernacle. The largest subsection of this largest part of the book of Exodus, then, deals with the instructions for and construction of the tabernacle, where the Lord met with His people and where they served Him in sacrifice and prayer. How important is this fact? One of the great Dutch Reformed theologians of the seventeenth century, Herman Witsius (1636–1708), expressed it this way: "God created the whole world in six days, but he used forty to instruct Moses about the tabernacle. Little over one chapter was needed to describe the structure of the world, but six were used for the tabernacle."[6] Clearly, the Holy Spirit wants us to notice that the tabernacle was extremely important to the faith and life of His old-covenant people—and, since it is part of inspired Scripture, to us.

With that in mind, how do we proceed to navigate through this largest section in the narrative of Exodus? As we work our way through these chapters, we will notice the following literary divisions. First, from 25:1 through 31:11, the Lord gave Moses *instruction* to build the tabernacle. Second, from 31:12 to 35:3, we find an interlude dealing with the golden calf narrative (which we will not deal with in this book).[7] Third, from 35:4 to 40:38, Moses recorded the actual *construction* of the tabernacle.

These details may seem boring, but they reveal the beautiful structure that the Holy Spirit gave to the book of Exodus. He inspired it, or breathed it out (2 Tim. 3:16). The details of the Word of God matter. For example, Jesus based an entire argument for the resurrection on the present tense of a verb (Luke 20:37–38), and Paul based an entire argument for Jesus being *the* seed of Abraham on a singular noun (Gal. 3:16).

It is clear, then, that we need to read and meditate on this portion of the Word of God purposefully and prayerfully. When we read the Word in a studious, contemplative, and prayerful way, we come to see not only the individual pearls of doctrine and application contained therein, but also how all of those pearls hang together like those on a necklace. The Word of God is as beautiful in its presentation as in its proclamation.

Reality

In saying all of this, I am assuming, as a Bible-believing Christian, that all the events related in these chapters really happened the way the text says they happened. These narratives are reality, not fantasy. Critical scholars, though, have sought to demonstrate the implausibility of these narratives by pointing to several "problems." Among these are alleged errors and alleged later additions by multiple editors and redactors. For instance, it has been said that all the materials listed in Exodus 38:24–31 would have been impossible to gather in the wilderness, that it would have been impossible to transport all these materials, and that a nomadic people certainly would not have had the skills necessary to construct the tabernacle. Likewise, some claim that the tabernacle was a myth that later editors added to the Bible as a way of giving a historical precedent for the construction of the temple. Both Jewish and Christian scholars have addressed these concerns with great force and ability, both literarily and historically.[8]

The most convincing reason for accepting these chapters as reality, though, is the fact that our Lord Jesus Christ spoke of this portion of Exodus as the Word of God. When did He do that? He did so when He taught His disciples about Himself from the Old Testament after His resurrection: "And beginning with *Moses* [that is, Genesis—Deuteronomy] and all the Prophets, he interpreted to them in all the Scriptures the things concerning himself" (Luke 24:27, emphasis added; cf. 24:44).

Following that tradition, the first martyr of the early church, Stephen, testified about the reality of this section of the Word when he said Moses "was in the congregation in the wilderness" and "received living oracles to give to us" (Acts 7:38). The words of Exodus 25–31 and 35–40 are among those "living oracles" (*logia zōnta*). Likewise, the writer to the Hebrews certainly had no question that the tabernacle narratives were part of the "living and active" Word of God (Heb. 4:12, *zōn . . . kai energēs*), accurate and historically reliable, when he quoted from them to show how Jesus fulfilled them (Hebrews 8–9). In fact, the writer said Moses "was instructed by God" when God said to him, "See that you make everything according to the pattern that was shown you on the mountain" (Heb. 8:5; cf. Ex. 25:9).

Finally, the Apostle Paul repeats the story within this section of Exodus of Moses' meeting with the Lord face to face, saying: "The Israelites could not gaze at Moses' face because of its glory, which was being brought to an end. . . . Moses . . . would put a veil over his face so that the Israelites might not gaze at the outcome of what was being brought to an end" (2 Cor. 3:7b, 13). He then equates the reading of the Old Testament with Moses himself: "For to this day, when they read the old covenant, that same veil remains unlifted, because only through Christ is it taken away. Yes, to this day whenever Moses is read a veil lies over their hearts" (2 Cor. 3:14b–15).

HERMENEUTICAL PRINCIPLES

Now that we know the overall story line and structure of the large section of Exodus dealing with the tabernacle, we need to determine how to interpret it. This is the task of hermeneutics, interpreting the text of Scripture in order to come to a true understanding of its meaning.[9] In order to do this, we have to engage exegesis. Exegesis is drawing out of the text what it means, as opposed to eisegesis, which is pouring into the text our own meaning and expectations. The ancient church father Hilary of Poitiers (300–368) described the process of hermeneutics and exegesis in his monumental treatise *On the Trinity* (1.18):

For he is the best student who waits till the words reveal their own meaning rather than imposes it, who takes more from the words than (puts) into them, and who does not force a semblance of meaning on the words, which he had determined to be the right one before starting to read. Since then we are going to speak of the things of God, let us leave to God knowledge of Himself and let us in pious reverence obey His words. For He is a fitting witness to Himself who is only known through Himself.[10]

In this section, I want to give a brief historical survey of how the tabernacle has been interpreted, then lay out some basic principles that will help us derive its true meaning.

History of Hermeneutics

Ancient interpreters looked at the tabernacle in a highly symbolic and allegorical way. Among these interpreters was the Jewish philosopher Philo of Alexandria (20 BC–AD 50). He saw in the tabernacle the universe in miniature. He arrived at this conclusion on the basis of his allegorical interpretation of the four kinds of materials used to construct the tabernacle, which he saw as the four elements of nature, and on the basis of his allegorical interpretation of the precious stones in the ephod, which he regarded as the signs of the Zodiac.[11]

Another example of this allegorical approach is found in the writings of the early church father Clement of Alexandria (150–215). He saw meanings behind the colors of the curtains: "For purple is from water, linen from the earth; blue, being dark, is like the air, as scarlet is like fire." He also said the altar of incense was the symbol of the earth, the courtyard symbolized the middlemost point of heaven and earth, the covering of the tabernacle was the barrier of popular unbelief, the lampstand represented the seven planets, the two cherubim were the two hemispheres, the golden mitre was the regal power of the Lord, and so on.[12]

Medieval expositors in particular applied this allegorical approach to the tabernacle. The Jewish rabbi Maimonides (1135–1204) interpreted the tabernacle as a symbol of a royal palace, with the priests symbolizing servants who offered honor through the ceremonial rites.[13] However, the allegorical approach found its greatest expression in the work of Bede the Venerable (673–735). Bede's *De tabernaculo*, "On the Tabernacle," was the first Christian exposition of the tabernacle narratives. In it, he followed what was known as the *quadriga*, the fourfold interpretation of Scripture.[14] This approach distinguished among the *historical* sense, which described literal things that happened; the *allegorical* sense, which described Christ and the sacraments; the *tropological* sense, which described how to live morally; and the *anagogical* sense, which described the heavenly and future state of things.[15]

What about Reformed Protestant theologians? In the seventeenth century, several interpreted the tabernacle. Johannes Cocceius[16] (1603–1669) said the tabernacle was the invisible church, while the outer court was the visible church. He also said the Holy Place was the church militant, while the Holy of Holies was the church triumphant.[17] One of Cocceius' contemporaries, the aforementioned Witsius, also interpreted the tabernacle as a symbol of the church: "The tabernacle, be it observed, was a figure of the Church; and the candlestick, of the Holy Spirit, to whom the Church is indebted for all her light."[18] Witsius went on to say that since the ark of the covenant was made of wood and gold, it was a type of Christ with His two natures.[19] In the nineteenth century, Brown wrote a wonderfully detailed explanation of the tabernacle's details, yet followed an unbounded allegorical approach. For example, he said the two silver tenons into which each board in the wall was placed represented faith, while the gold bars that ran across the boards were those who were leaning on Jesus for salvation, and so on.[20]

What is wrong with all of this? The main difficulty with such allegorical and symbolic interpretations is that they are highly subjective and arbitrary. Witsius saw in the wood and gold the humanity and divinity of our Lord Jesus Christ, but what keeps me from saying these elements really represented the suffering of Christ on the cross and His glorious resurrection? Who is correct? How can we know?

9

That brings us to principles of proper interpretation. In what follows, I offer several basic keys to interpreting the tabernacle narratives. These are in no way exhaustive, but I trust they are helpful.

Reading Them as Scripture

First, we need to read these stories as Holy Scripture. Jesus received the Law (Genesis, Exodus, Leviticus, Numbers, and Deuteronomy) as the prophetic Word of God (Matt. 11:13) and taught His disciples about Himself from these books (Luke 24:27, 44). When Paul reminded Timothy that from the days of his childhood, "you have been acquainted with the sacred writings [*hiera grammata*], which are able to make you wise for salvation through faith in Christ Jesus," he was referring to the books of the Old Testament (2 Tim. 3:15). These writings, just as much as the New Testament, are "breathed out by God [*theopneustos*] and profitable for teaching, for reproof, for correction, and for training in righteousness, that the man of God may be competent, equipped for every good work" (vv. 16–17).

This means that we need to read the story of the tabernacle, first, because it is the Word of God, and second, because reading it as such is profitable and a blessing to our souls (cf. Rev. 1:3). The Westminster Larger Catechism expresses this truth when it says that "the holy Scriptures are to be read with an high and reverent esteem of them; with a firm persuasion that they are the very word of God" (Q&A 157).

Reading Them Devotionally

Second, we need to read them devotionally. This means that our highest purpose in reading the Word is not to search for theological proof-texts or principles for successful living, but that we might be led to worship the triune God. The great psalm that extols the Word of God, Psalm 119, shows us how knowledge of God's Word leads us to praise Him:

> I will praise you with an upright heart, when I learn your righteous rules. (v. 7)

Blessed are you, O Lᴏʀᴅ; teach me your statutes! (v. 12)

Accept my freewill offerings of praise, O Lᴏʀᴅ, and teach me your rules. (v. 108)

Righteous are you, O Lᴏʀᴅ, and right are your rules. (v. 137)

Seven times a day I praise you for your righteous rules. (v. 164)

Martin Luther wrote that our approach to reading the Word was outlined in Psalm 119, consisting in prayer (*oratio*), meditation (*meditatio*), and spiritual conflict (*tentatio*).[21] The great poet of Israel, David, also spoke of this prayerful, meditative, and transforming reading of the Word when he said:

The law of the Lᴏʀᴅ is perfect, reviving the soul;
the testimony of the Lᴏʀᴅ is sure, making wise the simple;
the precepts of the Lᴏʀᴅ are right, rejoicing the heart;
the commandment of the Lᴏʀᴅ is pure, enlightening the eyes. . . .
More to be desired are they than gold, even much fine gold;
sweeter also than honey and drippings of the honeycomb.
(Ps. 19:7–8, 10)

When we read the Word, our souls are revived, we are made wise, we rejoice, we are enlightened, and we find what we desire most: the Lord Himself.

Gerald Bilkes writes that the church needs to recapture this reading of the Bible with the heart.[22] He says this involves recognizing the total claim of the Word of God; demanding the allegiance of our whole being; depending on grace so that our hearts may profit from the Word of God; and looking to the triune God to transcribe the Word of God on our hearts.

As we read the tabernacle narratives, we must be claimed by their authority, depend on the grace of the Holy Spirit to understand them, and expect God to inscribe their teaching on our hearts.

Reading Them through the Lens of the New Testament

Third, we need to read the tabernacle narratives through the lens of the New Testament. In reading the Old Testament, especially the tabernacle narratives, it is essential for us to look to the New Testament as the basis of our interpretation.[23] The dictum that Augustine (354–430) wrote in the year 419 must be our guide: *In Vetere Novum latet, et in Novo Vetus patet.* This means, "In the Old [Testament] the New [Testament] is concealed, and in the New [Testament] the Old [Testament] is revealed."[24] We need to realize that the Old Testament is incomplete. It is merely the first of two volumes, with the New Testament being the second. In the Old Testament, God spoke "at many times and in many ways" (Heb. 1:1), but when Jesus came in the flesh, God spoke through His Son, bringing that old revelation to completion (Heb. 1:2).

The Dutch commentator Willem Hendrik Gispen (1900–1986) applied this truth to the tabernacle narratives when he said, "When we consider the meaning of [the tabernacle] for us as Christians, we must stay with what the Scriptures, and especially the New Testament, say, and look at the tabernacle as a whole, rather than seeking a 'deeper' meaning in every loop, clasp, and crossbar."[25]

What is the reason for relying so much on the New Testament to understand the Old? The reason is the person and work of the Holy Spirit. As Robert Strimple wrote, "In the New Testament Christ's church has been given, by the inspiration of the Holy Spirit, that post-resurrection, post-Pentecost revelation that is absolutely authoritative, her infallible guide in all matters of faith and life."[26] The Spirit reveals the deep things of God (Rom. 8:1–27; 1 Cor. 1:18–2:16) and the realities of our redemption (2 Corinthians 3–4). As Paul told the Corinthians:

> Since we have such a hope, we are very bold, not like Moses, who would put a veil over his face so that the Israelites might not gaze

at the outcome of what was being brought to an end. But their minds were hardened. For to this day, when they read the old covenant, that same veil remains unlifted, because only through Christ is it taken away. Yes, to this day whenever Moses is read a veil lies over their hearts. But when one turns to the Lord, the veil is removed. Now the Lord is the Spirit, and where the Spirit of the Lord is, there is freedom. And we all, with unveiled face, beholding the glory of the Lord, are being transformed into the same image from one degree of glory to another. For this comes from the Lord who is the Spirit. (2 Cor. 3:12–18)

This veil that lies over the eyes of unbelieving hearts can be removed only by Jesus Christ working through the power of the Holy Spirit. This means that we desperately rely on the Holy Spirit, whose inspiration led to the writing of the New Testament, to help us properly understand the meaning of the Old Testament by His illumination.

Reading Them as Fulfilled in Jesus Christ

Fourth, we need to read the tabernacle narratives with the understanding that they are fulfilled in Christ. As Jesus said when He rebuked the Pharisees, "You search the Scriptures because you think that in them you have eternal life; and it is they that bear witness about me" (John 5:39). His rebuke was for those who thought "in-depth" Bible study, with all the obscure details, was itself saving; instead, He said, the study of Scripture must be centered in Him. In Witsius' words, Jesus is "the key of knowledge . . . without which nothing can be savingly understood in Moses and the prophets."[27]

Jesus demonstrated this to His disciples on the Emmaus road. After His resurrection, He led these downcast brothers through the Word of God to teach them of Himself: "And beginning with Moses and all the Prophets, he interpreted to them in all the Scriptures the things concerning himself" (Luke 24:27). He then returned to Jerusalem and spoke to those He had made Apostles: "Then he said to them, 'These are my words that I spoke to you while I was still with you, that everything

13

written about me in the Law of Moses and the Prophets and the Psalms must be fulfilled.' Then he opened their minds to understand the Scriptures" (Luke 24:44-45).

This Christ-centered approach to the Old Testament was not only a hallmark of ancient Christian interpretation, as the above quote from Augustine illustrates, it was how our Reformation forefathers read the Old Testament. Arguably the greatest of the seventeenth-century English Reformed theologians, John Owen (1616–1683), described this Christ-centered approach when he said:

> There is herein a *full manifestation* made of the wisdom of God, in all the holy institutions of the tabernacle and temple of old. Herein the veil is fully taken off from them, and that obscure representation of heavenly things is brought forth unto light and glory. It is true, this is done unto a great degree in the dispensation of the Gospel. By the coming of Christ in the flesh, and the discharge of his mediatory office in this world, the substance of what they did prefigure is accomplished; and in the revelations of the Gospel the nature and end of them is declared. Howbeit, they extended their signification also unto things within the veil, or the discharge of the priestly office of Christ in the heavenly sanctuary, Heb. ix. 24. Wherefore, as we have not yet a perfection of light to understand the depth of the mysteries contained in them; so themselves also were not absolutely fulfilled until the Lord Christ discharged his office in the holy place. This is the glory of the pattern which God showed unto Moses in the mount, made conspicuous and evident unto all. Therein especially do the saints of the Old Testament, who were exercised all their days in those typical institutions whose end and design they could not comprehend, see the manifold wisdom and goodness of God in them all, rejoicing in them for evermore.[28]

14

Reading Them Simply

Fifth, in contrast with the allegorical and highly symbolic approach described above, we need to read the tabernacle narratives simply, not speculatively. We have to realize that they are symbolic, but a symbol is not wild speculation, with every detail of shape, size, location, and color meaning something hidden.[29] The Reformers described how we are to read the Word, simply allowing its own words to give us its meaning, when they said *Scriptura Scripturae interpres*: "Scripture is the interpreter of Scripture."[30] When we allow the Word to guide our understanding, we can make a distinction between a symbol and an allegory. The difference is that while a symbol has one simple meaning and purpose, an allegory has many at one time.

What does it mean to read the Word and the tabernacle story simply? It means that we must read it theologically. In reading, then, we ask not about the hidden meaning of minor details such as the rings, the poles, and the boards of the tabernacle, or the color of the stones in the high priest's ephod, but questions such as, "What does this passage teach me about God, about my sins, about Christ's redemptive work, and about how I am to live for the glory of God?"[31] In the words of John Calvin:

> It would be puerile to make a collection of the *minutiae* wherewith some philosophize; since it was by no means the intention of God to include mysteries in every hook and loop; and even although no part were without a mystical meaning, which no one in his senses will admit, it is better to confess our ignorance than to indulge ourselves in frivolous conjectures. Of this sobriety, too, the author of the Epistle to the Hebrews is a fit master for us, who, although he professedly shews the analogy between the shadows of the Law and the truth manifested in Christ, yet sparingly touches upon some main points, and by this moderation restrains us from too curious disquisitions and deep speculations.[32]

Reading Them as Instructive Morally

Sixth, we need to read these narratives as instructive morally. One of the purposes of Scripture is to guide God's people in lives of godliness. The Scriptures were given "for reproof, for correction, and for training in righteousness" (2 Tim. 3:16). The Apostle Paul engaged in this reading of the Old Testament. In writing to the Corinthians, he drew on the Old Testament stories as the basis for moral catechesis. In the following passage, notice how Paul parallels the life of the Israelites in the wilderness with the life of new-covenant Christians:

> I want you to know, brothers, that our fathers were all under the cloud, and all passed through the sea, and all were baptized into Moses in the cloud and in the sea, and all ate the same spiritual food, and all drank the same spiritual drink. For they drank from the spiritual Rock that followed them, and the Rock was Christ. Nevertheless, with most of them God was not pleased, for they were overthrown in the wilderness. (1 Cor. 10:1–5)

Paul assumes here that the new-covenant church is the continuation of God's covenant of grace that He made with Israel. This is why Paul can say the Israelites were "our fathers." He even speaks to those who participated in the Lord's Supper by saying that their "fathers" ate "the same spiritual food" and drank "the same spiritual drink" because they partook of Christ. But God was displeased with the wilderness generation, and Paul goes on to say:

> Now these things took place as examples for us, that we might not desire evil as they did. Do not be idolaters as some of them were; as it is written, "The people sat down to eat and drink and rose up to play." We must not indulge in sexual immorality as some of them did, and twenty-three thousand fell in a single day. We must not put Christ to the test, as some of them did and were destroyed by serpents, nor grumble, as some of them did and were

16

destroyed by the Destroyer. Now these things happened to them as an example, but they were written down for our instruction, on whom the end of the ages has come. (Vv. 6–11)

These Old Testament stories are our "examples." The word Paul uses, *tupoi*, speaks of these stories as patterns or types of what happens to us.[33] Notice how Paul gives an exhortation and then bases it in an example: we should not "desire evil as they did" (v. 6); we should not be "idolaters as some of them were" (v. 7); we should not "indulge in sexual immorality as some of them did" (v. 8); we should not "put Christ to the test, as some of them did" (v. 9); and we should not "grumble, as some of them did" (v. 10).

While the tabernacle narratives may not present such obvious examples, we still must read them for the moral instruction they contain, for our holy God calls us to be holy as He is holy. This was not just an Old Testament exhortation (Lev. 11:44); it is also a New Testament command (1 Peter 1:16).

THE TABERNACLE AMONG THE TABERNACLES

One final hermeneutical key to understanding the tabernacle merits its own section. The tabernacle was not the first dwelling place of God with His people, nor would it be the last.[34] I would like to trace the theme of God's "tabernacling" (dwelling) among His people throughout Scripture to show the overall context of the tabernacle in the midst of Israel.

By means of such a survey, we will see that the Scriptures are like a rose, one that began to bud early in the Old Testament as God, the great Kingdom Builder, established His kingdom in the garden of Eden. Even when the Devil used Adam to desecrate this kingdom, the Scriptures continued to blossom as God began rebuilding His kingdom. He called Abram to be the father of a new kingdom-people who would live in a kingdom-place. He saved the Israelites from Egypt and brought them to that promised kingdom-place in the days of Joshua. Again, though it was defiled in the days of the judges, God reformed the church in the days of David and Solomon, giving His people a temple at which to worship. Finally, the rose of Scripture came to full bloom with the coming of our Lord—"God with us" (Matt. 1:23), "the Word" who was "made flesh and dwelt [tabernacled] among us" (John 1:14).

Beginning at the End–Revelation 21–22

We begin by going to the end of the Bible, Revelation 21–22. In the words of the contemporary New Testament scholar G. K. Beale, "Eschatology is protology: the goal of all redemptive history is to return to the primal condition of creation from which humankind fell and then go beyond it to a heightened state, which the first creation did not reach."[35] Since we live after "the fall and disobedience of our first parents, Adam and Eve, in Paradise" (HC, Q&A 7), to study what God did in the beginning is to study what God will do in the end, and vice versa. Revelation 21–22, then, vividly pictures the pinnacle of God's plan of creation, salvation, and human history.[36]

This pinnacle is painted in visionary pictures using the biblical and theological themes of the new heaven and new earth, the New Jerusalem, and the final pronouncement of God's covenant promise: "I will be your God, and you will be my people" (Lev. 26:12; Jer. 7:23; 11:4; 24:7; 30:22; Ezek. 11:20; 14:11; 36:28; 37:27). Everything God ever intended for His creation is described here in breathtaking terms that stretch "the limits of human vocabulary and thought."[37]

The end of the book of Revelation portrays the climax of creation, as the "first heaven and the first earth" (Rev. 21:1), which were created at the beginning (Genesis 1–2), are renewed, transformed, and purified. The new heaven and new earth, then, will be "the same heaven and earth, but gloriously rejuvenated, with no weeds, thorns or thistles, and so on."[38] God will not annihilate what He made and create another heaven and earth like the first, out of nothing (*ex nihilo*).[39] The Belgic Confession describes creation's climax, saying, "our Lord Jesus Christ will come from heaven, bodily and visibly, as he ascended, with great glory and majesty, to declare himself the judge of the living and the dead. He will burn this old world, in fire and flame, in order to cleanse it" (Art. 37).[40]

After seeing this glorious new creation, John wrote his vision of "the holy city, new Jerusalem" (Rev. 21:2). This city is not of this earth, but its origin is heavenly: it comes "out of heaven, from God." This vision of the New Jerusalem pictures the joining of the heavenly reality to the newly renewed heaven and earth. The New Jerusalem is the triumphant and glorified church of Jesus Christ described symbolically. It is a picture of God's people.[41] It is the reality of Paul's description of the cleansed and purified church: "Husbands, love your wives, as Christ loved the church and gave himself up for her, that he might sanctify her, having cleansed her by the washing of water with the word, so that he might present the church to himself in splendor, without spot or wrinkle or any such thing, that she might be holy and without blemish" (Eph. 5:25–27).

The people of God are described with other metaphors. Revelation 3:12 speaks of the overcomers being pillars in the temple of God, meaning that the people of God are the "literal" temple. Revelation 19:7–8 describes the marriage supper of the Lamb and notes that the bride "has made herself ready," being adorned in fine linen. The image of fine linen is then explained: "For the fine linen is the righteous deeds of the saints." The bride, then, is the church. This language is reflected in Revelation 21:2, which says "the holy city," New Jerusalem, has been "prepared as a bride adorned for her husband." In 21:9–27, John's vision of the New Jerusalem continues with more detail. An angel shows John "the Bride, the wife of the Lamb" (v. 9). As the angel takes him up to a high mountain, he again is shown "the holy city Jerusalem coming down out of heaven from God" (v. 10). So the bride of Christ, once again, is paralleled with the New Jerusalem.[42] In the words of Hebrews 12:23, the heavenly Jerusalem to which we have come is "the assembly of the firstborn who are enrolled in heaven."

Not only does John see the church coming down out of heaven, he learns that God is coming, too. Revelation 21–22 proclaims the climax of God's covenant bond with His people, which began in the garden.

Revelation 21:3–4 states the essence of God's relationship with His people and the heartbeat of history. Here we find the fulfillment of the redemptive-historical process of God coming into covenant with His people, to be their God and make them His people. John hears a "loud voice from the throne" that pronounces this climactic event: "Behold, the dwelling place of God is with man." This means that "He will dwell with [or, among] them, and they will be his people, and God himself will be with [or, among] them as their God." As the Old Testament speaks of Zion being restored (Isa. 35:10; 65:19), this obviously must entail a new dwelling place of God on earth.

But the climactic tabernacle of John's vision is not a structure called a tabernacle. Revelation 21:22 says, "And I saw no temple in the city, for its temple is the Lord God the Almighty and the Lamb." So John's description is characterizing what God's dwelling with His people will be like. The Immanuel promise characterizes God's tabernacle with His people. It means unbroken fellowship (Ex. 3:12; Lev. 26:11–12; Isa. 7:14) and a personal relationship (cf. Ex. 6:7; Deut. 14:2; 26:18–19) forever, in perfect fullness in the presence of the Lord Himself. It is "fully to enjoy him for ever" (WLC, Q&A 1).

The Garden as Tabernacle

Revelation 21 can describe God's dwelling among His people in the new heaven and new earth because He dwelt among His people in the first heaven and earth. We see this particularly in the garden of Eden (Gen. 2:9–14). In the description of the garden and its rivers, we read of gold (v. 11) and the precious stones bdellium and onyx (v. 12). Eden was adorned with beauty as the temple of God, the first true Holy Land, anticipating Israel's tabernacle and later its temple (Ex. 25:3, 7; 1 Kings 6:20–22, 28, 30, 32, 35).

God showed Himself to be powerful in creating the vast realms of space, sky, land, and seas, but also as an ingenious and creative artist who filled those forms.[43] The creation process recorded in Genesis 1:1–2:3 was a massive construction plan. God first subdued the darkness and deep of the original state and made earth a place suitable for habitation. In days one through three, He gave form to the earth. The psalmist describes this in terms of God's temple and palace:

Bless the LORD, O my soul!
O LORD my God, you are very great!
You are clothed with splendor and majesty,
covering yourself with light as with a garment,
stretching out the heavens like a tent.
He lays the beams of his chambers on the waters;
he makes the clouds his chariot;
he rides on the wings of the wind. . . .
From your lofty abode you water the mountains;
the earth is satisfied with the fruit of your work.
(Ps. 104:1–3, 13)

The prophet Isaiah echoes this view, saying, "It is he who sits above the circle of the earth, and its inhabitants are like grasshoppers; who stretches out the heavens like a curtain, and spreads them like a tent to dwell in" (Isa. 40:22).

In days four through six, God filled the form of the earth. The psalmist again describes this:

O LORD, how manifold are your works!
In wisdom have you made them all;
the earth is full of your creatures.
Here is the sea, great and wide,
which teems with creatures innumerable,
living things both small and great. (Ps. 104:24–25)

He then rested from His holy work. This form and fullness became His holy habitation, His dwelling among His people. It became the place where the pinnacle of His creation—Adam and Eve—enjoyed His presence.

21

David's House

After the creation account, we go on to read of God dwelling with Noah and his family in the ark (Genesis 6–9), with the patriarchs in their journeys (e.g., Gen. 31:3), and with the Israelites in Egypt (Ex. 2:23–25) and in the wilderness, both in the form of a pillar of cloud and fire (Ex. 13:21–22; Ps. 78:14), as well as in the tabernacle (Exodus 25–40).

We then read of another structure in which God dwelt with His people in the days of David. After he had finally been anointed over the tribe of Judah and eventually over all Israel (2 Samuel 5), King David was in his house enjoying the Lord's rest from his enemies (2 Sam. 7:1). This led David to desire to build a house for the Lord, seeing that He was the true King of Israel.

In the ancient Near Eastern world, whenever a god won a battle by means of his king, the king built a house for his god as a tribute. The Lord was the divine warrior who had triumphed over His enemies through David and granted rest to the land. Therefore, David desired to follow the accustomed pattern in grateful devotion. While he lived in a house, the Lord lived in a portable tent. When the Lord triumphed over Pharaoh and the gods of Egypt, His sanctuary was fitting for His people's transient existence. It had to be temporary because the people were a pilgrim people. But with the people settled in the land and David's throne established, a more permanent sanctuary was appropriate.

As the story unfolded, the Lord caught wind of David's desire to build Him a house (2 Sam. 7:4–17). The Lord then turned the tables on David—David would not build a house *for* the Lord but would receive a house *from* the Lord. The Lord used a literary device called a double entendre when he spoke of building a "house" for David. While David was thinking in an earthly manner, wanting to build an actual house for the Lord, the Lord was planning to build for David a familial house. It was as if God were saying, "You want to build a building for Me, but I am going to build a kingdom for you."

Why did God do this? In Deuteronomy 12, the Lord gave specific instructions about a central place of worship in the Land of Promise.

Six times He said He would "choose" the place where His name would dwell (Deut. 12:5, 11, 14, 18, 21, 26) and nine times He spoke of this place of His choosing as "there" (vv. 5 [twice], 6, 7, 11 [twice], 14 [twice], 21). The Lord is God and will not give His glory to another. He would choose the place and builder—not David. We see that in the language He used in 2 Samuel 7. It is unilateral, covenant language. The Lord said over and over again, "I will . . ." He promised to make David's name great (v. 9); to appoint a place for His people (v. 10); to plant His people (v. 10); to give David rest (v. 11); to make David a house (v. 11); to raise up David's son (v. 12); to establish that son's kingdom (v. 12); to establish that son's throne (v. 13); to be a father to that son (v. 14); and to discipline that son (v. 14).

This covenant promise was gracious, as the Lord reversed the typical ancient Near Eastern pattern of the earthly king building a house for the heavenly King. He did not receive a house from David, but granted one to him (v. 11). The Lord even promised that when David's son, Solomon, would sin, He would not cast him off in a covenant curse, but would discipline him as a son, saying, "my steadfast love will not depart from him" (v. 15). "Steadfast love" translates the Hebrew word for God's covenant faithfulness (*chesed*). We learn from this that God's dwelling among His people is a matter of grace, an immense privilege.

Solomon's Temple

What David desired to do, his son Solomon accomplished (1 Kings 7:51). The language of 1 Kings 6 indicates that the temple was a greater tabernacle because of this permanence. No longer would the Lord dwell in a portable tent, but in the permanence of a glorious temple. We learn also that the temple's greatness was beyond the tabernacle in the revelation of its dimensions. The tabernacle was thirty cubits long and ten cubits wide (Ex. 26:15–30).[44] The temple was sixty cubits long, twenty cubits wide, and thirty cubits high (1 Kings 6:2)—twice the size of the tabernacle. This expansion is seen even in the size of the Holy of Holies. In the tabernacle, it was ten cubits by ten cubits, according to ancient

23

tradition,[45] while in the temple it was twenty cubits by twenty cubits (1 Kings 6:20). This glory of the temple was eventually celebrated in the Psalms: "In Judah God is known; his name is great in Israel. His abode has been established in Salem, his dwelling place in Zion" (Ps. 76:1–2).

We see the continuation of the plan of God in the language used to describe the temple. The temple was a new garden of Eden. Why do I say this? First, there are creational themes in the descriptions of the temple. As 1 Kings 6–7 recounts the building of the temple, the word *finished* occurs seven times. Although not the same term used in Genesis 2:1, the creational theme is similar. First Kings 6:9a: "So he built the house and finished it." First Kings 6:14: "So Solomon built the house and finished it." First Kings 6:38b: "the house was finished." First Kings 7:1: "Solomon was building his own house thirteen years, and he finished his entire house" (Solomon's house was a part of the temple complex). First Kings 7:22: "Thus the work of the pillars was finished." First Kings 7:40: "So Hiram finished all the work that he did for King Solomon on the house of the LORD." First Kings 7:51: "Thus all the work that King Solomon did on the house of the LORD was finished."

We also see this creational, Edenic language in the descriptions of the materials and design of the temple. It was made of stone and then overlaid inside and out with cedar from Lebanon. Psalm 104 praises the Lord for creation, following the account of the six days of creation: "The trees of the LORD are watered abundantly, the cedars of Lebanon that he planted" (v. 16). Inside the temple were wooden carvings of gourds, flowers, and palm trees (1 Kings 6:18, 29). The wood was covered both inside and out with pure gold (1 Kings 6:20–22), which is described as being in the region of Eden in Genesis 2:11–12.

What was most striking about the temple as a new Eden was its appearance. The prophets reflected back on the appearance of Eden, saying in it was a mountain, a high place, where the Lord dwelled. From that mountain came the four rivers that watered the earth.[46] The prophet Ezekiel wrote: "You were in Eden, the garden of God . . . you were on the holy mountain of God" (Ezek. 28:13–14). But what does a mountain have to do with the temple, a building? Understand how the temple was constructed. In 1 Kings 6:5–6, we learn that there were three levels of side chambers against the temple, with the levels getting wider as they went higher. This means that this surrounding structure of the temple made the temple seem to be an inverted stepped pyramid, a ziggurat, or a high mountain. Unlike the ancient ziggurat structure, which pointed up to God as man tried to climb up to God, the temple pointed down because it was God's house on earth.

The common purpose of Eden, the tabernacle, and the temple was that the creature could have fellowship with the Creator. After Adam sinned, the Lord placed a cherub at the gate east of Eden to bar access to that holy place (Gen. 3:24). The temple had cherubim all around the walls (1 Kings 6:23–28), but we read of no swords in their hands. The temple was heaven on earth, for the Lord was giving His people a foretaste of their return to that primal Paradise.

After the temple was built, the Israelites brought the ark of the covenant into the Holy of Holies. As the priests placed it there and came out, "A cloud filled the house of the Lord" (1 Kings 8:10). This cloud was the Holy Spirit, who was at the first creation, hovering "over the face of the waters" (Gen. 1:2), and at the consecration ceremony of the tabernacle (Ex. 40:34).

The Prophets

We move from the high point of the temple's erection to the low point of its destruction, as interpreted by the prophets. In many ways, Ezekiel 10 is the low point of the history of God's people. A people created for the Lord's own glory and pleasure from all other peoples transgressed the covenant just as Adam did (Hos. 6:7). Like Adam, they sought the freedom to worship a god in their own image. Like Adam, they were excommunicated from the presence of God.

Second Kings 24–25 chronicles these last days of the southern kingdom of Judah. In those days, the Babylonian kingdom, under the leadership of the great Nebuchadnezzar, besieged Judah. There were three successive waves of assault, in 605, 597, and 586 BC. According to the curses of the covenant as described in Deuteronomy 28, the city of Jerusalem was destroyed, the temple was desecrated, and the people were dispersed to the nations. Second Kings 25:9 says the house of the Lord was burned to the ground, and 25:21b says, "So Judah was taken into exile out of its land." Deuteronomy 28:68 compares this dispersion to being taken by ships back to Egypt—the last place God's people wanted to go.

The Scriptures are clear that God decreed the destruction of the temple because of His people's sin. Second Kings 24:3 says, "Surely this came upon Judah at the command of the LORD, to remove them out of his sight, for the sins of Manasseh." Second Kings 24:20 says, "For because of the anger of the LORD it came to the point in Jerusalem and Judah that he cast them out from his presence."

As we turn back to Ezekiel 10, we are given a glimpse of the meaning of all of this from God's point of view. Here is the Lord's seminary course on the significance of the invasion by Babylon. It is a vision of God's chariot-throne, held up by the cherubim (v. 1). In this vision, Ezekiel sees a "man" who takes coals of fire to cast them onto Jerusalem (v. 2). In the story of God's dealings with the world, fire is associated with His judgments (Gen. 19:23–28). Judah, then, became like Sodom and Gomorrah (Isa. 1:10). The church had become like the world, and God had had enough of His worldly church. In the later words of Jesus to the church in Laodicea, He was ready to "spit you out of my mouth" (Rev. 3:16).

Then, the worst of all the covenant curses is depicted: the Lord deserts Jerusalem. In Ezekiel 10:18, we see that the glory of the Lord, His *chabod*, goes out from the temple. This is a visual sign of the Holy Spirit, who hovered over the face of the deep (Gen. 1:2); who led the people into the wilderness (Exodus 13); who filled the tabernacle (Exodus 40); and who filled the temple of Solomon (1 Kings 8:10).[47]

In Ezekiel 10:19, the cherubim mount the chariot of the Lord to take this glory elsewhere. It goes to the east gate of the temple. The temple was the typological return to Eden, to the presence of the Lord, so to go east was to follow Adam and Eve's footsteps away from the Lord (Gen.

3:23–24). In Ezekiel, the Lord goes east, away from Eden, leaving the temple *ichabod*, without glory (cf. 1 Sam. 4:19–22).

Yet, while this was a curse on the whole nation, we see the gospel purpose of it for the remnant chosen by grace. Not only did the glory of the Lord go east, the people of Judah also went east. The Lord led His people into exile in Babylon. The Lord deserted the temple and the city but not His people. As the saying goes, while we may feel that God has slipped out of our hands, we have not slipped out of His. He became an alien in a strange land with His remnant. The words of Ezekiel 11:16 are touching: "Though I removed them far off among the nations, and though I scattered them among the countries, yet I have been a sanctuary to them for a while."

There is also a promise of the *chabod* of the Lord returning. Haggai 1:1–15 speaks about the rebuilding of the temple of the Lord. While the people of God were in Babylon, the Lord raised up the Persians, who defeated the Babylonian kingdom. Cyrus, the great king of Persia, decreed in 538 BC that the Jews could return to Jerusalem and rebuild the temple:

> In the first year of Cyrus king of Persia, that the word of the LORD by the mouth of Jeremiah might be fulfilled, the LORD stirred up the spirit of Cyrus king of Persia, so that he made a proclamation throughout all his kingdom and also put it in writing: "Thus says Cyrus king of Persia: The LORD, the God of heaven, has given me all the kingdoms of the earth, and he has charged me to build him a house at Jerusalem, which is in Judah. Whoever is among you of all his people, may his God be with him, and let him go up to Jerusalem, which is in Judah, and rebuild the house of the LORD, the God of Israel—he is the God who is in Jerusalem. And let each survivor, in whatever place he sojourns, be assisted by the men of his place with silver and gold, with goods and with beasts, besides freewill offerings for the house of God that is in Jerusalem." (Ezra 1:1–4)

Then, in Ezra 2, we read that fifty thousand people returned. Those who returned offered eleven hundred pounds of gold and six thousand pounds of silver (Ezra 2), and immediately began rebuilding the ruins of the altar and foundation of the temple (Ezra 3).

This is where the prophet Haggai picks up the story. He tells us that the Jews stopped rebuilding the house of the Lord (Ezra 4:24) and built their own homes instead (Hag. 1:3–11). The year was 520 BC, and the Lord had called Haggai to command the people to finish rebuilding the Lord's house.

First, Haggai confronted the complacency of the Jews in not rebuilding the temple (1:2–4). He spoke in the name of the "LORD of hosts" (v. 2), which should give us a clue that Israel was in for the rebuke of the law. This title is used fourteen times in Haggai, and like its use more than two hundred times elsewhere in Scripture, it has the intention of explaining the Lord's anger, judgment, and kingly right to rebuke His people. It declared that He is the Lord of the heavenly armies and would come in judgment on the Israelites if they remained disobedient.

God referred to Israel as "these people" (v. 2a), not the expected, "My people." This was a sign of His displeasure, because "these people" were saying "the time has not yet come to rebuild the house of the LORD" (v. 2b). "These people" had become complacent with the work of the Lord; therefore, the Lord asked them, "Is it a time for you yourselves to dwell in your paneled houses, while this house lies in ruins?" (v. 4). Their complacency was a result of their priorities, which were nothing but selfish, and therefore idolatrous.

Israel's complacency led Haggai to pronounce the curse for not rebuilding (vv. 5–6, 9–11). While "these people" said, "The time has not yet come to rebuild," the Lord said, "Consider your ways" (v. 5). Literally, the Lord said, "Set your hearts upon your ways" (*siymu levavchem al-darecheychem*; cf. Hag. 1:7). The issue was their hearts and attitudes.

Because their hearts were complacent, selfish, and idolatrous, the Lord sent the curses of the old covenant from Leviticus 26 and Deuteronomy 28 upon them: "You have sown much, and harvested little. You eat, but

28

you never have enough; you drink, but you never have your fill. You clothe yourselves, but no one is warm. And he who earns wages does so to put them into a bag with holes" (v. 6). The Lord sent the covenant judgments of poor harvest (Deut. 28:38–40), insufficient food (Deut. 28:48), and drought (Deut. 28:23–24). In their complacency, their lives had become characterized by consumerism. Although they worked hard and played harder, they never had enough. The curse was pronounced and summarized in Haggai 1:9 and 1:11 with a pun: while the Lord's house lay in "ruins" (*charav*), so Israel's land suffered "drought" (*chorev*).

In the midst of all of this, Haggai, speaking in the name of the Lord, gave the command to rebuild (vv. 7–8). "These people" were humbled by the law and now were called to repentance: "Consider your ways." They were to change their heart attitudes from complacence to performance, and rebuild what they had started so many years before. Notice the verbs used in verse 8: "go up . . . bring . . . build." Why? It was not to earn their salvation or to do some sort of penance, but to set things in their proper order: Israel the servant would bring honor to her King. As the Lord said, giving two reasons for rebuilding, "That I may take pleasure in it and that I may be glorified."

Repentance leads to good works, and so Haggai describes for us the Israelites' commitment to rebuild: everyone "obeyed the voice of the Lord their God," and "feared the Lord" (1:12), and everyone "worked on the house of the Lord of hosts, their God" (v. 14). As Matthew Henry said, "A holy fear of God will have a great influence upon our obedience to him."[48] To fear the Lord is to acknowledge one's sin, to turn from it in true repentance, and to commit oneself to the Word of God.

Finally, Haggai pronounced comfort during the rebuilding. After they were humbled by the law, moved to repentance, and began living in obedience as they worked on the house of the Lord, the Lord spoke a word of comfort, a word of gospel: "I am with you" (v. 13).

Here is the most wonderful thing. While they rebuilt the Lord's house, the people were only rebuilding something like a child's model of a temple to come. They were providing an illustration of what the Lord would do when He made His advent on this earth, when "the latter glory of this house shall be greater than the former" (Hag. 2:9).

The Coming of the Lord

With the coming of the Lord, the idea of God dwelling among His people became personal. In the words of John, "And the Word became flesh and *dwelt* among us" (John 1:14a, emphasis added). The connection between the word *skēnē*, translated here as "dwelt," and the Old Testament tabernacle is clear, as the Septuagint used the same word for "tabernacle" or "tent."[49] This is why John could write of Jesus: "And we have seen his glory" (John 1:14b). Jesus was the glory of God that filled the temple in human form.

This was not an abstract idea, but a personal reality, so much so that John could also write: "That which was from the beginning, which we have heard, which we have seen with our eyes, which we looked upon and have touched with our hands, concerning the word of life—the life was made manifest, and we have seen it, and testify to it and proclaim to you the eternal life, which was with the Father and was made manifest to us" (1 John 1:1–2).

When the Lord came to earth, He also explicitly pronounced Himself to be the reality of the temple, saying, "Destroy this temple, and in three days I will raise it up" (John 2:19). Later, He told the Samaritan woman at the well: "The hour is coming when neither on this mountain nor in Jerusalem will you worship the Father. . . . But the hour is coming, and now is here, when the true worshipers will worship the Father in spirit and truth" (John 4:21, 23). Since Jesus is the temple, this true worship occurs whenever just two or three are gathered together in His name (Matt. 18:20) and wherever His people are found among all the nations of the earth (Zeph. 2:11b; Mal. 1:11).

God's Dwelling in the Church

The Lord still dwells among His people. Despite His ascension into heaven, He promised His church, "And behold, I am with you always, to the end of the age" (Matt. 28:20). Because God still dwells among His people, the Apostle Paul tells us that Jews and Gentiles alike, who belong to Jesus Christ, are now members in God's household (Eph. 2:19), which has Christ as its cornerstone, the Apostles and prophets as its foundation, and believers as the living stones that God uses to build it (vv. 20–22; cf. 1 Peter 2:5). Thus, in this age, the church of Jesus Christ is the living temple of God by the Spirit in the world. Whereas the dwelling for God by the Spirit was once in lifeless materials of wood, stone, and metal, now it is in the living people of the Lord.

In the book of Revelation, John also describes the church as having been redeemed in order to become the new temple of God. Just as Israel's first exodus involved the Lord's victory over the gods of Egypt (Ex. 12:12), leading to His setting up His dwelling among His people, so John describes our redemption using this imagery of "the Song of Moses"— exodus, victory, and God dwelling among us (Rev. 15:3–4). As Paul says elsewhere, God's dwelling is now among the church corporately (1 Cor. 3:9–17; cf. 2 Cor. 6:16–18) and individually (1 Cor. 6:19).

The church, then, is the tabernacle, temple, and dwelling place of God. In the words of 1 Peter 2:4–10, we are the living stones Christ uses to build His new temple. The gathering of the stones means local church assemblies are temples of worship (v. 5) and places where His witness to the world goes out (v. 10). We are also the priests (vv. 5, 9) who assemble in this temple to offer sacrifices that are acceptable to the Lord (v. 5; cf. Rom. 12:2; Heb. 13:15). All of this is true on the basis of the work of Christ, who has sent His Spirit to His church in this age. Thus, the temple and its sacrifices are now "spiritual," that is, created by and in reliance on the Holy Spirit.

OUR RESPONSE

As we read the tabernacle story in light of the above, how should we respond to what God teaches us? Our first response must be to pray that the Holy Spirit will open our eyes, just as He did with the disciples of

Jesus on the Emmaus Road in Luke 24. Hilary of Poitiers exemplified this response when he offered this prayer in one of his writings: "Our minds are born with dull and clouded vision, our feeble intellect is penned within the barriers of an impassable ignorance concerning things Divine; but the study of Thy revelation elevates our soul to the comprehension of sacred truth, and submission to the faith is the path to a certainty beyond the reach of unassisted reason."[50] In the historical Reformed liturgies of the sixteenth century, the "prayer for illumination" was an important element of worship. For example, in Martin Bucer's Strassburg Liturgy of 1539, he prayed the following:

> Almighty, gracious Father, forasmuch as our whole salvation depends upon our true understanding of thy holy Word, grant to all of us that our hearts, being freed from worldly affairs, may hear and apprehend thy holy Word with all diligence and faith, that we may rightly understand thy gracious will, cherish it, and live by it with all earnestness, to thy praise and honor; through our Lord Jesus Christ. Amen.[51]

In the liturgy of the Dutch Reformed Churches, first published in the 1566 Psalter of Petrus Dathenus, the minister would pray:

> O heavenly Father, Thy Word is perfect, restoring the soul, making wise the simple, and enlightening the eyes of the blind, and a power of God unto salvation for every one that believes. We, however, are by nature blind and incapable of doing anything good, and Thou wilt succor only those who have a broken and contrite heart and who revere Thy Word. We beseech Thee, therefore, that Thou wilt illumine our darkened minds with Thy Holy Spirit and give us a humble heart, free from all haughtiness and carnal wisdom, in order that we, hearing Thy Word, may rightly understand it and may regulate our lives accordingly.[52]

We need to plead for the Holy Spirit to work on us and in us like this as we read the tabernacle story.

Our second response must be to pray that the Holy Spirit will transform us more and more into the image of Jesus Christ. In the words of *The Book of Common Prayer*, we need to pray to the Lord, "That it may please thee to give to all thy people increase of grace to hear meekly thy Word, and to receive it with pure affection, and to bring forth the fruits of the Spirit; we beseech thee to hear us, good Lord."[53] Paul contrasted the blindness of those who read the Old Testament in an unbelieving way with those whose eyes have been opened (2 Cor. 3:16). This opening comes from the Lord through the power of His Spirit, who also transforms us more and more: "Now the Lord is the Spirit, and where the Spirit of the Lord is, there is freedom. And we all, with unveiled face, beholding the glory of the Lord, are being transformed into the same image from one degree of glory to another. For this comes from the Lord who is the Spirit" (2 Cor. 3:17–18).

Our third response must be to seek to know the Lord experientially through the Word. We must not read the Word merely for information's sake, but that we might be drawn closer and closer, face to face, with our Lord in the bond of covenant fellowship. Jesus expressed this when He spoke of abiding in Him by faith and abiding in His words: "If you abide in me, and my words abide in you" (John 15:7). To know the Lord, to be "in me," goes together with knowing His Word; to know His Word is to know Him.

Our fourth and final response must be to seek to experience the love of God in Jesus Christ as we read and meditate on the tabernacle story. Our prayer must be Paul's prayer for the Ephesians:

> For this reason I bow my knees before the Father, from whom every family in heaven and on earth is named, that according to the riches of his glory he may grant you to be strengthened with power through his Spirit in your inner being, so that Christ may

dwell in your hearts through faith—that you, being rooted and grounded in love, may have strength to comprehend with all the saints what is the breadth and length and height and depth, and to know the love of Christ that surpasses knowledge, that you may be filled with all the fullness of God. (Eph. 3:14–19)

As you read and meditate on the tabernacle narratives with me, I pray that you may come to see that it is not something obscure that happened thousands of years ago. Instead, I pray you will read these narratives as *your* family story. This is how Peter challenged his readers throughout Asia Minor, which was hundreds of miles from Jerusalem, in the middle of the first century, several decades after our Lord's ministry. He said that the Holy Spirit had revealed to the prophets "that they were serving not themselves but you, in the things that have now been announced to you through those who preached the good news to you by the Holy Spirit sent from heaven, things into which angels long to look" (1 Peter 1:12).

Ultimately, we need to meditate on this, our family story, because we have the same God as our forefathers. The same God who said to them, "I may dwell in their midst" (Ex. 25:8), says to us today, "In [Christ] you also are being built together into a dwelling place for God by the Spirit" (Eph. 2:22). Just as He did for our forefathers, God has come to dwell among us that we might have a relationship with Him based on His amazing grace.

CONTRIBUTIONS TO
BUILD THE TABERNACLE

Exodus 25:1–7; 35:4–29

The Lᴏʀᴅ said to Moses, "Speak to the people of Israel, that they take for me a contribution. From every man whose heart moves him you shall receive the contribution for me. And this is the contribution that you shall receive from them: gold, silver, and bronze, blue and purple and scarlet yarns and fine twined linen, goats' hair, tanned rams' skins, goatskins, acacia wood, oil for the lamps, spices for the anointing oil and for the fragrant incense, onyx stones, and stones for setting, for the ephod and for the breastpiece." (Ex. 25:1–7)

"Grace is free, airtime isn't." I remember Michael Horton making this statement on the radio program *The White Horse Inn* back when I was in college.[1] It was a witty way to let listeners know that the show could not continue without the financial support of those who listened. As anyone involved in any nonprofit service knows, he was right. In order for Christians to build anything that will spread the good news of Jesus Christ, whether a radio program, a magazine, or a church building, we need to join in sacrificial giving.

The situation was the same with our Israelite forefathers in the wilderness. The Israelites knew that their God had created everything out of nothing (Gen. 1:1). Because of that, He owns the cattle on a thousand hills and does not need man's gifts (Ps. 50:10). Therefore, God could have created a house for His name out of nothing. Yet God determined that the tabernacle was to be created through the ordinary means of His people's giving. For this reason, the tabernacle narratives do not begin with a mallet, chisel, or measuring line, but with an offering plate.

As we begin our meditations on the tabernacle, we turn to Exodus 25:1–7 and its parallel in Exodus 35:4–29. These sections teach us about Israel's contributions to build the tabernacle. Three truths in these passages teach us much about our giving in the church today: the motivation, the ministry, and the materials.

THE MOTIVATION

First, we learn about the *motivation* for the contributions. The Lord instructed Moses (Ex. 25:1) to command the people to give a contribution (v. 2, *terumah*), that is, some portion of their possessions that was dedicated for sacred service.[2] This is what we call, in common Christian parlance, an offering. But in calling for a contribution, the Lord made clear that it was to be driven by a right motivation. It was to come "from every man whose heart moves him" (v. 2). Those whose hearts had been stirred by the plagues on the Egyptians, the exodus from Egypt, and the Red Sea crossing would want to give freely.

We see another beautiful picture of this in the example of David and Israel. Just before the building of the temple of the LORD, there was another offering. David made a contribution "because of my devotion to the house of my God" (1 Chron. 29:3). Next, he challenged the people to be generous, asking, "Who then will offer willingly, consecrating himself today to the LORD?" (v. 5) We then read of Israel's "freewill offerings" (v. 6) and of their joy in giving them: "Then the people rejoiced because they had given willingly, for with a whole heart they had offered freely to the LORD" (v. 9).

Digging deeper, we are struck by the language in Exodus 35:4–29. This section begins, "This is the thing that the LORD has commanded" (v. 4). Thus, there is a wonderful juxtaposition of what we normally think of as two contradictory ideas: heartfelt offering and God's command. We see these two ideas in the last verse of this passage, which says that the people brought what "the LORD had commanded by Moses . . . as a freewill offering to the LORD" (v. 29). All too often, we set up in our minds a contrast between duty and delight when it comes to serving the Lord. For instance, we contrast form and freedom when it comes to liturgy and worship as if form quenches all freedom or as if freedom cannot have form. But according to this text, there is no contradiction between what we must do and what we want to do as God's people. The movement of the Israelites' redeemed hearts to give the Lord an offering was in complete unison with the Lord's will for their lives.

This is how the Christian life routinely works for the regenerated and justified child of God. Paul says it like this: "But thanks be to God, that you who were once slaves of sin have become obedient from the heart to the standard of teaching to which you were committed, and, having been set free from sin, have become slaves of righteousness . . . slaves of God" (Rom. 6:17–18, 22). We once did not serve God and in fact *could not* serve Him because of our rebellious hearts (Rom. 8:7–8), but now that He has taken hold of us we can and want to serve Him according to His commands in His Word. We have become "obedient from the heart." Because of the Lord's grace that has changed our lives, we can now delight in the duties of the Lord, which *The Book of Common Prayer* says "is perfect freedom."[3]

We see this theme expressed in much more detail in Exodus 35. We read that "whoever is of a generous heart" (v. 5) was to bring an offering. Giving was to be with full willingness and generosity. As John Calvin (1509–1564) said of this passage, "All Scripture teaches us that no obedience is pleasing to God except what is voluntary."[4] We then read that "everyone whose heart stirred him and everyone whose spirit moved him" (v. 21), and "all who were of a willing heart" (v. 22), gave to the offering.

For the people of God in the new covenant, giving is to be just as willing and generous. Paul writes:

> The point is this: whoever sows sparingly will also reap sparingly, and whoever sows bountifully will also reap bountifully. Each one must give as he has decided in his heart, not reluctantly or under compulsion, for God loves a cheerful giver. And God is able to make all grace abound to you, so that having all sufficiency in all things at all times, you may abound in every good work. As it is written, "He has distributed freely, he has given to the poor; his righteousness endures forever." He who supplies seed to the sower and bread for food will supply and multiply your seed for sowing and increase the harvest of your righteousness. You will be enriched in every way to be generous in every way, which through us will produce thanksgiving to God. (2 Cor. 9:6–11)

What moved the hearts of the Israelites to be willing and generous? It was the operation of the Holy Spirit, who applied the gracious work of God to their hearts. He saved them from Egypt (Exodus 1–14), He provided for them during their journey in the wilderness (Exodus 15–18), and He entered into a sacred covenant relationship with them (Exodus 19–24). In a word, grace led to gratitude; mercy moved their hearts. For the Israelites, then, the motivation for their contribution was their redemption from Egypt, from slavery, and from certain death.

It is the same with us: We "present [our] bodies as a living sacrifice, holy and acceptable to God" because of "the mercies of God" (Rom. 12:1). We give thanks to God because of the lavishness of the grace He has given to us (Eph. 1:8). Paul fleshes out this idea of mercy and grace for the Corinthians: "For you know the grace of our Lord Jesus

Christ, that though he was rich, yet for your sake he became poor, so that you by his poverty might become rich" (2 Cor. 8:9). Our motivation for giving is the grace of God in giving us His Son, Jesus Christ. There can be no other motivation; certainly not merit or compulsion. As the medieval commentator Bede the Venerable (672–735) said against the Pelagians, who believed man had the ability to save himself apart from God's grace: "We bring the firstfruits of our possessions to the Lord when, if we do anything good, we truthfully attribute it all to divine grace."[5] Our gratitude must be motivated by grace alone.

THE MINISTRY

Second, we learn about the *ministry* supported by the contributions. Moses' words taught the Israelites that by giving for the construction of the tabernacle, they were participating in its *ministry*. What does this mean?

Moses certainly did not mean what so much of popular Christianity believes today: that every member of the church is a minister in the church.[6] There is only one ministry, properly speaking, and that is the ministry of Word and sacrament. It is true that all members of Christ's church belong to the priesthood of believers, but this is not the same as the ministry. Likewise, although not all the Israelites were priests, all the Israelites participated in the ministry of the priesthood. The Jewish scholar Nahum Sarna (1923–2005), writing about the tabernacle narratives, said the tabernacle was "a cooperative enterprise" that involved all Israel, from the greatest to the weakest member.[7]

Moses writes that Israel's contributions of gold, silver, and bronze (Ex. 25:3), blue, purple, and scarlet yarns and fine twined linen (v. 4), goats' hair, tanned rams' skins, and goatskins (vv. 4–5), acacia wood (v. 5), oil (v. 6), spices (v. 6), and onyx stones and stones for setting (v. 7) were "to be used for the tent of meeting, and for all its service, and for the holy garments" (Ex. 35:21). As noted earlier, the Creator of the heavens and the earth did not need the Israelites' contributions to build a tabernacle. Paul states it in this way: "The God who made the world and everything in it, being Lord of heaven and earth, does not live in temples made by man, nor is he served by human hands, as though he needed anything, since he himself gives to all mankind life and breath and everything" (Acts 17:24–25). However, God chose to work through the means of the contributions of His people. Calvin pointed out that it was God who "daily rained down manna from heaven; yet he would have every one, from the very least to the greatest, bring together, in testimony of their piety, whatever was necessary for the sacred work."[8] He did not need them, but He invited them to participate in the ministry of the tabernacle.

We see this idea continued in the New Testament. As members of the priesthood of all believers, all believers have a vital function in the life of the Christian ministry. Paul describes the giving of the Philippians to support his work as a "partnership" in the gospel ministry: "I thank my God in all my remembrance of you, always in every prayer of mine for you all making my prayer with joy, because of *your partnership in the gospel* from the first day until now" (Phil. 1:3–5, emphasis added). Later, he says that besides the Philippians, "no church entered into *partnership with me* in giving and receiving, except you only" (Phil. 4:15, emphasis added). The Greek word that is translated as "partnership" in these verses is *koinōnia.* This word denotes fellowship, closeness, and an intimate relationship.[9] While not all believers are ministers, all believers participate in the ministries of their pastors.

What Exodus 25 and 35 and the Apostle Paul teach us, then, is that every member of the body of believers who gives of his or her talent, time, and treasure toward the ministry of the gospel, whether in the tabernacle, in Philippi, or today in the church, is a partner in the ministry. The Israelites' contributions were "to be used for the tent of meeting, and for all its service, and for the holy garments" (Ex. 35:21). While believers are taught in this passage that without the ministry there would be no church, this text also teaches ministers that without the members of the church there would be no one to minister to and no one to support ministers.

THE MATERIALS

Third, we learn about the *materials* that were contributed. The Lord commanded the Israelites to give "gold, silver, and bronze, blue and purple and scarlet yarns and fine twined linen, goats' hair, tanned rams' skins, goatskins,[10] acacia wood, oil for the lamps, spices for the anointing oil and for the fragrant incense, onyx stones, and stones for setting, for the ephod and for the breastpiece" (25:3–7). These offerings can be divided into seven distinct categories: metals, dyed yarns, fabrics, timber, oil, spices, and gems.[11] The metals of gold, silver, and bronze are listed in order of preciousness and from most expensive to least expensive. The yarns are also ordered this way.[12]

But how could former slaves in Egypt who had become nomads in the wilderness contribute such costly materials? The answer, again, is the lavish grace of God.

Before the night of the Passover, the Lord instructed the Israelites to ask their Egyptian neighbors "for silver and gold jewelry" (Ex. 11:2). When Israel left Egypt, "The people of Israel had also done as Moses told them, for they had asked the Egyptians for silver and gold jewelry and for clothing. And the Lord had given the people favor [*hēn*] in the sight of the Egyptians, so they let them have what they asked. Thus they plundered the Egyptians" (12:35–36).[13] By the favor, or grace, of the Lord, Israel received the wealth of Egypt. Also, on their journey, the Israelites engaged in a war against Amalek (17:8–16). Their success, no doubt, increased their plunder. All of these tangible materials were to be part of the offering the Israelites gave to build a glorious tabernacle that would be the house of God in their midst.[14]

How does this passage speak to us? What materials does the Lord use in the new covenant to build His "holy temple" (Eph. 2:21)? The materials used now are people—you and I. The New Testament clearly proclaims that the dwelling place of God is now the people of God. Peter writes, "You yourselves like living stones are being built up as a spiritual house" (1 Peter 2:5). Paul adds, "In him you also are being built together into a dwelling place for God by the Spirit" (Eph. 2:22). Elsewhere, Paul speaks of the church as the temple of God, citing Leviticus 26:12 and Isaiah 52:11:

> Do not be unequally yoked with unbelievers. For what partnership has righteousness with lawlessness? Or what fellowship has light with darkness? What accord has Christ with Belial? Or what portion does a believer share with an unbeliever? What agreement has the temple of God with idols? For we are the temple of the living God; as God said, "I will make my dwelling among them and walk among them, and I will be their God, and they shall be my people. Therefore go out from their midst, and be separate from them, says the Lord, and touch no unclean thing; then I will welcome you, and I will be a father to you, and you shall be sons and daughters to me, says the Lord Almighty." (2 Cor. 6:14–18)

There is more to the new-covenant fulfillment of the materials of the tabernacle. While the Exodus narratives speak of the Israelites building the house of God with their own hands, who now is described as the builder of the house of God? In the new covenant, God Himself is the builder of the tabernacle, the church:

> Therefore . . . consider Jesus . . . who was faithful to him who appointed him, just as Moses also was faithful in all God's house. For Jesus has been counted worthy of more glory than Moses—as much more glory as the builder of a house has more honor than the house itself. (For every house is built by someone, but the builder of all things is God.) Now Moses was faithful in all God's house as a servant, to testify to the things that were to be spoken later, but Christ is faithful over God's house as a son. And we are his house if indeed we hold fast our confidence and our boasting in our hope. (Heb. 3:1–6)

In light of these verses, I encourage you to examine your heart by reflecting on questions such as these: Am I a part of this house today? Have I died to myself that I might live to God? Have I turned away from living a life of sin and self, and turned to Jesus Christ to live a life for His glory and honor? If you can answer yes to these questions, you should be assured that you are a part of the Lord's tabernacle, in which He dwells among us. You are one of the living stones hewn out of the nations by God's grace alone.

If you are a member of Christ's house, Exodus 25 calls you to contribute to building the means of His dwelling today. Contribute willingly and generously to the church, being motivated by the gospel of Jesus Christ that has saved you from all of your sins. Contribute to the ministry of the church because you desire to partner with it in your locale and to see more and more living stones adorn its walls. Contribute because you are the very material with which the Lord Himself builds, with His own hands, His church throughout the world. As one writer stated it:

> New Testament Israelites are invited to bring gifts for the building of a greater temple than the tabernacle, and that all may enjoy the privilege of giving, the very smallest offerings are acceptable. As the hair and the skins brought by some who may not have had jewels to bestow were as necessary for the construction of the sacred structure as the more costly offerings of their richer brethren, so the coppers of the poor, or of little children, are as needful to assist in building the spiritual edifice as the sovereigns of the wealthy.[15]

Grace is free; therefore, freely give.

THE TABERNACLE
IN THE WILDERNESS

Exodus 25:8-9

"And let them make me a sanctuary, that I may dwell in their midst. Exactly as I show you concerning the pattern of the tabernacle, and of all its furniture, so you shall make it." (Ex. 25:8–9)

After leaving Egypt (Ex. 12:33–42), the Israelites travelled through the wilderness for a couple of months until they came to Mount Sinai. So Israel left Egypt geographically and chronologically, but they also needed to leave it spiritually and theologically. They had experienced the reality that they were the "treasured possession" of the Lord (Ex. 19:5), but they had no Bibles. They had become a "kingdom of priests" (Ex. 19:6), but they had no catechisms. They had become a "holy nation" (Ex. 19:6), but they had no Sunday school. How would the Lord teach a congregation that no doubt numbered two to three million souls (cf. Num. 1:45, 47) to leave behind the idolatry they had seen and experienced in Egypt, and to cling in faith to Him alone, having no other gods before Him (Ex. 20:3)? How would He instruct them to leave the false worship they had seen in Egypt and participate in the pure worship of God alone, having no carved images (Ex. 20:4)? The answer to these questions was the tabernacle.

The book of Hebrews tells us that the priests of the tabernacle ministered in "a copy [*hupodeigmati*] and shadow [*skia*] of the heavenly things" (Heb. 8:5; cf. 9:23). When the writer of this epistle says that the tabernacle was a copy and a shadow, he means that it was derived from something else. A copy is made from an original and a shadow is cast from something of substance.

In Hebrews 9:24, he says something even more telling: "holy places made with hands . . . are copies of the true things [*antitupa tōn alēthinonōn*]."[1] The tabernacle was, literally, an antitype. Behind an antitype is always its type. What is the type of the tabernacle? The apostolic author says the tabernacle is an antitype of the "true things."[2] The Greek word *alethinos* refers not to something that is true cognitively but to something that is true genuinely or ideally.[3] In this case, the genuine article is heaven: "For Christ has entered, not into holy places made with hands, which are copies of the true things, *but into heaven itself*" (v. 24a, emphasis added).

When you were a child, you no doubt drew pictures for your mother and father. Most likely you used crayons. However, your crayon drawing of your house was not really your house. It was just a drawing of what was genuine. In the tabernacle, God provided His people with a very large crayon drawing. It was designed to teach Israel about what it meant for God to dwell among them and to lift their hearts to heaven, to the reality of the tabernacle. Above all, the drawing was to help the people of God know Him. As Tremper Longman III says, "Even before we explore the Christological dimensions [of the text] we . . . learn more about the nature of God and our relationship with him."[4] All the narratives about the tabernacle and its furnishings, then, are "visual aids of spiritual realities."[5] God revealed Himself to sinners through the tabernacle to draw them into relationship with Himself.[6]

Of course, many argue that this is all just myth. After all, many temples were raised in the ancient Near East. For example, the ancient king of Lagash in Sumeria, Gudea, built a temple for the god Ningirsu after receiving its design in a dream. The Babylonian creation story, *Enuma elish*, includes the instructions for Marduk's temple. The Egyptians' temples have the same sort of history.[7] Like the tabernacle narratives, these stories taught that temples were divinely initiated.

But while we might be tempted to read Exodus as an account of another ancient religious building project, our story is different. As Nahum Sarna explains, ancient extra-biblical temple instructions were given in the context of existing earthly temples; one god would tell his followers to build him a temple according to the example of another god's temple. With this in mind, Sarna notes: "Our narrative, however, knows nothing of any prior history to the institution, which is presented as an innovation so unprecedented that without divine instructions, verbal and visual, it would be unintelligible. In other words, the narrative in this way deliberately disconnects and dissociates the Tabernacle from anything that is in Israel's world of experience."[8]

Thus, the tabernacle in the wilderness taught the Israelites new realities in God's redemptive plan for His people. Three key truths were communicated in this crayon drawing: holiness, helpfulness, and heavenliness. These realities are extremely relevant to us as new-covenant Christians, too, but as we will see, we no longer have merely a crayon drawing to aid our understanding, but the real thing itself.

HOLINESS

First, the tabernacle taught the people about *holiness*. God said, "Let them make me a sanctuary" (Ex. 25:8). The Hebrew term for "sanctuary" (*miqdash*) denotes that the tabernacle was a holy place. The book of Hebrews tells us, "Even the first covenant had regulations for worship and an earthly place of holiness" (Heb. 9:1). The tabernacle was that "earthly place of holiness" (*hagion kosmikon*), because, as we saw above, it was a copy and shadow of the genuine place of holiness, heaven.

47

But if the tabernacle was just an "earthly place," how did it communicate lessons about holiness. It did so in three ways.

First, the tabernacle taught the people about holiness because it was the place of God's holy presence in their midst. In Exodus 26–40, the word *holy* is used forty-eight times. Holiness was the theme of this building project. Its holiness, though, was found not in itself but in the Lord alone: "And let them make me a sanctuary that I may dwell in their midst" (Ex. 25:8). Apart from the Lord, the tabernacle was merely a tent. It was like the lifeless clay the Lord God formed into the shape of a man before breathing into it His breath of life (Gen. 2:7); like a valley of dry bones with no souls within (Ezek. 37:1–17); and like a whitewashed sepulcher with only dead men's bones inside (Matt. 23:27). The tabernacle was holy when God's presence filled it. Thus, the people learned that God Himself is holy.

Second, the tabernacle taught about holiness by its placement. In the camp of the Israelites, there were concentric circles of increasing holiness, from the unholy places outside the camp to the inner sanctum of the Holy of Holies at the center of the camp. Outside the camp was the place of the unholy peoples, including those Israelites rendered ritually unclean (e.g., Lev. 13:45–46). Inside the camp was where the holy nation dwelt. Then, behind the curtain of the tabernacle courtyard was a holier place. The Holy Place and the Most Holy Place, that is, the Holy of Holies, were each holier still.[9] This arrangement taught the people that God in His holiness is different from fallen man.

It also was meant to communicate to the Israelites that although they were journeying through the wilderness, Mount Sinai was still in their midst. As Sarna says, the tabernacle was "a living extension of Mount Sinai."[10] At Sinai, the people had gathered at the foot of the mountain (Ex. 19:20–25), the elders had ascended to the middle of the mountain (24:1–8), and Moses had ascended to the top (19:20). Likewise, the people were permitted access to the courtyard, the priests to the Holy Place, and the high priest to the Holy of Holies. In fact, the ancient expositor Theodoret of Cyrus said one of the reasons God commanded the tabernacle was to represent earth and heaven to His people. Just as there is the earth, the firmament (sky), and heaven, so there is the Holy Place, the veil, and the Holy of Holies.[11]

Third, the tabernacle taught the people about holiness by means of the materials used in its construction. Again, moving from the tabernacle's exterior to its interior, we find concentric circles of ever-increasing worth, preciousness, and, thus, holiness. The outer court had an unadorned curtain and the courtyard furniture used bronze sockets with wood poles. But inside the Holy Place, the materials were pure gold and silver. Finally, the Holy of Holies housed the ark, which was overlaid with pure gold inside and out.[12] Thus, the people of Israel learned that holiness is of surpassing worth. All of this taught the holy nation of Israel that their Lord was a holy God.

Yet the holiness of the tabernacle did not end there. God did not set up the tabernacle merely to be gazed upon as a spectacle. Its holiness—His holiness—was meant to affect His people practically. When they saw and participated in the tabernacle's services, the Lord intended to teach them the necessity of worshiping Him in holiness: "Among those who are near me I will be sanctified, and before all the people I will be glorified" (Lev. 10:3). The psalmist would later summarize what God wanted to teach the people: "Worship the LORD in the splendor of holiness; tremble before him, all the earth!" (Ps. 96:9).

He also intended to teach them the necessity of being holy themselves. The Lord applied all of this to His people when He said: "For I am the LORD your God. Consecrate yourselves therefore, and be holy, for I am holy. You shall not defile yourselves with any swarming thing that crawls on the ground. For I am the LORD who brought you up out of the land of Egypt to be your God. You shall therefore be holy, for I am holy" (Lev. 11:44–45). The tabernacle taught that God is holy; therefore, His people need to be holy. In other words, theology had to become biography. Theology, what we believe about God, still must become personal.

What God intended to teach His people then, He also desires to teach His people today. In particular, when we assemble for worship under the new covenant, we still go to the tabernacle to worship in heaven:

For you have not come to what may be touched, a blazing fire and darkness and gloom and a tempest and the sound of a trumpet and a voice whose words made the hearers beg that no further messages be spoken to them. For they could not endure the order that was given, "If even a beast touches the mountain, it shall be stoned." Indeed, so terrifying was the sight that Moses said, "I tremble with fear." But you have come to Mount Zion and to the city of the living God, the heavenly Jerusalem, and to innumerable angels in festal gathering, and to the assembly of the firstborn who are enrolled in heaven, and to God, the judge of all, and to the spirits of the righteous made perfect, and to Jesus, the mediator of a new covenant, and to the sprinkled blood that speaks a better word than the blood of Abel. (Heb. 12:18–24)

We still worship a holy God in a holy manner: "Therefore let us be grateful for receiving a kingdom that cannot be shaken, and thus let us offer to God acceptable worship, with reverence and awe, for our God is a consuming fire" (Heb. 12:28–29). Worshiping in the heavenly tabernacle also teaches us more clearly and thoroughly how holy our God is and how important holiness is for us. Are you striving for "the holiness without which no one will see the Lord" (Heb. 12:14)? Do you seek to be "holy in all your conduct" since "he who called you is holy" (1 Peter 1:15)? As those who come to the heavenly tabernacle, you must.

HELPFULNESS

Second, the tabernacle taught the people their only source of *help*. As we saw above, the term *sanctuary* (*miqdash*) meant that the tabernacle was the place where God's holiness was located and accessed. Another of the terms for this structure is "tent of meeting" (*'ohel moed*), which appears thirty-five times in the book of Exodus. One example is Exodus 29:42. In speaking of the morning and evening sacrifice of two lambs, the Lord said, "It shall be a regular burnt offering throughout your generations at the entrance of the tent of meeting before the LORD, where I will meet with you, to speak to you there." The Lord gave the tabernacle to His people not only to exhibit His holiness and their need to be holy, but also as a means by which He could meet with them to help their unholiness.

This is yet another indication that the story of Scripture is about how human beings, who were expelled from the presence of God in the garden of Eden after the fall of Adam and Eve, can return to the garden and dwell once again with God.[13] The tabernacle expressed visibly what the Old Testament taught verbally: "And let them make me a sanctuary, that I may dwell in their midst" (Ex. 25:8; cf. Ex. 29:45; Lev. 26:11–12; Ezek. 37:27; Zech. 2:10). The New Testament teaches that living in the presence of God is the fruit of our relationship with God through Christ, a relationship that will culminate in the new heavens and new earth (2 Cor. 6:16; Rev. 21:3).

Meeting with His people was God's way of helping them in their sins, ignorance, and disobedience. But how exactly was the tabernacle helpful?

First, it provided a tangible way for the people to relate to their God through sacrifice and prayer. The tabernacle was a way of re-creating the situation that existed in the garden of Eden, where the Lord God dwelt with His people, Adam and Eve.[14] Thus, the tabernacle was His way of bringing them to that original peace and fellowship with Him. John Calvin described this help when he said that although God "could not be enclosed in the tabernacle . . . in His indulgence for the infirmities of an ignorant people, He desired to testify the presence of His grace and help by a visible symbol."[15] As the Lord's son (Ex. 4:22), Israel needed its Father's help.

Second, the tabernacle taught the people about God's gracious condescension to them. The Israelites, who dwelt in tents (Ex. 16:16), now had their God in a tent alongside them. As Geerhardus Vos wrote, the tabernacle was "to satisfy God's desire to have a mutual identification of lot between Himself and them." Further, it "helps us to feel somewhat of the inner warmth and God-centered affection."[16] The Hebrew word *mishkan*, used by God to say, "I may *dwell* in their midst" (Ex. 25:8), has the connotation of a temporary dwelling such as nomads used.[17] This means that the Lord of Israel, the God of the universe, had become a pilgrim alongside His people in the desert.

The Lord had made this promise before. When Jacob had his dream of the staircase that spanned heaven and earth, with angels ascending and descending it, we read, "And behold, the LORD stood above it" (Gen. 28:13), meaning that God stood above the staircase. All of our English translations render this verse this way, yet some include a marginal note saying that this verse can also be translated "the LORD stood *beside* him." The phrase used here (*nitsav 'alayv*) is used elsewhere in Genesis and Exodus to speak of intimate closeness, of being beside someone (Gen. 18:2; 24:13; Ex. 18:14).[18] Hence, Jacob exclaimed, "Surely the Lord is in this place" (Gen. 28:16). The Lord did not come to Jacob as *El Shaddai*, God Almighty, as He did in Abram's dream (Gen. 17:1), but as the Lord. He came and stood next to Jacob, speaking words of gracious comfort, affirming to Jacob that his was the chosen line and that He would do everything He had promised. Then the Lord applied this promise, saying: "I am with you and will keep you wherever you go, and will bring you back to this land. For I will not leave you" (Gen. 28:15a). When Jacob was disillusioned by life's hard circumstances, when he was running because of his sin, when he was as far from God as he could get, his Savior was right next to him. He heard a wonderful promise of help, and Israel could see the same promise in the tabernacle: "I am with you."

New-covenant Christians also need this help. The tabernacle of Israel proclaims to us that God is near to us and available for us, but the New Testament tells us that God incarnate is an even more present help in trouble: "Therefore he had to be made like his brothers in every respect, so that he might become a merciful and faithful high priest in the service of God, to make propitiation for the sins of the people. For because he himself has suffered when tempted, he is able to help those who are being tempted" (Heb. 2:17–18). To seek His help, simply follow the words of Hebrews 4:16, which say to all of us, "Let us then with confidence draw near to the throne of grace, that we may receive mercy and find grace to help in time of need." You may be thinking, "But I am a sinner." What is your sin? Know that the Lord is near in grace. What is your burden? Experience His gracious nearness through prayer. What is your struggle? Go and approach Him in prayer and trust.

HEAVENLINESS

Third, the tabernacle taught the people about *heaven*. The pious worshiper would leave his tent somewhere in the Israelite camp to draw near to the Lord in the tabernacle. He would approach the curtain between the camp and the courtyard, then move into the courtyard itself. By doing this, he would move from earth to heaven, from this age to the life of the world to come.[19] If the worshiper happened to see the curtain that separated the Holy Place from the courtyard moved away by a ministering priest or by the wind, he would glimpse again the beautiful colors, the golden brilliance, and the smoke that he had seen on Sinai. Even more, he would see the cherubim on the inner curtain, guarding the way into the Holy of Holies, just as the cherubim guarded the gate east of Eden (Gen. 3:24).

Our text emphasizes the heavenliness of the tabernacle when it says God told the people to build it "exactly as I show you concerning the pattern" (Ex. 25:9). Of this phrase, the medieval English theologian Bede, likely writing with Hebrews 9:24 in mind, said, "Thus the tabernacle that was shown to Moses on the mountain is that heavenly city and celestial homeland."[20] The tabernacle revealed a picture of heaven (cf. 1 Chron. 28:11–19).

Thus, as we have seen, the tabernacle was a copy of the authentic article, a shadow of something of substance, an earthly picture of the heavenly reality. In studying the tabernacle, we meditate on a crayon drawing that our souls might have the benefit of the genuine article. This leads us to contemplate the reality of the shadow, the heavenly that has come to take the place of the earthly. As Stephen said in his only recorded sermon: "The Most High does not dwell in houses made by hands, as the prophet says, 'Heaven is my throne, and the earth is my footstool. What kind of house will you build for me, says the Lord, or what is the place of my rest? Did not my hand make all these things?'" (Acts 7:48–50).

The tabernacle narrative in Exodus 25:8–9 is a part of that law that is "but a shadow of the good things to come" (Heb. 10:1). Now, those things have come. The tabernacle testified to the souls of believing Israelites that a holy God would one day come and dwell in the midst of sinners to remove their sins. It testified that the world of sinners needs the help only the Lord can give. It testified that God had to come to earth from heaven, that we who are on the earth might be brought to heaven. In short, the tabernacle testified of Jesus Christ.

Our Lord Jesus Christ is the fulfillment of the tabernacle. He said of Himself, "something greater than the temple is here" (Matt. 12:6), while His beloved disciple, the Apostle John, said so dramatically of Him, "And the Word became flesh and dwelt [that is, "tabernacled"] among us" (John 1:14).[21] The tabernacle was one of the "precious and very great promises" (2 Peter 1:4) that the Old Testament made concerning the coming incarnation of God Himself.[22] In the words of Herman Witsius:

> Amongst the precious promises with which the God of heaven was graciously pleased to favour the people of Israel, that in which he assured them that he should "walk in the midst of them," is entitled to hold a distinguished place. The Lord made good this promise in various ways, and by several steps. 1st, He caused the tabernacle of the congregation to be erected, and the ark of the testimony and covenant to be made, and gave them to Israel as symbols of his special presence.[23]

The ultimate fulfillment of the promise, of course, was the coming of the Lord in the flesh. Do you see Him today even clearer than the psalmist? "One thing have I asked of the LORD, that will I seek after: that I may dwell in the house of the LORD all the days of my life, to gaze upon the beauty of the LORD and to inquire in his temple" (Ps. 27:4). Does your heart cry out for Him in a greater way than the psalmist? "As a deer pants for flowing streams, so pants my soul for you, O God. My soul thirsts for God, for the living God. When shall I come and appear before God?" (Ps. 42:1–2). Do you long for Him as the psalmist? "O God, you are my God; earnestly I seek you; my soul thirsts for you; my flesh faints for you, as in a dry and weary land where there is no water. So I have looked upon you in the sanctuary, beholding your power and glory" (Ps. 63:1–2). Do you desire to be with Jesus as the psalmist wanted to be with the Lord? "Whom have I in heaven but you? And there is nothing on earth that I desire besides you. My flesh and my heart may fail, but God is the strength of my heart and my portion forever" (Ps. 73:25–26).

The tabernacle was God's drawing to His people then; now we have this image in flesh and blood—Jesus Christ.

THE ARK
OF THE COVENANT

Exodus 25:10-22; 37:1-9

"They shall make an ark of acacia wood. Two cubits and a half shall be its length, a cubit and a half its breadth, and a cubit and a half its height. You shall overlay it with pure gold, inside and outside shall you overlay it, and you shall make on it a molding of gold around it. You shall cast four rings of gold for it and put them on its four feet, two rings on the one side of it, and two rings on the other side of it. You shall make poles of acacia wood and overlay them with gold. And you shall put the poles into the rings on the sides of the ark to carry the ark by them. The poles shall remain in the rings of the ark; they shall not be taken from it. And you shall put into the ark the testimony that I shall give you. You shall make a mercy seat of pure gold. Two cubits and a half shall be its length, and a cubit and a half its breadth. And you shall make two cherubim of gold; of hammered work shall you make them, on the two ends of the mercy seat. Make one cherub on the one end, and one cherub on the other end. Of one piece with the mercy seat shall you make the cherubim on its two ends. The cherubim shall spread out their wings above, overshadowing the mercy seat with their wings, their faces one to another; toward the mercy seat shall the faces of the cherubim be. And you shall put the mercy seat on the top of

57

the ark, and in the ark you shall put the testimony that I shall give you. There I will meet with you, and from above the mercy seat, from between the two cherubim that are on the ark of the testimony, I will speak with you about all that I will give you in commandment for the people of Israel." (Ex. 25:10–22)

We normally save the best for last. Doing so adds excitement and suspense to our lives. For example, during Christmas, we exchange many gifts, but we usually hold back the most meaningful gifts to be opened last. When we read well-written books, we know the drama will keep building until the climactic conclusion brings it to a resolution, so we resist the temptation to read the end until we have read what comes before. Even our Lord Jesus Christ operated this way. He once attended a wedding in Cana in Galilee. When all the wine at the reception had been drunk, our Lord turned water into wine. The master of the feast then tasted it and said to the bridegroom, whom he thought had provided the wine: "Everyone serves the good wine first, and when people have drunk freely, then the poor wine. But you have kept the good wine [*kalon oinon*] until now" (John 2:1–11).

What does saving the best for last have to do with the tabernacle? Remember, as an Israelite approached the tabernacle, he first came to a white curtain that encircled the courtyard. As he entered the courtyard, the first thing he saw was an elevated bronze altar and, beyond that, a bronze basin for ritual washing. Then there was the tabernacle itself, with its tall curtain. Inside was the table of bread on the right and the menorah for light on the left. Straight ahead was the altar of incense, then the veil embroidered with cherubim. Last of all, concealed behind the veil, where no Israelite except the high priest might go one day each year, was the ark of the covenant (*'aron berith*), also called "the ark of the covenant of the Lord" (Deut. 10:8, *'aron berith YHWH*). This was the last piece of furniture seen in the tabernacle, and its most important.

Yet even though the ark was the last thing a visitor to the tabernacle would encounter, it was not the last thing the Lord mentioned in the instructions for the tabernacle. After saying to Moses, "Let them make for me a sanctuary" (Ex. 25:8), God began to give the instructions for the tabernacle in the rest of chapters 25 through 31. The most important piece of furniture in the tabernacle, the ark of the covenant, was not saved for last; it was listed *first*. It got the prime place in the narrative.[1] Nahum Sarna notes this when he writes that the tabernacle instruction narrative moves from the inside of the tabernacle to the outside and from the most important parts to the least important parts.[2]

Such arks were important pieces of furniture in other ancient religions surrounding the Israelites.[3] In other cultures, though, the arks contained images of their deities. In Israel, the only objects within the ark of the covenant were those God provided and commanded—a sample of the manna with which the Lord fed the Israelites (Ex. 16:32–34; Heb. 9:4), Aaron's staff that budded with almonds (Num. 17:1–11; Heb. 9:4), and the tablets of the law (Ex. 25:16, 21; 40:20; Deut. 10:2; 31:26; Heb. 9:4). The placing of the tablets of "the testimony" (*ha 'edut*) within the ark mirrored the common legal practice in the ancient world of storing national treaties in sacred arks, testifying to the documents' importance and signifying that the deities witnessed to the terms and implemented the stipulations.[4] In ancient practice, a copy of such a treaty was placed in the sacred place of the lesser kingdom that offered itself in obedience to the greater kingdom. In Israel, the astounding truth was that both copies were kept at the Lord's feet in the ark, testifying that the Lord would be the covenant-keeper in His relationship with Israel.[5] He entered a covenant with them on the basis of His grace (Deut. 7:6–8). He would keep them in that covenant on the basis of His grace (Jer. 31:3).

Why was this ark so important that it was listed as the first piece of furniture in the tabernacle of the Israelites? Moreover, why is it important for us to understand this and to appropriate it to our spiritual benefit? The ark was important, both for the Israelites and for us, because it was the place of presence, the place of propitiation, and the place of pleading.

THE PLACE OF PRESENCE

First, the ark of the covenant was *the place of presence*. While the Lord was present among His people in the exodus (Ex. 13:17–18, 21–22), He localized this presence in the tabernacle for the benefit of His sinful people. As we have seen, the tabernacle was constructed so that the Lord would be among His people: "And let them make me a sanctuary, that I may dwell in their midst" (Ex. 25:8). But in an even more specific way, the ark served as the place of the presence of God. As we read in our text,

THE ARK OF THE COVENANT

The ark of the covenant (Ex. 25:10–22; 37:1–9) was the only piece of furniture in the Most Holy Place; the ark and its contents were kept hidden from view at all times. The ark itself was a wooden chest, overlaid with pure gold, measuring 3.75 feet long, 2.25 feet wide, and 2.25 feet high (1.1 m x 0.7 m x 0.7 m). It contained within it the two stone tablets of the testimony (the Ten Commandments). The author of Hebrews adds that it also contained "a golden urn holding the manna, and Aaron's staff that budded" (Heb. 9:4). The ark was not to be touched by human hands. Two wooden poles, overlaid with gold, were used to transport it and were not to be removed from the ark. The mercy seat, or atonement cover, was a solid golden slab that fitted perfectly on top of the ark. The golden cherubim, which were hammered out of the same piece of gold, had wings outstretched over the mercy seat and faces that looked downward (in reverent awe). It was here, from between the cherubim, that God spoke to Moses, the representative of the people of Israel. Ancient iconography often depicts cherubim as having a lion-like body, wings, and a human face.

From *ESV Study Bible*, ©2008.
All rights reserved.

"*There* I will meet with you . . . *on* the ark of the testimony, I will speak with you" (Ex. 25:22; emphasis added).

Here is such a mind-blowing idea about the God of the Bible that we have to pause for a moment. The eternal God who is not constrained by the existence of time, the infinite God who is not bound by the constraints of space, the transcendent God who dwells above and beyond all time and space, and the immense God who fills all time and space condescended to the weakness of His people and became manifest for their benefit in one locale. This God is not bound by time, but He bound Himself to the time-bound experience of His people. This God is not bound by space, but He bound Himself to this box. He is above all creational constraints, but He bound Himself to them. He is everywhere, but He was *there*.

The psalmist set this truth about the nature of Israel's God to song so that His people could celebrate Him:

> The LORD is high above all nations,
> and his glory is above the heavens!
> Who is like the LORD our God,
> who is seated on high,
> who looks far down
> on the heavens and the earth? (Ps. 113:4–6)

What a God we have. What a God has us. He chose to stoop very low and to humble Himself very far for the sake of His wandering people in the wilderness. Even more, He chose to stoop and to humble Himself for us in His Son, Jesus Christ, and then to stoop as low as death: "he humbled himself by becoming obedient to the point of death, even death on a cross" (Phil. 2:8).

These benefits were found at the ark and in the entire apparatus of the tabernacle. As the nineteenth-century Old Testament scholar C. F. Keil said, "The furniture was the divinely-appointed media for the realization of the covenant fellowship, through which the people could not only render their stipulated services to God in terms of the covenant, but also in turn receive at His hands those blessings of salvation which, in that same covenant, He had pledged Himself to bestow upon His people."[6]

So, how was the Lord present for His people at the ark of the covenant? First, God's presence was visibly demonstrated by the fact that the ark was *the throne of God*. Why did the ark have "four rings of gold . . . on its four feet" (Ex. 25:12) and two poles that went through those rings (Ex. 25:13–14)? Of course, these features were there for the practical purpose of transporting the ark (v. 14) throughout the wilderness wandering. But because the poles went through rings at the feet of the ark, and because the poles were held at shoulder height, the priests carried this symbol of the Lord's presence even as an earthly king would have been carried—above his people. This is in stark contrast to how Uzzah and his brother carried the ark from Baale-judah to Jerusalem (2 Sam. 6:1–11). Instead of carrying it above the people on the poles God commanded to be made for this purpose, they transported the ark on an ox cart. Instead of treating it as the throne of the king, they treated it as something common.

In this narrative, we also learn of the mercy seat (Ex. 25:17, *kapporet*), which was the lid of the ark. On top of this lid were two cherubim of gold (v. 18), kneeling under the feet of the Lord. We hear in our narrative that the Lord met with His people and spoke to them "from above the mercy seat, from between the two cherubim" (v. 22). Thus, the ark was also the footstool of the Lord's throne.[7] In Psalm 80, this fact was celebrated in song. "Give ear, O Shepherd of Israel, you who lead Joseph like a flock! You who are *enthroned* upon the cherubim, shine forth" (emphasis added). Again, in Psalm 99:1 we read: "The LORD reigns; let the peoples tremble! He sits *enthroned* upon the cherubim; let the earth quake!" (emphasis added). David clearly explained this when he told the leaders of his people: "Hear me, my brothers and my people. I had it in my heart to build a house of rest for the ark of the covenant of the LORD and for the footstool of our God" (1 Chron. 28:2). When Jeremiah called on the people to repent, he said: "In those days, declares the LORD, they shall no more say, 'The ark of the covenant of the LORD.' . . . At that time Jerusalem shall be called the throne of the LORD" (Jer. 3:16–17a).

Does this mean that Israel's God was contained in the ark or limited by it? Absolutely not. Unlike the gods of the surrounding nations, the God of Israel could not be contained. Solomon would later say of the temple: "But will God indeed dwell on the earth? Behold, heaven and the highest heaven cannot contain you; how much less this house that I have built!" (1 Kings 8:27). The ark taught the Israelites that while God could not be contained—since His throne is in heaven itself (Pss. 11:4; 123:1; Isa. 40:22) and earth is His footstool (Isa. 66:1)—yet He condescended to dwell among them. The tabernacle visually exhibited this, as it was the house of the Lord, while the Holy of Holies was the throne room of God, and the ark of the covenant was both His throne and His footstool. The King graciously dwelt in Israel's midst.

Second, God's presence was visibly demonstrated by *the cloud of glory*. Clouds are a recurring theme in Genesis and Exodus. In the sight of Abram, the Lord passed through a row of animal carcasses as "a smoking fire pot and a flaming torch" (Gen. 15:17). Later, when the Lord brought His people out of Egypt and into the wilderness, He appeared to them as "the pillar of cloud by day and the pillar of fire by night" to lead them and to protect them from Pharaoh's armies (Ex. 13:22). As they camped at the foot of Mount Sinai, the Lord said to Moses, "the LORD will come down on Mount Sinai in the sight of all the people" (Ex. 19:11). How did He come down for them to see?

> On the morning of the third day there were thunders and lightnings *and a thick cloud* on the mountain and a very loud trumpet blast, so that all the people in the camp trembled. Then Moses brought the people out of the camp to meet God, and they took their stand at the foot of the mountain. Now Mount Sinai was *wrapped in smoke* because the LORD had descended on it in fire. *The smoke of it went up like the smoke of a kiln, and the whole mountain trembled greatly.* And as the sound of the

trumpet grew louder and louder, Moses spoke, and God answered him in thunder. The LORD came down on Mount Sinai, to the top of the mountain. And the LORD called Moses to the top of the mountain, and Moses went up. . . . Now when all the people saw the thunder and the flashes of lightning and the sound of the trumpet and *the mountain smoking*, the people were afraid and trembled, and they stood far off and said to Moses, "You speak to us, and we will listen; but do not let God speak to us, lest we die." Moses said to the people, "Do not fear, for God has come to test you, that the fear of him may be before you, that you may not sin." The people stood far off, while Moses drew near to the thick darkness where God was. (Ex. 19:16–20; 20:18–21, emphasis added)

This cloud would appear again at the end of the narrative, when the tabernacle was finally erected. We read:

The cloud covered the tent of meeting, and the glory of the LORD filled the tabernacle. And Moses was not able to enter the tent of meeting because the cloud settled on it, and the glory of the LORD filled the tabernacle. Throughout all their journeys, whenever the cloud was taken up from over the tabernacle, the people of Israel would set out. But if the cloud was not taken up, then they did not set out till the day that it was taken up. For the cloud of the LORD was on the tabernacle by day, and fire was in it by night, in the sight of all the house of Israel throughout all their journeys. (Ex. 40:34–38)

How was this cloud related to the ark? According to Leviticus 16:2, Moses told Aaron not to enter the Holy of Holies at any time he pleased because if he did he would surely die. What reason did Moses gave? Aaron would die because "I will appear in the cloud over the mercy seat" (Lev. 16:2). In the tabernacle, the Lord was enshrouded in the cloud of

His glory, just as He was in Isaiah's vision (Isa. 6:1–5). It was as if He were saying to the transgressor that He was "coming on the clouds of heaven with power and great glory" (Matt. 24:30).

The fact that the ark was the place of the Lord's presence among His people brought great assurance to the people of God. This high, lofty, majestic, and resplendent King dwelt among His grumbling, complaining, bickering, and sinful people (Ex. 15:24; 16:2, 8, 9, 12; 17:2). Does that sound familiar? We, too, are grumbling, complaining, bickering, and sinful people. Thankfully, God is not far off in another land, but He is near to us who are sinners. The promise to the new-covenant believer is that the Lord is near to us by the power of the Holy Spirit, who dwells in us (1 Cor. 6:19), even as Jesus promised His helpful presence (John 14:16). The assurance His nearness brings was described by the prophet Isaiah much later in this history of salvation. Just as God accompanied Israel when they wandered in a wilderness, so, too, He was with them in the days of their restoration from exile. Thus, the prophet said, "In all their affliction he was afflicted" (Isa. 63:9).

THE PLACE OF PROPITIATION

Second, the ark was *the place of propitiation*. How could a holy God dwell in the midst of a sinful people? Further, how could a sinful people ever hope to approach a holy God and not be destroyed, as were Nadab and Abihu (Lev. 10:1–3)? That brings us to an unusual but important theological term that we need to know and experience: *propitiation*.

To understand this word, think about how a mother and father become angry when a child sins. How does the child persuade his parents to cease to be angry and become happy with him? In our home, our children have to sit in a timeout, then tell us what they did wrong, and finally ask for forgiveness. Then we give big hugs and kisses. That's propitiation. It means turning away anger. In the Bible, propitiation is an act by which God's wrath is turned away from us. The imagery is expressed in Psalm 85, which says,

LORD, you were favorable to your land;
    you restored the fortunes of Jacob.
You forgave the iniquity of your people;
    you covered all their sin.
You withdrew all your wrath;
    you turned from your hot anger. (vv. 1–3)[8]

Toward this end, God gave a distinct set of instructions for the ark's lid (Ex. 25:17–22), called the *kapporet* in Hebrew. When the Old Testament was translated into Latin, this word was translated as *propitiatorium*, which means "the place of propitiation." The standard English translation is "the mercy seat" (KJV).

This lid, then, was the place of propitiation, the place where the wrath of God was turned away from His people. As John Calvin wrote about the mercy seat: "God was propitiated towards believers by the covering of the Law, so as to shew Himself favorable to them by hearing their vows and prayers. For as long as the law stands forth before God's face it subjects us to His wrath and curse; and hence it is necessary that the blotting out of our guilt should be interposed, so that God may be reconciled with us."[9] But while there was a morning and an evening sacrifice on the altar in the courtyard every day, as well as the offerings of the individual worshipers, these merely covered over sins and pointed forward to one great propitiatory sacrifice. In contrast, there was only one day a year when sacrificial blood was offered on the *kapporet* to propitiate the wrath of almighty God. As Leviticus 16 describes in great detail, on the annual Day of Atonement, propitiation was made by means of a substitutionary sacrifice.

As new-covenant believers, we know that these annual sacrifices were only pictures of the propitiation of God's wrath. We see the powerlessness of the animal sacrifices in Hebrews 9:13–14, which says: "For if the blood of goats and bulls, and the sprinkling of defiled persons with the ashes of a heifer, sanctify for the purification of the flesh, how much more will the blood of Christ, who through the eternal Spirit offered himself without blemish to God, purify our conscience from dead works to serve the living God." Just as Jesus alone can cleanse the soul and conscience, He alone can turn away the wrath of God, since He is our propitiation (Rom. 3:25; 1 John 2:2; 4:10).

The Lord is present in our midst in public worship just as He was in the tabernacle, but is He present to judge or to save? In a more personal way, will He look on our sins or will He look on Jesus Christ in our place? The Lord provided the Israelites a place of propitiation on the ark's lid, and He still provides a place today. That "place" is Jesus Christ. He offers Himself to us. He turns away the wrath of God from us. He cleanses us of our sins. He cancels them out. He nullifies their power. He brings us into the presence of God blameless and acceptable. Confess your sins to Him and believe that Jesus Christ will propitiate God's wrath against you. In this way, you shall be saved.

THE PLACE OF PLEADING

Third, the ark was *the place of pleading*. This was a benefit that came to the people of God because of propitiation. Because of the sacrifices that were offered on the mercy seat in their place, the people of God could plead with the Lord in prayer, knowing that He would answer them.

In reflecting on the psalms as we sing them through year in and year out in my congregation's evening service, I have been struck by one interesting section of the Psalter, psalms 60 through 85. It is amazing to count the number of times the theme of restoration and revival occurs. Let me give just one psalm as an illustration. In Psalm 80, Asaph prays three times for the Lord to "restore us . . . that we may be saved" (Ps. 80:3, 7, 19). These prayers need to be read in the light of the very beginning of the psalm. In verses 1–2, Asaph prays for the restoration and revival of the church on the basis of the ark of the covenant. He prays, in effect: "Lord, we look to You to restore and revive us because You dwell upon the ark. You are present there and You have promised that You may be propitiated there. Now come and save us."

Let me exhort you, on the basis of the fact that the ark's reality is with us in Jesus Christ, to plead with the Lord as your forefathers did in their prayers. There are numerous areas in which we need to plead with Him in the name of Jesus. Plead with the Lord that He would restore, reform, and revive His church in our time. We are so worldly that we have let the world dictate what the church should be. We need to cry out in repentance with the psalmist:

> O God, the nations have come into your inheritance;
>> they have defiled your holy temple;
>> they have laid Jerusalem in ruins. . . .
> How long, O Lord? Will you be angry forever?
>> Will your jealousy burn like fire? (Ps. 79:1, 5)

Plead with the Lord for your own forgiveness. When you come before Him in prayer, be struck by the depth of your sins. Be repentant in sincerity of heart:

> Do not remember against us our former iniquities;
>> let your compassion come speedily to meet us,
>> for we are brought very low.
> Help us, O God of our salvation,
>> for the glory of your name;
> deliver us, and atone for our sins,
>> for your name's sake! (vv. 8–9)

When you confess, also call on the Lord to keep His promise that "if we confess our sins, he is faithful and just to forgive us our sins and to cleanse us from all unrighteousness" (1 John 1:9). How is He both faithful and just? It is through Jesus Christ. In Him, we receive God's faithfulness while He received God's justice. This promise is celebrated in the Lord's Supper, which visibly communicates to us that "He was condemned to die that we might be pardoned, that He endured the suffering and death of the cross that we might live through Him, and that He was once for-saken by God that we might forever be accepted by Him."[10]

Furthermore, plead with the Lord for the salvation of your children. Whether you agree or disagree with the doctrine and practice of infant baptism, we all agree that our children need the Lord. Pray that the Lord would make His promises a reality in the souls of your children, that they, too, will be saved when they turn to the Lord. Pray every night that the Lord would give them new hearts. Pray every night that the Lord would give you the energy to catechize them and lead them to Christ. Pray according to the psalmist's vision:

> He established a testimony in Jacob
> > and appointed a law in Israel,
> which he commanded our fathers
> > to teach to their children,
> that the next generation might know them,
> > the children yet unborn,
> and arise and tell them to their children,
> > so that they should set their hope in God
> and not forget the works of God,
> > but keep his commandments. (Ps. 78:5–7)

Plead with the Lord for the salvation of the lost. Pray for the hun-dreds, thousands, and millions of people you live near, work with, interact with, and know as friends who do not know the Lord. Pray that the Lord's blessing would be on you, that you might be a blessing to the world:

> May God be gracious to us and bless us
> > and make his face to shine upon us,
> that your way may be known on earth,
> > your saving power among all nations.
> Let the peoples praise you, O God;
> > let all the peoples praise you!

Let the nations be glad and sing for joy,
  for you judge the peoples with equity
  and guide the nations upon earth. (Ps. 67:1–4)

Pray with confidence, knowing that the Lord Jesus Christ's sacrifice "is the only and most perfect sacrifice and satisfaction for sin, and is of infinite worth and value, abundantly sufficient to expiate the sins of the whole world" (CD 2.5). Pray that He will convict sinners of their sins and convert their hearts to receive His satisfaction for their sins. Pray that He will bring people into your life so you can share the gospel with them and bring them to church.

We need to be restored. We need to be reformed. We need to be revived. To this end, may the Holy Spirit lead us to experience the realities of the ark—the presence of Christ, the propitiation provided by Christ, and the pleading on the basis of Christ.

THE TABLE WITH BREAD

Exodus 25:23-30; 37:10-16

"You shall make a table of acacia wood. Two cubits shall be its length, a cubit its breadth, and a cubit and a half its height. You shall overlay it with pure gold and make a molding of gold around it. And you shall make a rim around it a handbreadth wide, and a molding of gold around the rim. And you shall make for it four rings of gold, and fasten the rings to the four corners at its four legs. Close to the frame the rings shall lie, as holders for the poles to carry the table. You shall make the poles of acacia wood, and overlay them with gold, and the table shall be carried with these. And you shall make its plates and dishes for incense, and its flagons and bowls with which to pour drink offerings; you shall make them of pure gold. And you shall set the bread of the Presence on the table before me regularly." (Ex. 25:23–30)

There is something about a good meal with friends that I find about as satisfying as anything else at this point in my life. To enjoy delectable food, palate-stimulating drink, laughter among friends, and

a oneness of heart with those closest to you is a deeply satisfying experience. Many of you, no doubt, can testify to this experience.

This should not come as a surprise to us. When the Scriptures seek to
describe the nature of our fellowship with God, they often use the imagery of a meal. Abraham ate with the Lord (Gen. 18:1–8). Moses and the
elders of Israel ate with Him (Ex. 24:9–11). When the prophets wanted to
describe the Lord's reinstitution of fellowship with His backslidden people,
they said it would be a day in which His people would be served "a feast
of rich food, a feast of well-aged wine, of rich food full of marrow, of aged
wine well refined" (Isa. 25:6). The psalmist responds to this promise, saying, "My soul will be satisfied as with fat and rich food, and my mouth will
praise you with joyful lips" (Ps. 63:5). In the new covenant, Jesus instituted
a meal for His people to celebrate "until he comes" (1 Cor. 11:26; cf. Matt.
26:26–29), and the early church devoted itself to the enjoyment of that
Communion feast (Acts 2:42). Even our heavenly experience in the presence of God is described as a large wedding banquet for the husband, our
Lord Jesus Christ, and His bride, the church (Rev. 19:1–8).

Keep this in mind as you imagine entering into the tabernacle proper
and looking to your right to see *the table with bread.* Upon that small table
lay the holy bread and four holy utensils, all intended to communicate that
the Lord desires to unite with His people in a satisfying fellowship meal.

The bread that lay on the table was called "the bread of the Presence" (Ex. 25:30, *lehem panim*) because it was in the presence of God,
"before me" (v. 30, *le-panay*). Likewise, the table was called "the table
of the Presence" (Num. 4:7, NIV, *shulhan ha-panim*), because it, too, was
in the Lord's presence. Another term used to describe it was "the table
for the showbread" (2 Chron. 29:18, *shulhan ha-ma'arechet*) because the
rows of bread were displayed on it.[1] Finally, it was called "the pure table"
(Lev. 24:6, KJV, *ha-shulhan ha-tahor*), because it was overlaid with "pure
gold" (Ex. 25:24).

As we meditate on this table and the bread that was set upon it, we must
lift up our hearts beyond them to Jesus Christ, their reality and significance.
In the words of the historical liturgy of the Dutch Reformed churches:

That we, then, may be nourished with Christ, the true heavenly bread, let us not cling with our hearts unto the external bread and wine but lift them up on high in heaven, where Christ Jesus is, our Advocate, at the right hand of His heavenly Father, whither also the articles of our Christian faith direct us; not doubting that we shall be nourished and refreshed in our souls, with His body and blood, through the working of the Holy Spirit, as truly as we receive the holy bread and drink in remembrance of Him.[2]

We can do this by looking at this table with bread from three vantage points: its presentation, its preservation, and its participation.

ITS PRESENTATION

First, we need to meditate on the table's *presentation*. The Lord commanded Moses to build a table that was the equivalent of three feet long, one and a half feet wide, and two feet, three inches high (Ex. 25:23). Also, Moses was to make four kinds of utensils to use in the service of this table: "plates and dishes for incense, and . . . flagons and bowls with which to pour drink offerings" (Ex. 25:29).[3] Regarding the use of the table, God told Moses to "set the bread of the Presence on the table before me regularly" (25:30). Notice, then, that this table was to serve as a place of presentation for the holy bread before the Lord. This was to be done "regularly." The Hebrew term translated as "regularly" (*tamid*) conveys the idea of something happening at constant, perpetual intervals, which is normally associated in the Old Testament law with each morning and evening (cf. Num. 28:1–8).

Later in the Pentateuch, more details are given about this table and the bread that was placed on it. In Leviticus 24:5–9 we have the fullest account. There we learn that twelve loaves of bread were placed on the table (v. 5). What is the significance of twelve loaves? The number no doubt is symbolic of the twelve tribes of Israel, that is, all of the people of God.[4] Furthermore, frankincense was poured on the loaves so they might be "a memorial portion as a food offering to the Lord" (v. 7). The word *memorial* translates the same Hebrew word that is rendered in Exodus 25 as "regularly." These loaves, then, were to be offered regularly, constantly. This ritual of presenting the showbread was so important that it was even described as a *berith 'olam*, as a "covenant forever" (v. 8).

What do all these details mean? The presentation of the bread on the table teaches us about both grace and gratitude. It speaks of grace because by placing the twelve loaves on the table, the priest symbolically offered up the people to the Lord, and they were accepted as a sweet-smelling offering to Him. This is a wonderful type and shadow of our Lord Jesus Christ, our High Priest, who offers us "without spot or wrinkle or any such thing" to God (Eph. 5:27). When the book of Hebrews expounds in detail our Lord's high priestly ministry in chapter 2, it quotes Isaiah 8:18, which says, "Behold, I and the children whom the LORD has given me . . . " (v. 2). Our Lord "ever lives to make intercession" for us (Heb. 7:25), presenting us, His people, before the throne of the Father in heaven.

The presentation of the bread on the table also speaks of gratitude. Like the Israelites who were symbolized by the twelve loaves, God calls us to offer ourselves as living sacrifices on His heavenly altar (Rom. 12:1–2). How can we do anything less? We are to do this because we belong wholly to Him: "You are not your own, for you were bought with a price" (1 Cor. 6:19–20). We belong to the Lord constantly, forever: "I, with body and soul, both in life and in death, am not my own, but belong to my faithful Savior Jesus Christ" (HC, Q&A 1). Our lives, then, are lived before Him, before His shining face (*coram Deo*).[5]

ITS PRESERVATION

Second, we need to meditate on the bread's *preservation*. It was presented on the table before the Lord, stacked in two rows of six loaves each (Lev. 24:6). What do we learn from this seemingly obscure detail?

In the first place, the bread on the table was "to remind Israel of its sustaining God."[6] The priests offered bread to the Lord because He had provided it for them in the miracle of manna (Exodus 16), which was His providential provision of their "daily bread" (Matt. 6:11). By giving them bread, the Lord sustained His people with the most basic staple of earthly life. The Psalms celebrate this provision: "Man ate of the bread of the angels; he sent them food in abundance" (Ps. 78:25), and, "He . . . gives food to all flesh, for his steadfast love endures forever" (Ps. 136:25).

Second, the table included a feature to protect the presented bread. The tabletop was not just a flat surface. Notice God's command: "And you shall make a rim around it a handbreadth wide, and a molding of gold around the rim" (Ex. 25:25). This feature was unique to the table of bread.[7] Around the top edge of the table, then, was something like a crown molding. Why did God command this unique feature? While it no doubt shows the creativity of God and the fact that He cares about the finer details of craftsmanship to show forth His beauty and glory, there was something much more significant about this molding.

THE TABLE WITH BREAD

The wooden table, overlaid with pure gold (Ex. 25:23–30; 37:10–16), was 3 feet long, 1.5 feet wide, and 2.25 feet high (1 m x 0.5 m x 0.7 m). It held the 12 loaves (Lev. 24:5–9) of the bread of the Presence, which were holy (1 Sam. 21:4). Wooden poles, overlaid with gold, were inserted through the rings of the table when the table was transported.

Simply put, this crown molding was intended to keep the bread and all the holy utensils from falling off the table. This unique and utilitarian detail might not strike us as significant, but it is. This is a wonderful picture of the care of God for His people. Just as He kept the bread and utensils from falling away, so He keeps His people, symbolized by the bread, ever before His presence. God is always exerting His preserving power over His people, who are bound by nature to fall away from Him. The Canons of Dort speak of the real possibility of our falling away from the grace of the Lord, if we were left to ourselves in our sins: "Because of these remnants of sin dwelling in them and also because of the temptations of the world and Satan, those who have been converted could not remain standing in this grace if left to their own resources" (5.3). The Canons add: "So it is not by their own merits or strength but by God's undeserved mercy that they neither forfeit faith and grace totally nor remain in their downfalls to the end and are lost. With respect to themselves this not only easily could happen; but also undoubtedly would happen" (5.8).

This illustrates that those of us who are Reformed Christians should not get caught up in talking about merely the perseverance of the saints, about believers being "once saved, always saved," or about issues related to human will or ability. When we do this, we miss the beauty of the gospel. Instead, what we believe about our ultimate salvation should be a reflection of what we believe about the very nature of God Himself. The perseverance of the saints is rooted in God's preservation of the saints. This divine preservation, which we see under the type and shadow of the law's ceremonies in the table of bread, is a tremendous gospel comfort that is fulfilled for believers in the work of Jesus Christ:

> "I give them eternal life, and they will never perish, and no one will snatch them out of my hand. My Father, who has given them to me, is greater than all, and no one is able to snatch them out of the Father's hand." (John 10:28–29)

> Blessed be the God and Father of our Lord Jesus Christ! According to his great mercy, he has caused us to be born again to a living

hope . . . who by God's power are being guarded through faith for a salvation ready to be revealed in the last time. (1 Peter 1:3, 5)

[God] is able to keep you from stumbling and to present you blameless before the presence of his glory with great joy. (Jude 24)

In drawing this truth out of the well of God's Word, we must acknowledge a sobering fact. We should not imagine that because the twelve loaves were preserved by means of the rim around the tabletop that God preserved every single Israelite. We know the all-too-sad reality that not all Israel—that is, the corporate, covenant people—is Israel, that is, the true people of God (Rom. 9:6). In new-covenant terms, not all in the church are the elect; not all who are in the church are of the church. As the Belgic Confession reminds us, "the company of hypocrites who are mixed among the good in the church . . . nonetheless are not part of it, even though they are physically there" (Art. 29).

How is this comforting, then? The table of bread was like a visible sermon that the priests were to use to explain to the people the distinction between the church that is visible and the church that is invisible (cf. WCF 25), between the church in its administration and the church in its essence. It was as if it were saying that only the one who trusts in the Lord who preserved the bread is actually preserved from eternal death. In other words, only those who trust in the Lord Jesus Christ, who is "the living bread that came down from heaven" (John 6:51), and who do so with a true faith, are preserved by God for eternal glory. This is why Peter extols God for His preserving work in the context both of His power and the faith of His people, "who by God's power are being guarded *through faith*" (1 Peter 1:5, emphasis added).

ITS PARTICIPATION

Third, as we consider the table with bread, we also need to meditate on its *participation*. The bread was set before the Lord regularly, as we have

seen from Exodus 25:30.[8] Was the bread, once offered, miraculously preserved for all time? Or was it allowed to stay on the table until it went
bad, after which the priests threw it away?

Exodus 25 does not answer these questions, but clarity appears in
Leviticus 24. Here we learn that every Sabbath the priests brought bread
into the Holy Place as an offering from the people (v. 8). Imagine being
an Israelite and seeing this ritual Sabbath after Sabbath. You would see
new bread go in, but you would not see old bread come out. Where did
the bread go? We learn the answer to this question when we read, "And
it shall be for Aaron and his sons, and they shall eat it in a holy place,
since it is for him a most holy portion out of the Lord's food offerings, a
perpetual due" (v. 9).

In short, the Aaronic priesthood participated in a weekly meal that
consisted of this holy bread. They ate it in the Holy Place, that is, in the
presence of the Lord. We might say, as new-covenant Christians, that
they celebrated Holy Communion with their Lord every week on behalf
of the people of God. The blessing for us in the new covenant is that all
of us as God's people are called priests, which means that all of us get to
eat of the Lord's bread and have intimate communion with Him.[9]

What does all this mean for us? When the seed of the woman who was
to crush the Serpent's head (Gen. 3:15), the son of Abraham who was to
bless all the nations (Gen. 12:3), and the son of Judah who was to wield
the scepter (Gen. 49:10) would finally come, something wonderful would
happen. No longer would there be an exclusive priesthood that would exclusively partake of the holy bread exclusively in the Holy Place before the holy
Lord. When the Lord would come, all His people would be priests, all would
partake of His holy bread, and all would do so in His holy presence.

That day is here. Listen to these promises: "You yourselves like living
stones are being built up as a spiritual house, to be a holy priesthood" (1
Peter 2:5a). As priests, we are called out of the world and into the heavenly tabernacle to feed on the true manna and the holy bread, which are
signs of the reality Jesus Christ is: "Do not labor for the food that per-
ishes, but for the food that endures to eternal life. . . . My Father gives

you the true bread from heaven. . . . I am the bread of life; whoever comes to me shall not hunger, and whoever believes in me shall never thirst" (John 6:27, 32, 35).

Are you hungry today? Do you desire to be satisfied in your soul? Do you long for wholeness? Then believe in Jesus Christ by faith and feed your faith by communing with His body and His blood as often as you are able. In the words of J. C. Ryle (1816–1900):

> We shall all do well to remember the charge of the Apostle Paul: *"Forsake not the assembling of yourselves together, as the manner of some is"* (Heb. 10:25). Never to be absent from God's house on Sundays, without good reason—never to miss the Lord's Supper when administered in our own congregation—never to let our place be empty when means of grace are going on, this is one way to be a growing and prosperous Christian. The very sermon that we needlessly miss, may contain a precious word in season for our souls. The very assembly for prayer and praise from which we stay away, may be the very gathering that would have cheered, established, and revived our hearts. We little know how dependent our spiritual health is on little, regular, habitual helps, and how much we suffer if we miss our medicine.[10]

Our hunger is satisfied when by faith we partake of Christ, the true bread from heaven (John 6). He is presented before us to feed upon every time we gather in His presence for holy worship when His Word is rightly preached and His Communion is celebrated. He is the bread that preserves us, of which we can say, "The Body of our Lord Jesus Christ, which was given for thee. . . . The Blood of our Lord Jesus Christ, which was shed for thee to preserve thy body and soul unto everlasting life."[11] He is the One with whom we participate in close fellowship, as with a friend: "The cup of blessing that we bless, is it not a participation in the blood of Christ? The bread that we break, is it not a participation in the body of Christ?" (1 Cor. 10:16).

THE LAMPSTAND OF GOLD

Exodus 25:31-40; 27:20-21;
37:17-24

"You shall make a lampstand of pure gold. The lampstand shall be made of hammered work: its base, its stem, its cups, its calyxes, and its flowers shall be of one piece with it. And there shall be six branches going out of its sides, three branches of the lampstand out of one side of it and three branches of the lampstand out of the other side of it; three cups made like almond blossoms, each with calyx and flower, on one branch, and three cups made like almond blossoms, each with calyx and flower, on the other branch—so for the six branches going out of the lampstand. And on the lampstand itself there shall be four cups made like almond blossoms, with their calyxes and flowers, and a calyx of one piece with it under each pair of the six branches going out from the lampstand. Their calyxes and their branches shall be of one piece with it, the whole of it a single piece of hammered work of pure gold. You shall make seven lamps for it. And the lamps shall be set up so as to give light on the space in front of it. Its tongs and their trays shall be of pure gold. It shall be made, with all these utensils, out of a talent of pure gold. And see that you make them after the pattern for them, which is being shown you on the mountain." (Ex. 25:31–40)

"You shall command the people of Israel that they bring to you pure beaten olive oil for the light, that a lamp may regularly be set up to burn. In the tent of meeting, outside the veil that is before the testimony, Aaron and his sons shall tend it from evening to morning before the LORD. It shall be a statute forever to be observed throughout their generations by the people of Israel." (Ex. 27:20–21)

Imagine you are taking an ordinary walk through the camp of Israel in the wilderness. As you walk, you weave your way through the maze of tents in which your brothers and sisters sleep. Then you reach the tabernacle complex and pass through the large entrance curtain of the courtyard. You walk past the high bronze altar of sacrifice and then past the bronze laver just in front of the tabernacle proper. Finally, you pass the first veil and come into the first room, the Holy Place. What do you see? On your right is the table with bread, on which we focused in the last chapter. Looking over to your left, you see a large *lampstand of gold*.

This lampstand was something like a tall golden candelabra. On each side of the central stem were three more lamps branching out of it. In these seven lamps, oil was burned constantly to give light. It was made of pure gold (Ex. 25:31, *zahav tahor*), while the table for bread, by comparison, was made of wood and only overlaid with gold.

In beginning to meditate on the purpose and meaning of this piece of furniture, we have to ask why we need light. The answer should be simple. We need light so that we can see clearly in darkness. It was no different for the priests who ministered inside the tabernacle. They needed a source of light within the tabernacle as they ministered before the Lord, especially in the evening. After all, the tabernacle was enclosed with curtains and was filled with the smoke of the altar of incense. The lampstand (*menorah*) gave the priests the light they needed so that they could "serve [the Lord] day and night in his temple" (Rev. 7:15), as the church does in heaven.

Of course, for us, the lampstand had a deeper significance. As we look behind the veil and into the Holy Place, we do so as Christians, which means we need to lift up our hearts beyond the lampstand to its spiritual significance and substance, Jesus Christ. To do this, let us consider three functions it served: It gave light to show the Savior, to show salvation, and to show service.

LIGHT TO SHOW THE SAVIOR

First, the lampstand of gold gave *light to show the Savior*. The Lord commanded Moses to make the lampstand out of one piece of gold, with cups made like almond blossoms. He also commanded him to collect pure beaten olive oil for the lamps, as would be fitting for use in the holy house of God. The lampstand, then, came from God: "And see that you make them after the pattern for them, which is being shown you on the mountain" (Ex. 25:40). These stipulations reveal God's concern that the priests have light to perform their duties, His desire for beauty and glory in the place of His worship, and His insistence that His worship be done precisely according to His Word. But what, ultimately, was the lampstand about?

The lampstand also had a symbolic purpose.[1] To begin to understand that purpose, remember that the interior of the tabernacle was like heaven on earth. Why do I say this? It was like heaven on earth because the curtains of blue, purple, and scarlet yarns were visible only from inside the tabernacle. Further, these curtains had cherubim woven into them, as if they were flying in heaven. Also, the great veil between the Holy Place and the Holy of Holies had cherubim woven into it, a reminder of the cherubim stationed at the gate of the garden of Eden to guard the holy place of God. Finally, the smoke from the altar of incense that filled the tabernacle was like the smoke that covered the Lord's presence on Mount Sinai: "Behold, I am coming to you in a thick cloud" (Ex. 19:9; cf. 19:16, 18; 20:18).

Inside this microcosm of heaven stood the lampstand, which was in the shape of a trunk with six branches coming from it—like a tree.

THE LAMPSTAND OF GOLD

The golden lampstand (Ex. 25:31–40) was made of pure gold, hammered out of one solid piece. Resting on a base, the central stem had six branches, three on either side, together carrying seven lamps. The lampstand with its branches was modeled on a flowering almond tree.

Here in the midst of heaven on earth was a symbol of the tree of life that stood in the earthly paradise, Eden (Gen. 2:9). Because of his sin, Adam was barred from that tree, and so are we, his descendants. The New Testament makes clear that only those whose spiritual eyes have been enlightened by God and who embrace the good news for sinners are granted access to the tree of life (Rev. 2:7).

The light that this "tree" gave the priests was even more symbolic. Throughout Scripture, the Lord Himself is associated with light. God passed through the rows of animal sacrifices as "a smoking fire pot and a flaming torch" in the days of Abram (Gen. 15:17). Likewise, when Moses met God on Mount Sinai, God appeared to him as a burning bush (Ex. 3). Furthermore, God led the Israelites in the pillar of fire by night in the days of the exodus and wilderness journey (Ex. 13:21–22). Where there is light, there is the Lord.

Listen to how the psalms later captured the truth that God is the light of His people:

When we are in distress because of our enemies, we can pray, "Lift up the light of your face upon us, O Lord!" (Ps. 4:6b).

When we are afraid, we can pray confidently: "The Lord is my light and my salvation; whom shall I fear? The Lord is the stronghold of my life; of whom shall I be afraid?" (Ps. 27:1).

When we contrast our lives with the wicked, we can pray, "For with you is the fountain of life; in your light do we see light" (Ps. 36:9).

When the world accuses us of wickedness, we can go to our Advocate, praying: "Vindicate me, O God, and defend my cause against an ungodly people, from the deceitful and unjust man deliver me! Send out your light and your truth; let them lead me; let them bring me to your holy hill and to your dwelling!" (Ps. 43:1, 3).

When we look back on our salvation, just as the Israelites looked back on their entrance to the Promised Land, we can pray, "for not by their own sword did they win the land, nor did their own arm save them, but your right hand and your arm, and the light of your face, for you delighted in them" (Ps. 44:3).

When we come to holy worship on the Lord's Day, we can pray, "Blessed are the people who know the festal shout, who walk, O Lord, in the light of your face" (Ps. 89:15).

The new-covenant fulfillment of this symbolism should be clear to us—Jesus Christ.[2] Our Lord Jesus said of Himself: "I am the light of the world" (John 8:12). The Apostle John writes of our Savior's coming into the world, "The light shines in the darkness" (John 1:5). Later, John described our Lord in this way: "Then I turned to see the voice that was speaking to me, and on turning I saw seven golden lampstands, and in the midst of the lampstands one like a son of man, clothed with a long robe and with a golden sash around his chest. The hairs of his head were white, like white wool, like snow. His eyes were like a flame of fire" (Rev. 1:12–14).

Where light is described in the New Testament, there is Jesus. The lampstand of gold in the tabernacle was ultimately intended to point the priests and the people to the truth that one day there would be no need of a lamp because the Lord Himself would come and provide the light.

LIGHT TO SHOW SALVATION

Second, the lampstand gave *light to show salvation*. Its light was not only a symbol of the Lord, it taught the priests and the Israelites a spiritual truth for them in their time and place. It taught that just as the priests could not minister without the Lord's light, so no one can truly see and understand God's ways without the Lord enlightening the heart and soul: "Open my eyes, that I may behold wondrous things out of your law" (Ps. 119:18). This was a wonderful way of communicating a spiritual truth.

Although we are born with our physical eyes open, the "eyes" of our hearts are blinded by the darkness of our sin (Eph. 4:18). When you stand in the darkness, can you see? Your eyes are open and you might be able to see the outlines of furniture or other objects. However, you cannot really "see." Likewise, all of us are born in spiritual darkness, without the ability to find God on our own: "No one seeks for God" (Rom. 3:11; cf. John 6:44, 65). All of us are born depraved and sinful: "no one does good, not even one" (v. 12). The lampstand taught the Israelites that they were in the dark by nature and that they needed the Lord to shine on them if they were to understand anything about Him and be saved.

Listen to how the Apostle Paul describes our situation: "Now this I say and testify in the Lord, that you must no longer walk as the Gentiles do, in the futility of their minds. They are darkened in their understanding, alienated from the life of God because of the ignorance that is in them, due to their hardness of heart. They have become callous and have given themselves up to sensuality, greedy to practice every kind of impurity" (Eph. 4:17–19). The words Paul uses here—*futility, darkened, alienated, ignorance, hardness, callous, sensuality, greedy, impurity*—show that this is not a good place to be, to say the least.

Sadly, there is nothing we can do about it. Our eyes are so darkened by our sin that even the little glimmers of light we see we try to cover and snuff out. As Paul said, "the wrath of God is revealed from heaven against all ungodliness and unrighteousness of men, who by their unrighteousness *suppress the truth*" (Rom. 1:18, emphasis added). Without the intervention of the Lord, shining the light of His Holy Spirit on our hearts, we live in a world of spiritual darkness.

The lampstand of gold was a visual reminder to the people of God that they were by nature blind and in the dark. It was also a reminder that the remedy was the Lord alone. The lampstand said: "You need to be regenerated. You need to be given new life. You need to be converted. You need to be changed. You need the Lord to shine His light on you so that you can see Him, so that you can find Him, and so that you can embrace Him." As the psalmist said, "in your light do we see light" (Ps. 36:9b). This is why when Jesus said, "I am the light of the world," He went on to say, "Whoever follows me will not walk in darkness, but will have the light of life" (John 8:12). As the Canons of the Synod of Dort confess about humanity:

> Man was originally created in the image of God and was furnished in his mind with a true and salutary knowledge of his Creator and things spiritual, in his will and heart with righteousness, and in all his emotions with purity; indeed, the whole man was holy. However, rebelling against God at the devil's instigation and by his own free will, he deprived himself of these outstanding gifts. Rather, in their place he brought upon himself blindness, terrible darkness, futility, and distortion of judgment in his mind; perversity, defiance, and hardness in his heart and will; and finally impurity in all his emotions. (3/4.1)

Jesus is the answer. He is the light. Paul elaborated on this when he said that the gospel is "veiled . . . to those who are perishing [since] the god of this world has blinded the minds of the unbelievers, to keep them from seeing the light of the gospel of the glory of Christ" (2 Cor. 4:3–4). But then he added, "For God, who said, 'Let light shine out of darkness,' has shone in our hearts to give the light of the knowledge of the glory of God in the face of Jesus Christ" (v. 6).

Since the Lord Jesus Christ is the answer to our darkness, pray to Him today. What should you pray? The words of the psalmist need to become your words: "Restore us, O God; let your face shine, that we may be saved" (Ps. 80:3).

LIGHT TO SHOW SERVICE

Third, the lampstand gave *light to show service*. As the priests came to understand and began to teach the people the significance of the lamp-stand as a sign of the Lord's presence and the salvation He alone could give, they had to be struck by how blessed they were. They dwelt within the borders of the holy assembly. Outside their camp was the realm of the unholy world. But the lampstand showed Israel that it was called to serve the world. The light that dwelt within their midst was to be shined outside their camp into the dark world.

As the prophets reminded Israel over and over again in the midst of their failures, God had given them a high calling to serve the nations. How? They were to serve the Lord by serving their neighbors, being bright lights in the midst of thick darkness. One of the great prophetic statements of Israel's calling is in Isaiah 60:1–3, where we read:

> Arise, shine, for your light has come,
>   and the glory of the LORD has risen upon you.
> For behold, darkness shall cover the earth,
>   and thick darkness the peoples;

but the Lord will arise upon you,
    and his glory will be seen upon you.
And nations shall come to your light,
    and kings to the brightness of your rising.

Because Israel failed to be that light, the Lord sent His Son, the one Isaiah called "your light." He came to a world lost in "thick darkness." Isaiah foretold that His light would attract the nations in the unholy world to come within the holy camp:

It shall come to pass in the latter days
that the mountain of the house of the Lord
    shall be established as the highest of the mountains,
    and shall be lifted up above the hills;
and all the nations shall flow to it,
    and many peoples shall come, and say:
"Come, let us go up to the mountain of the Lord,
    to the house of the God of Jacob,
that he may teach us his ways
    and that we may walk in his paths." (2:2–3)

This imagery of the people of God being the light of the world continues in the New Testament. When our Lord came to His people Israel, He described their leaders as "the blind [who] lead the blind" (Matt. 15:14). Despite their high privilege of having been "entrusted with the oracles of God" (Rom. 3:2) and claiming to be "a guide to the blind, a light to those who are in darkness, an instructor of the foolish, a teacher of children" (Rom. 2:19–20), the teachers of the law did not teach themselves (v. 21).

But we have been enlightened and are to lead the world to the true light, Christ. The beloved Apostle John wrote to the churches of Asia Minor that our Lord walks among the lampstands, that is, the churches

(Rev. 1:13). Because He has come and because He still walks in the midst of His people, He calls the church today to be light in darkness. Our Lord clearly said that we as the church are to be "the light of the world" (Matt. 5:14; Phil. 2:15). We must become in practice what He has declared us to be in principle. This is why He went on to say that we are to let the light of our good works of service in His name shine before men (Matt. 5:16).

One of the ways we can fulfill the calling that Israel had, as symbolized by the lampstand, is to teach the world the way to worship the one true God purely. We need to make it known that He desires to be worshiped "in spirit and truth" (John 4:24). As John Calvin said, the lampstand taught the Israelites "that they were directed by God Himself as to how they were to worship Him aright, and that a light was set before their eyes which might disperse all the darkness of error . . . lest they should obscure the very worship of God with their gross inventions, [and] that, intent on the instruction of the Law, they might with a pure and enlightened mind seek after God in all the ceremonies."[3] With all the religions available to people in our global village, our light has a chance to teach that the triune God is to be worshiped and served only through the Son in the power and fellowship of the Holy Spirit.

Like the light of the lampstand, then, the shining of our light before the world is a perpetual obligation, even as the lampstand was "regularly . . . set up to burn" (Ex. 27:20, *tamid*). We serve the Lord as His light by shining the light of His Word upon the Savior and His way of salvation. May the Lord shine through us in a dark world; may the world's eyes be opened to the true light.

THE CONSTRUCTION
OF THE TABERNACLE

Exodus 26; 35:30–36:38;
38:21–31

"Moreover, you shall make the tabernacle with ten curtains of fine twined linen and blue and purple and scarlet yarns; you shall make them with cherubim skillfully worked into them. . . . And you shall make fifty clasps of gold, and couple the curtains one to the other with the clasps, so that the tabernacle may be a single whole. You shall also make curtains of goats' hair for a tent over the tabernacle; eleven curtains shall you make. . . . You shall make fifty loops on the edge of the curtain that is outermost in one set, and fifty loops on the edge of the curtain that is outermost in the second set. You shall make fifty clasps of bronze, and put the clasps into the loops, and couple the tent together that it may be a single whole. . . . And you shall make for the tent a covering of tanned rams' skins and a covering of goatskins on top. You shall make upright frames for the tabernacle of acacia wood. . . . There shall be two tenons in each frame, for fitting together. So shall you do for all the frames of the tabernacle. . . . You shall overlay the frames with gold and shall make their rings of gold for holders for the bars, and you shall overlay the bars with gold. Then you shall erect the tabernacle according to the plan for it that you were shown on the mountain. And you shall make a veil of blue and purple and scarlet yarns and fine twined linen. It shall be made with cherubim skillfully worked into it. And you shall hang it on four pillars of acacia overlaid with gold, with hooks of gold, on four bases of silver. And you shall hang the veil from the clasps, and bring the ark of the testimony in there within the veil. And the veil shall separate for you the Holy Place from the Most Holy. You shall put the mercy seat on the ark of the testimony in the Most Holy Place. And you shall set the table outside the veil, and the lampstand on the south side of the tabernacle opposite the table, and you shall put the table on the north side. You shall make a screen for the entrance of the tent, of blue and purple and scarlet yarns and fine twined linen, embroidered with needlework. And you shall make for the screen five pillars of acacia, and overlay them with gold. Their hooks shall be of gold, and you shall cast five bases of bronze for them." (Ex. 26:1–37)

When we gather with the sacred assembly in our various locations, where are we worshiping? In one sense, the answer is obvious: we worship where our feet are. We could even give a physical address. But when we as God's people in the new covenant worship Him as He commands in His Word, we are worshiping in the tabernacle. You might object, "But I thought Jesus put an end to old-covenant ceremonies." Yes, He did. But He also brings us to experience the reality to which the ceremonies of the tabernacle pointed. Therefore, we still worship in the tabernacle of God.

The author of the epistle to the Hebrews explains the location of Christian worship:

Therefore, brothers, since we have confidence to enter the holy places by the blood of Jesus, by the new and living way that he opened for us through the curtain, that is, through his flesh, and since we have a great priest over the house of God, let us draw near with a true heart in full assurance of faith, with our hearts sprinkled clean from an evil conscience and our bodies washed with pure water. (10:19–22)

As Christians, then, we enter the courtyard, move past the bronze altar and the bronze basin for washing, pass the first veil into the Holy Place, and go even farther—beyond the great curtain into the very Holy of Holies. We do this because, on the cross, Jesus tore the veil in two (Matt. 27:51). We do this because Jesus' flesh was offered as a sacrifice on the bronze altar and His blood washes us as the water in the bronze laver cleansed the people in the tabernacle. Because of His work, we "enter the holy places," "through the curtain," and "draw near."

As we turn to the narrative of *the construction of the tabernacle*, we will return to two of the points we considered when we looked at the instructions for the tabernacle's building, with some elaboration. We will learn in more depth what it is to worship in the presence of God as we consider the tabernacle's holiness and heavenliness.

ITS HOLINESS

First, we encounter the tabernacle's *holiness*. To worship in the tabernacle was to worship in a holy place and to experience the holy presence of God. This is seen in the materials used for its construction. There were four layers of curtains, going from innermost to outermost: linen (Ex. 26:1–6), goats' hair (vv. 7–13), rams' skin (v. 14), and the aforementioned *tahash* skin (Ex. 26:14).[1] It is fascinating that the Lord put the most unattractive curtains on the outside and the most attractive on the inside. John J. Davis writes, "From a purely aesthetic point of view the tabernacle could not be considered a thing of beauty, at least not from the outside."[2]

This is typical of God, who often cloaks His glory in simplicity, His power in weakness, and His wisdom in foolishness to confound the unbeliever but to comfort the believer (cf. 1 Cor. 1:18–31). Ultimately, He cloaked His majesty in flesh as His Son, Jesus Christ, took on ordinary humanity: "He had no form or majesty that we should look at him, and no beauty that we should desire him" (Isa. 53:2b). In a sense, then, to come to the tabernacle was to come to the holy God Himself, hidden under the veils of the ordinary and earthly.

THE TABERNACLE

The entire tent was 45 feet (13.7 m) long, 15 feet (4.6 m) wide, and 15 feet (4.6 m) high. It was a wooden skeletal structure, overlaid with gold, with no solid roof or front wall (Ex. 26:15–29). Five wooden bars (overlaid with gold) passed through rings attached to each frame (Ex. 26:26–30).

The Most Holy Place was a 15-foot (4.6-m) cube, containing only the ark of the covenant (Ex. 25:10–22; 37:1–9). It was here that Yahweh would descend to meet with His people in a cloud theophany (divine appearance). The high priest could enter only once a year, on the Day of Atonement (see note on Heb. 9:7).

The Holy Place of the tabernacle tent was 30 feet (9.1 m) long, 15 feet (4.6 m) wide, and 15 feet (4.6 m) high.

The table for the bread of the Presence (Ex. 25:23–30)

The veil that formed the entrance to the tabernacle was similar to the veil separating the Holy Place from the Most Holy Place, except that cherubim were not embroidered on it. It was suspended on five golden pillars (Ex. 26:36–37).

The framed structure was covered by four layers of cloth and skin (Ex. 26:1–14).

The golden lampstand (Ex. 25:31–40; 37:17–24)

The altar of incense (Ex. 30:1–10; 37:25–29)

The veil separating the Most Holy Place from the Holy Place was made from blue, purple, and scarlet dyed yarns woven with fine twined linen and embroidered with cherubim (Ex. 26:31–33). It was hung on four golden pillars.

94

The innermost layer was made up of ten curtains of "fine twined linen" (*mashzar*), a phrase that refers not just to ordinary linen but to the particular linen produced by a highly specialized technique of weaving for the Lord's tabernacle. The "screen" (Ex. 26:36) around the tabernacle complex was also made of "fine twined linen," but with the qualification that it was "embroidered with needlework" (*ma'aseh rokem*), a term that signifies that it was less intricate than the inner curtain.[3] These curtains were made with "blue and purple and scarlet yarns," not just bland, ordinary colors, and they had "cherubim skillfully worked into them" (Ex. 26:1, *keruvim ma'aseh hoshev*). These angels reminded the people that the place wherein they stood was holy ground.

The clasps that held the curtains together were made of gold (v. 6), and the frames of the tabernacle (v. 29) and the bars that ran along the walls to give them stability were overlaid with gold (v. 29). The base of the tabernacle was a series of blocks made of silver (v. 19).

The veil (v. 31, *parokhet*), which served to "separate . . . the Holy Place from the Most Holy" (v. 33), was made of "fine twined linen" with "cherubim skillfully worked into it" (v. 31). Elsewhere it is called "the veil of the screen" (Ex. 35:12; 39:34; 40:21; Num. 4:5, *parokhet ha-masakh*), "the veil of the testimony" (Lev. 24:3, *parokhet ha-'edut*), and "the veil of the sanctuary" (Lev. 4:6, *parokhet ha-kodesh*) because it walled off the Holy of Holies, where the ark of the covenant was kept. This veil taught "how reverently God's majesty must be regarded, and with what seriousness holy things are to be engaged in, so that they may not approach God's presence without fear, nor boldly break in upon the mysteries of things sacred."[4]

The fact that the camp was separated from the courtyard by a large screen all around, and that the tabernacle was itself set apart from the courtyard by its curtains, signifies the holiness of the tabernacle and its services. To come into the presence of God, then, is to come into the presence of His holiness.

This knowledge needs to lead new-covenant believers to practical action. We can learn from this that we must prepare our minds, our bodies, and our souls for worship. As the English Puritan John Dod (1549–1645) said, "That policie and discretion which we see in naturall men about the market of their bodies, we must learne about the market of our souls . . . if ever we will make good markets for our souls, we must be preparing our hearts."[5] How should we go about preparing each of these aspects of our humanity?

We need to prepare *our minds*. As you leave worship on the Lord's Day and then go about your life in the world, begin to look forward to the next Lord's Day. As the week draws near to its end, know that the "Sunday" coming up is, in reality, "the Lord's Day" (Rev. 1:10).

We need to prepare *our bodies*. Sunday morning must begin Saturday night. To prepare for the Lord's Day, you need to get to bed at a decent hour and get enough sleep so that you will be refreshed and ready to worship.[6] When the Israelites were about to meet God, they prepared their outward appearance by cleansing their garments (Ex. 19:9–11). How much more should we prepare our outward persons in the new and better covenant?

We need to prepare *our souls*. All through the week we need to be meditating on what we heard on the Lord's Day and anticipating meeting again with the Lord the next Lord's Day. Do you look forward to gathering with the saints? Do you long to hear the Word, receive the sacraments, sing psalms and hymns, and pray publicly? The Puritan George Swinnock expressed the benefit of preparing for the Lord's Day and the Lord's service when he said, "If thou wouldst thus leave thy heart with God on the Saturday night, thou shouldst find it with him in the Lord's day morning."[7]

As Christians, our heart's desire should be that of David: "One thing have I asked of the LORD, that will I seek after: that I may dwell in the house of the LORD all the days of my life, to gaze upon the beauty of the LORD and to inquire in his temple" (Ps. 27:4). Our attitude ought to be that of the sons of Korah: "How lovely is your dwelling place, O LORD of hosts! My soul longs, yes, faints for the courts of the LORD; my heart and flesh sing for joy to the living God. . . . For a day in your courts is better than a thousand elsewhere. I would rather be a doorkeeper in the house of my God than dwell in the tents of wickedness" (Ps. 84:1–2, 10). It is amazing to consider that we live in the reality of what these psalms anticipated. The Israelites lived in the time of anticipation, but we live in the time of participation.[8] There should be no greater anticipation among Christians than coming into God's holy presence.

ITS HEAVENLINESS

Second, we encounter the tabernacle's *heavenliness*. To worship in the tabernacle was to worship in a heavenly place and to experience the heavenly presence of God. Worship in the presence of God is and should be otherworldly. There are at least three ways in which the tabernacle was heavenly.

First, to enter the tabernacle was to enter a different world. The courtyard was screened off from the camp, and the tabernacle itself was screened off from laypeople. To enter into either of these areas was to enter a different and special realm.

Likewise, when we, as new-covenant believers, enter worship, we are entering heaven. Why would we even think of getting out of our seats in the middle of holy worship to take a restroom break, to get a drink of water, or to take a phone call? Is God boring? Have we heard His Word so much that we do not need to hear it again? We should prepare ourselves for heavenly worship in the most mundane and practical of ways, such as turning off our mobile devices and using the restroom before we go in. Likewise, we can help our children understand the distinctiveness of worship by not giving them water and juice before entering.

Second, to build the tabernacle, Moses and all those gifted by the Holy Spirit had to follow God's instructions. Four times in the tabernacle narratives we hear these or similar words: "According to the plan for it that you were shown on the mountain" (Ex. 25:9; 25:40; 26:30; 27:4). God stressed that Moses had to make the tabernacle exactly as God wanted it to be made. There was no place for creativity. There was no place for variation to "keep it fresh." God is an exacting, precise, and specific God. Because of that, He gave very specific instructions for the tabernacle, that it might reflect the heavenly reality in which God exists and that He desires us to experience.

Likewise, our worship is heavenly, at least to the extent it is conducted according to the Lord's Word.[9] If God had not given us instructions, our worship would be chaos. Each of us would want something completely different. But God in His Word teaches us to do three necessary things when we come together on the Lord's Day. He wants us to read and to preach His Word, He wants us to celebrate His sacraments, and He wants us to pray (Acts 2:42).

One of the most striking ways we can experience and practice the heavenliness of worship is by singing the biblical psalms in a dignified and joyful way. The psalms are God's words, not ours. We should not have a band that makes a worship service resemble a concert. Getting more specific, we should not have heavy-metal services or country-music services. These things are of this world; they are creations of our own heads and hands. But worship is not about us and our particular tastes and preferences. It is about God. He taught His people this truth in the construction of the tabernacle.

All this means that we cannot evaluate worship by the standards of the world. We crave entertainment. We have our Facebook pages, our Twitter accounts, our iPods full of our favorite songs, our favorite radio stations on presets in our cars, our email, which we access via our iPhones and Blackberrys, and so on. But God is not a commodity; He is not something to entertain us. He is not just another thing in a long line of things. He says the whole Lord's Day is His day, and especially when we step into worship, He says, "Mine."

Third, the rear of the tabernacle was to the west (Ex. 26:22, 27), literally, "seaward" (*yammah*), that is, toward the Mediterranean Sea. As an Israelite approached the screen entrance to the courtyard, the veil of the tabernacle, and the great veil of the Holy of Holies, he moved from east to west. This arrangement reminded the people that even the sun offered its worship to the Lord as it arose every morning: "Praise him, sun and moon, praise him, all you shining stars!" (Ps. 148:3). Since the Israelites had their backs to the east and their faces to the west as they came into God's presence, they showed they were not worshipers of the sun, which rose in the east every morning, but of the Creator of the sun.[10] As the psalmist would later sing: "Yours is the day, yours also the night; *you have established* the heavenly lights and *the sun*" (Ps. 74:16, emphasis added).

What's the big deal with this? After Adam sinned against God, "the Lord God sent him out from the garden of Eden to work the ground from which he was taken. He drove out the man, and at the east of the garden of Eden he placed the cherubim and a flaming sword that turned every way to guard the way to the tree of life" (Gen. 3:23–24). Adam and his wife were sent to the east. The garden, which was like heaven on earth, was to the west. To go east in Scripture, then, is to go away from the presence of God. To go west is to go toward His presence. The Israelites were granted access into the earthly microcosm of what God forbade Adam and Eve from entering. As they approached the heavenly presence of God, they came into the courtyard, while the priests went into the Holy Place and the high priest went into the Holy of Holies. As the high priest entered the Holy of Holies, he passed beyond the cherubim on the great veil—the image of the cherubim at the entrance to Eden.

Now, in the new covenant, that veil is torn asunder (Matt. 27:51). As we come to worship, we enter that paradise as well. We leave the world and enter heaven for a time, to commune with our God.

God gave the tabernacle to bring His people into His holy and heavenly presence. In doing so, God came to the aid of His people. When the people witnessed God in smoke and thunder on Mount Sinai, they were terrified (Ex. 19:16). Rightly so, for they were wretched, vile, and helpless sinners, as are we. God's holiness should frighten us. His heavenliness should cause reverence and awe within us. Who can stand before Him? Who can walk into God's presence on his own merits? No one can; we are too sinful. But God is a God who helps the helpless, who finds the lost, who gives sight to the blind, who cleanses the filthy. He provided Israel a means to have its sins removed, to have fellowship with the Lord, and to worship Him in the tabernacle. He also has given us access to His presence through Christ and worship that is in Spirit and truth.

Do you desire to be clean so that you can enter the Holy of Holies? Do you long for heavenly life beyond the sin, frustration, and futility of this life? There is only one way to receive this, just as there was only one way among the Israelites. They had to enter the courtyard, offer a sacrifice at the bronze altar, and be cleansed in the bronze laver. Then they had to have a priest enter the Holy Place for them, be enlightened by the lamp-stand, be fed by the bread of the presence, and be lifted up by the altar of incense. Finally, they needed the high priest to enter the Holy of Holies to offer a great sacrifice once a year on top of the ark of the covenant.

For us, the way is Jesus Christ. Just as the wise men from the east came west at His birth to worship Him, so you must come to Jesus Christ. You must come to Him with your sins, but sorrowing for them; you must come with your doubts, yet believing in Him. "Let us then with confidence draw near to the [holy and heavenly] throne of grace, that we may receive mercy and find grace to help in time of need" (Heb. 4:16). I pray you will come.

THE ALTAR OF BRONZE

Exodus 27:1–8; 38:1–7

"You shall make the altar of acacia wood, five cubits long and five cubits broad. The altar shall be square, and its height shall be three cubits. And you shall make horns for it on its four corners; its horns shall be of one piece with it, and you shall overlay it with bronze. You shall make pots for it to receive its ashes, and shovels and basins and forks and fire pans. You shall make all its utensils of bronze. You shall also make for it a grating, a network of bronze, and on the net you shall make four bronze rings at its four corners. And you shall set it under the ledge of the altar so that the net extends halfway down the altar. And you shall make poles for the altar, poles of acacia wood, and overlay them with bronze. And the poles shall be put through the rings, so that the poles are on the two sides of the altar when it is carried. You shall make it hollow, with boards. As it has been shown you on the mountain, so shall it be made." (Ex. 27:1–8)

"My God is a God of love! He would never punish people eternally for their sins. That was what the Old Testament God did. I believe in the New Testament God."

Have you heard this sentiment expressed by a loved one, friend, or acquaintance? The view that God's love overrules His justice is an ancient heresy called Marcionism (cf. BC, Art. 9), but it remains prevalent in churches today. Both testaments emphasize that there is only one God (Deut. 6:4; 1 Cor. 8:6), that He never changes (Mal. 3:6; Heb. 13:8), and that He is *both* just and merciful (Ps. 85:10; Rom. 3:26; 1 John 1:9). Nevertheless, many people today, even Christians, fundamentally misunderstand the nature of God. The church that Jesus built to be in the world but not of the world (John 17:14–15) has become very worldly, at least in the Western world. People's beliefs are formed more by preference and sentimentality than by the truth of God's Word.

In July 2009, Harvard University Professor Henry Louis Gates was mistakenly arrested after he forced open the jammed door of his Cambridge, Massachusetts, house. The charge against Gates was soon dropped, but a controversy ensued when the Cambridge police force was accused of racial profiling in the arrest of Gates, who is black. To resolve the controversy, U.S. President Barack Obama invited Gates and the arresting officer, Sgt. James Crowley, to the so-called "White House Beer Summit." Obama's action represented a microcosm of our culture's belief that there is no accountability for actions, no need for remorse, and no need to confess sins against one another in order to bring about reconciliation. Instead, this photo-op affirmed that sitting down over a beer and putting on a smile will do the trick of covering over strife, real or pretend.

Why do I bring all this up? I do so because we have come to a pair of passages that fundamentally challenge our weak ideas about the nature of who God is, who we are, and our predicament before God. They are narratives of the instructions for and construction of *the altar of bronze.*

Altars are a fundamental part of biblical religion. The patriarch Abram built altars (Gen. 12:7, 8; 13:18) and so did Moses (Ex. 17:15; 24:4). They were piles of dirt or stone that served as places to sacrifice and supplicate the Lord. God continued this practice in the tabernacle narratives by commanding Moses to build an altar in the midst of His people, in the courtyard of the tabernacle. He intended this altar to teach the Israelites their need for satisfaction, confession, and substitution. New-covenant believers desperately need these lessons, too, for we have the very same needs as our forefathers in the wilderness.

102

SATISFACTION

First, the altar of bronze taught the Israelites their need for *satisfaction*. Imagine again the camp of Israel in the desert. All the tribes camped in a circle around the tabernacle (Numbers 2). When a worshiper brought a sacrificial animal, he approached the courtyard, which was formed by a white curtain that went around the entire tabernacle (Ex. 27:9–19). After passing this curtain and entering the courtyard, the first thing he saw was "the altar of burnt offering" (Ex. 38:1, *mizbah ha-'olah*) and its fire.

This fire teaches us an important truth about God. In Leviticus 6, we find "the law of the burnt offering." Notice what it says about the fire:

> The burnt offering shall be on the hearth on the altar all night until the morning, and *the fire of the altar shall be kept burning on it.* And the priest shall put on his linen garment and put his linen undergarment on his body, and he shall take up the ashes to which the fire has reduced the burnt offering on the altar and put them beside the altar. Then he shall take off his garments and put

THE ALTAR OF BRONZE

The bronze altar for burnt offerings (Ex. 27:1–8; 38:1–7) stood in the outer courtyard with its poles removed. It was a hollow wooden box, overlaid with bronze, measuring 4.5 feet high and 7.5 feet long and wide (1.4 m x 2.3 m x 2.3 m). There was a bronze grating on the top and on the sides of the altar.

on other garments and carry the ashes outside the camp to a clean place. *The fire on the altar shall be kept burning on it*; it shall not go out. The priest shall burn wood on it every morning, and he shall arrange the burnt offering on it and shall burn on it the fat of the peace offerings. *Fire shall be kept burning on the altar continually; it shall not go out.*" (vv. 9b–13, emphasis added)

The fire on the bronze altar never went out. We can imagine the priests constantly crying out: "Feed the fire! Fan the flame!"[1] The fire of the altar needed to be satisfied constantly lest it be extinguished.

But how did the fire begin? When the first offerings in the tabernacle were placed on the altar, we read that "fire came out from before the LORD and consumed the burnt offering and the pieces of fat on the altar, and when all the people saw it, they shouted and fell on their faces" (9:24). God Himself lit the insatiable fire that was to burn constantly.

The fire on the altar, which the worshipers saw first as they entered the courtyard, then, was a picture of God Himself as a "consuming fire" (Heb. 12:28). This means that since God is righteous (that is, upright) and holy (that is, pure), being without sin, He must punish sin or He would cease to be God. Like the fire of the altar, He must be satisfied. The Heidelberg Catechism expresses this truth clearly:

Q. 10. Will God allow such disobedience and apostasy to go unpunished?
A. Certainly not, but He is terribly displeased with our inborn as well as our actual sins, and will punish them in just judgment in time and eternity, as He has declared: "Cursed is everyone that continueth not in all things which are written in the book of the law to do them."

Q. 11. But is not God also merciful?
A. God is indeed merciful, but He is likewise just; His justice therefore requires that sin which is committed against the most

high majesty of God, be punished with extreme, that is, with everlasting punishment both of body and soul.

As sinners, then, we need to satisfy God's justice. If we do not, we cannot enter His presence. Again, the Heidelberg Catechism addresses this subject:

Q. 12. Since, then, by the righteous judgment of God we deserve temporal and eternal punishment, how may we escape this punishment and be again received into favor?
A. God wills that His justice be satisfied; therefore, we must make full satisfaction to that justice, either by ourselves or by another.

The catechism then goes on to narrow down who is qualified to make this satisfaction to God:

Q. 13. Can we ourselves make this satisfaction?
A. Certainly not; on the contrary, we daily increase our guilt.

Q. 14. Can any mere creature make satisfaction for us?
A. None; for first, God will not punish any other creature for the sin which man committed; and further, no mere creature can sustain the burden of God's eternal wrath against sin and redeem others from it.

Q. 15. What kind of mediator and redeemer, then, must we seek?
A. One who is a true and righteous man, and yet more powerful than all creatures; that is, one who is also true God.

In the Old Testament, the Lord taught His children this truth in a graphic, earthly way—through the numerous sacrifices of bulls, goats, sheep, and birds. His intense wrath and justice were satisfied only temporarily by these animal sacrifices. This satisfaction is still required for sinful humans to enter the perfect presence of God.

CONFESSION

Second, the altar of bronze taught the Israelites their need for *confession*. Among other sacrifices, the burnt offering (Leviticus 1) and the sin offering (Leviticus 4) were offered on this altar. It seems likely that when the Levitical priests offered these sacrifices, they also offered urgent prayers of confession. Just as Samuel did when he made a sacrifice, we can surmise that the priests "cried out to the LORD for Israel, and the LORD answered" (1 Sam. 7:9).

We see a connection between the sacrifices offered on the bronze altar and confession of sins elsewhere in Scripture. We read that when an Israelite brought a burnt offering, he would lay his hands on the animal (Lev. 1:4). Likewise, when a sin offering was made, the worshiper would lay his hands on the animal, whether he was a priest (4:4), a leader (v. 24), or one of the people (v. 29). If the whole congregation had sinned, the elders would lay their hands on the animal (v. 15).

What was the purpose of this laying on of hands? In the "scapegoat" ritual on the Day of Atonement, the high priest would lay his hands on the animal's head and "confess . . . all the iniquities of the people of Israel" (Lev. 16:21).[2] Gordon Wenham says of the laying on of hands: "It was at this point that the worshipper said his prayer. The laying on of hands is associated with praying in Lev. 16:21 (cf. Deut. 21:6–9) as well as in later Jewish tradition. This is an important theological principle. Sacrifice without prayer is useless. All a man's powers must be active in divine worship, heart and mouth as well as hands and feet."[3]

This is a vital truth for us to hear. The contemporary church focuses heavily on the love of God, on being accepted by God, and other positive-sounding doctrines, but it has lost the biblical doctrine of repentance. The word *repentance* in our English New Testaments usually translates the Greek word *metanoeō*, which literally means a change of mind.[4] It is a U-turn that leads one away from self to the Savior in faith.

This confession, or repentance, is twofold. First, there is an initial repentance from sin and confession of sin when a person is converted.

One of the most vivid descriptions of this step is in 1 Thessalonians 1:9, where Paul reports what he had heard about the Thessalonians: "you turned to God from idols to serve the living and true God." The word Paul uses here, *epistrephō,* denotes not only a change of mind but a total turning away from idols to the one true and living God.[5] This is what an Israelite needed to do upon entering the tabernacle courtyard for the first time.

This is also what we need to do today in order to enter the presence of God and be welcomed by Him. We cannot be accepted by God apart from repentance. John the Baptist taught this: "Repent, for the kingdom of heaven is at hand" (Matt. 3:2); Jesus taught this: "I have not come to call the righteous but sinners to repentance" (Luke 5:32; cf. Matt. 4:17); Peter taught this: "Repent therefore, and turn again, that your sins may be blotted out, that times of refreshing may come from the presence of the Lord" (Acts 3:19–20a); and Paul taught this: "The times of ignorance God overlooked, but now he commands all people everywhere to repent" (Acts 17:30).

This initial repentance is explained fully in the Westminster Larger Catechism:

Q. 76. What is repentance unto life?
A. Repentance unto life is a saving grace, wrought in the heart of a sinner by the Spirit and word of God, whereby, out of the sight and sense, not only of the danger, but also of the filthiness and odiousness of his sins, and upon the apprehension of God's mercy in Christ to such as are penitent, he so grieves for and hates his sins, as that he turns from them all to God, purposing and endeavouring constantly to walk with him in all the ways of new obedience.

But it is crucial to understand that this necessary repentance is not merely a formal repentance, a formal turning away from sin. It is not merely a change of mind, as if one were to say, "Well, I hear what he's saying today so I'll say with my lips that I turn to God." This repentance must be a true confession of sins. We need to be grieved by our sins. We need to hate them because they are filthy and odious to God. We need to renounce our own wills. We need to turn from ourselves and give ourselves up totally to Jesus Christ.

Second, there is an ongoing confession and repentance that we need to practice each day of our Christian lives. The contemporary church has largely forgotten this repentance. Many think: "I confessed my sins and I was saved, so let's move on. I don't need to hear this stuff again." If that is your attitude, you have not yet confessed your sin of ignorance and pride. You need to "repent of [your] particular sins, particularly" (WCF 15.5). Even as Christians, we must constantly hear the words of the Apostle John: "If we [that is, Christians] confess our sins [not just in the past, but continually], he is faithful and just to forgive us our sins and to cleanse us from all unrighteousness" (1 John 1:9).

Our children do not have to tell us they are sorry for their misbehavior only once. As often as they sin and disobey, they need to show that they are sorry and to be honest about what they have done. It was the same with the worshipers who constantly went in and out of the tabernacle courtyard. They had to confess their sins constantly. Likewise, the historical Christian church has had a very healthy practice of setting aside time in weekly worship to confess sins. One example of this is found in *The Book of Common Prayer*:

> Almighty and most merciful Father, we have erred, and strayed from thy ways like lost sheep. We have followed too much the devices and desires of our own hearts. We have offended against thy holy laws. We have left undone those things which we ought to have done; and we have done those things which we ought not to have done; and there is no health in us. But thou, O Lord, have mercy upon us, miserable offenders. Spare thou those, O God, who confess their faults. Restore thou those who are penitent; according to thy promises declared unto mankind

in Christ Jesus our Lord. And grant, O most merciful Father, for his sake; that we may hereafter live a godly, righteous, and sober life, to the glory of thy holy Name. Amen.[6]

This ongoing repentance is itself twofold: death and resurrection, dying and living. The language used to describe the altar in the parallel chapter, Exodus 38, vividly portrays this. There it is called not merely "the altar" (27:1) but "the altar of burnt offering" (38:1). The burnt offering (*'olah*) is also known as the whole burnt offering because the entire animal was offered and burnt on the altar (Leviticus 1). It was a picture that the worshiper, as identified with the sacrifice (v. 4), had to die completely. But it was also known as the ascension offering because its smoke would ascend to God "with a pleasing aroma to the LORD" (vv. 9, 13, 17). This meant it was a picture that the worshiper ascended into heaven to be accepted by the Lord. From this we learn that we must constantly be confessing, lamenting our sinful natures and our sinful thoughts, words, and deeds to God. We must die to self. Likewise, we must constantly be seeking to live our new life in Christ for the glory of God. We must live to God.

Here is how the Heidelberg Catechism explains this twofold repentance:

Q. 88. In how many things does true repentance or conversion consist?
A. In two things: the dying of the old man, and the making alive of the new.

Q. 89. What is the dying of the old man?
A. Heartfelt sorrow for sin, causing us to hate and turn from it always more and more.

Q. 90. What is the making alive of the new man?
A. Heartfelt joy in God through Christ, causing us to take delight in living according to the will of God in all good works.

When we stand before God in worship—indeed, in all our times—
we are before a God whose justice must be satisfied, so we must come
before Him and confess our sins with heartfelt sorrow for them, hating
them and turning from them. But what is the remedy?

SUBSTITUTION

Third, the altar of bronze taught the Israelites their need for *substitution*. It showed them that something or someone must take their place,
because no person can pay for his or her own sins.

This altar had "horns for it on its four corners" (Ex. 27:2), and the
psalmist described their purpose: "Bind the festal sacrifice with cords, up
to the horns of the altar!" (Ps. 118:27). The substitute animal was tied
to the altar before it was burned, providing a vivid picture of the punishment each sinner deserved. But God is gracious as well as just, and He
provided a means for His justice to be satisfied in sacrifices. The various
sacrifices listed in Leviticus 1–7 were given so that the worshiper—the
sinner—would not have to be consumed by the raging fire of God's wrath
and justice. God showed His grace toward His people not only in prescribing the plethora of sacrifices but also in accepting them, "that [the
worshiper] may be accepted before the LORD" (Lev. 1:3).

But for faithful Israelites, there was a gnawing reality that constantly
came back to them: their impersonal sacrifices of animals could never
take away their personal sins completely. Animals that did not sin could
not pay for the Israelites' very personal and very real sins in the sight of
almighty God. As the author of the letter to the Hebrews writes:

> For since the law has but a shadow of the good things to come
> instead of the true form of these realities, it can never, by the same
> sacrifices that are continually offered every year, make perfect
> those who draw near. Otherwise, would they not have ceased
> to be offered, since the worshipers, having once been cleansed,
> would no longer have any consciousness of sins? But in these

sacrifices there is a reminder of sins every year. For it is impossible for the blood of bulls and goats to take away sins. (10:1–4)

It is the same today. Do you ever get that nagging feeling that you are just not doing enough? You need to be a better person, to be more generous with your time and money, to be more patient, more loving, more forgiving—and the list goes on. You have these feelings because you are guilty. But there is nothing you can do to take away that guilt; there is no point in trying harder.

This is why God sent His Son, Jesus Christ, to be the Substitute for sinners. God cannot merely overlook, forget, or cover up our sins with a generic sense of love and "moving on." No, our sins must be satisfied. Our sins must be genuinely confessed. And our sins must be placed on a substitute, because we cannot pay for them:

> But when Christ appeared as a high priest of the good things that have come, then through the greater and more perfect tent (not made with hands, that is, not of this creation) he entered once for all into the holy places, not by means of the blood of goats and calves but by means of his own blood, thus securing an eternal redemption. For if the blood of goats and bulls, and the sprinkling of defiled persons with the ashes of a heifer, sanctify for the purification of the flesh, how much more will the blood of Christ, who through the eternal Spirit offered himself without blemish to God, purify our conscience from dead works to serve the living God. (Heb. 9:11–14)

Because of the once-for-all substitution of our Lord Jesus Christ on the cross, a substitution that we experience through means of initial and ongoing confession of our sins, we can have the assurance that a full and final satisfaction has been made for all our transgressions. In this way, God's justice is turned away from us, while His love and grace are fully poured out upon us.

111

THE LORD'S COURTYARD

Exodus 27:9-19; 38:9-20

"You shall make the court of the tabernacle. On the south side the court shall have hangings of fine twined linen a hundred cubits long for one side. Its twenty pillars and their twenty bases shall be of bronze, but the hooks of the pillars and their fillets shall be of silver. And likewise for its length on the north side there shall be hangings a hundred cubits long, its pillars twenty and their bases twenty, of bronze, but the hooks of the pillars and their fillets shall be of silver. And for the breadth of the court on the west side there shall be hangings for fifty cubits, with ten pillars and ten bases. The breadth of the court on the front to the east shall be fifty cubits. The hangings for the one side of the gate shall be fifteen cubits, with their three pillars and three bases. On the other side the hangings shall be fifteen cubits, with their three pillars and three bases. For the gate of the court there shall be a screen twenty cubits long, of blue and purple and scarlet yarns and fine twined linen, embroidered with needlework. It shall have four pillars and with them four bases. All the pillars around the court shall be filleted with silver. Their hooks shall be of silver, and their bases of bronze. The length of the court shall be a hundred cubits, the breadth fifty, and the height five cubits, with hangings of fine twined linen and bases of bronze. All the utensils of the tabernacle for every use, and all its pegs and all the pegs of the court, shall be of bronze." (Ex. 27:9–19)

Recently, the journal *First Things* published an article that asked, "Why are so many people getting tattoos today?"[1] As one who does not have any tattoos but who ministers to many who do, I found the author's thesis fascinating. He said many people are getting tattoos because we are living in a "liquid society," and they are seeking stability and permanence. Whether or not this thesis is true in every situation, there is no doubt that clothing fads, political trends, jobs, and even hope and love are not permanent in today's Western culture. People do want to feel a sense of stability and security in this life while feeling a sense of transcendence from life. Apparently, tattoos can fill that need for some.

The wonderful thing about the Christian message concerning Jesus is that it has an answer for this deep human longing—whether one has a tattoo or not. The reason for this longing for permanence and transcendence, and the reason the world cannot provide them, is very simple: sin. We live in what we Christians call a fallen world. This means that the world as God created it and intended it to be has been marred by our sin. We live in a sin-torn world that will always disappoint, always frustrate, and always sadden us. The Apostle Paul said this world has been "subjected to futility, not willingly, but because of him who subjected it, in hope that the creation itself will be set free from its bondage to corruption and obtain the freedom of the glory of the children of God. For we know that the whole creation has been groaning together in the pains of childbirth until now" (Rom. 8:20–22). Is it any wonder the Christian life was described by our Reformation forefathers as "nothing but a constant death?"[2]

The way the world is today is the way the world was in the days of our forefathers, the Israelites. They, too, knew the frustrations of a fallen world. They, too, needed stability and a sense of belonging to something bigger than themselves. The passage before us describes the way the Lord brought permanence and transcendence to His people while they wandered in the desert for forty years. He taught them about it by means of *the Lord's courtyard.*

114

As we meditate on this passage, note two key points about the courtyard (*hatsar*) of the tabernacle that spoke truth to the Israelites and that speak truth to us today: It provided a place of *permanence* and a place of *access*.

PERMANENCE

First, the Lord's courtyard provided a place of *permanence*. Israel's whole existence was one of turbulence, not permanence. Their fathers wandered the earth like Adam, who was "east of the garden of Eden" (Gen. 3:24), and "acknowledged that they were strangers and exiles on the earth" (Heb. 11:13), with only temporary altars at which to worship (e.g., Gen. 12:7, 8). While in Egypt, their hearts longed for the land promised to Abraham, and "God heard their groaning" (Ex. 2:24). After the exodus, they still had no permanent home, as God cursed them with forty years of wandering in the desert because of their sin (Num. 13:25–14:38).

Yet the Lord provided for them. So, everywhere they stopped in their journey, the courtyard's pillars and bases of bronze were planted (e.g., Ex. 27:10–12).[3] Its bronze pillars were propped up. The great curtainlike walls that surrounded the tabernacle area were unfurled. This courtyard gave the tribes a point of reference around which to pitch their tents, as each tribe was assigned a location in relation to the tent of the Lord (Numbers 2).

But this place of holiness was only semipermanent. It looked forward to a day of true permanence. Eventually it gave way to the place of permanent holiness in the temple on Mount Zion, "the city of the great King" (Ps. 48:2). The mountain that supported the temple of the Lord was so special that the sons of Korah prayed, "On the holy mount stands the city he founded; the LORD loves the gates of Zion more than all the dwelling places of Jacob" (Ps. 87:1–2). God knows the needs of His people. He knows we are weak. He knows we need permanence, stability, and structure.

I hope you are saying to yourself: "But we don't live in Jerusalem. There is no temple. Neither do we live in the desert. There is no tabernacle courtyard. Can there be any permanence for us given that these verses describe what happened long ago?" We find the answer in John 4,

THE TABERNACLE AND COURTYARD

The tabernacle was a portable temple—a "tent of meeting"—within a movable courtyard (Exodus 25–31; 35–40). It was constructed after the pattern that Yahweh revealed to Moses on Mount Sinai, and was assembled in the desert as Moses led the Israelites from Egypt to the Promised Land. For an enlargement of the tent itself, see p. 94. The tabernacle courtyard was 150 feet (46 m) long and 75 feet (23 m) wide, totaling 11,250 square feet (1,045 square meters).

The Most Holy Place of the tabernacle tent was a 15-foot (4.6-m) cube, containing only the ark of the covenant (Ex. 25:10–22; 37:1–9). It was here that Yahweh would descend to meet with his people in a cloud theophany (divine appearance).

The Holy Place of the tabernacle tent was 30 feet (9.1 m) long, 15 feet (4.6 m) wide, and 15 feet (4.6 m) high. It housed the table (Ex. 25:23–30), the golden lampstand (Ex. 25:31–40; 37:17–24), and the altar of incense (Ex. 30:1–10; 37:25–29).

The framed structure was covered by four layers of cloth and skin (Ex. 26:1–14).

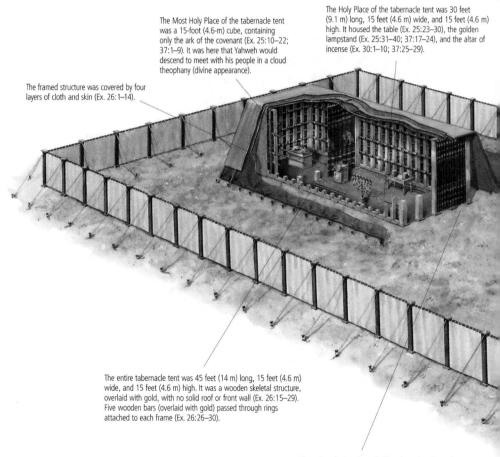

The entire tabernacle tent was 45 feet (14 m) long, 15 feet (4.6 m) wide, and 15 feet (4.6 m) high. It was a wooden skeletal structure, overlaid with gold, with no solid roof or front wall (Ex. 26:15–29). Five wooden bars (overlaid with gold) passed through rings attached to each frame (Ex. 26:26–30).

The veil separating the Holy Place from the tabernacle courtyard was similar to the veil separating the Holy Place from the Most Holy Place, except that cherubim were not embroidered on it (Ex. 26:36–37). It hung on five golden pillars.

Tabernacle and Court Architectural Plan

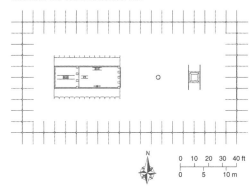

N

0 10 20 30 40 ft
0   5   10 m

The bronze basin with its stand was for ceremonial washings (Ex. 30:17–21; 38:8).

The bronze altar, also known as the altar of burnt offering (Ex. 27:1–8; 38:1–7), was made from a hollow wooden box (7.5 feet/2.3 m long and wide, and 4.5 feet/1.4 m high), overlaid with bronze. It had four horns at its corners. It was transported by means of two poles on its journey through the wilderness.

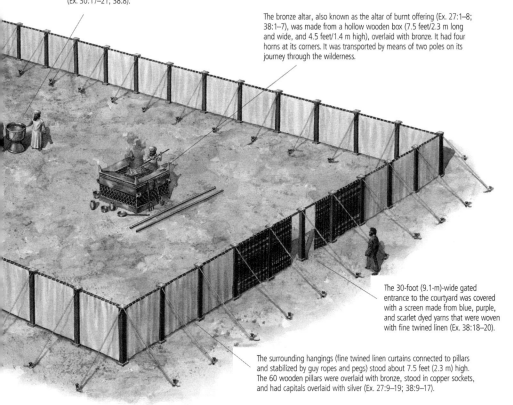

The 30-foot (9.1-m)-wide gated entrance to the courtyard was covered with a screen made from blue, purple, and scarlet dyed yarns that were woven with fine twined linen (Ex. 38:18–20).

The surrounding hangings (fine twined linen curtains connected to pillars and stabilized by guy ropes and pegs) stood about 7.5 feet (2.3 m) high. The 60 wooden pillars were overlaid with bronze, stood in copper sockets, and had capitals overlaid with silver (Ex. 27:9–19; 38:9–17).

117

which records a conversation our Lord had with a woman. Jesus was a Jew and she was a Samaritan, part of a mixed race created by the Assyrians, who wanted to breed the Jews out of the land. Part of their conversation went like this:

> [The woman said,] "Our fathers worshiped on this mountain, but you say that in Jerusalem is the place where people ought to worship." Jesus said to her, "Woman, believe me, the hour is coming when neither on this mountain nor in Jerusalem will you worship the Father. You worship what you do not know; we worship what we know, for salvation is from the Jews. But the hour is coming, and is now here, when the true worshipers will worship the Father in spirit and truth, for the Father is seeking such people to worship him. God is spirit, and those who worship him must worship in spirit and truth." (vv. 20–24)

Jesus was saying that there would no longer be one holy mountain here or another holy mountain there. There would not be one permanent, fixed, holy place on the earth where everyone would go to worship God in "the beauty of holiness" (Ps. 29:2, KJV). Instead, He said, worship of the Father would occur "in spirit," that is, in the Holy Spirit, and "in truth," that is, in Christ.

Do you understand what this means? When we ask our children the basic catechism question, "Where is God," they answer. "God is everywhere."[4] Because of that truth, wherever we gather together in the name of the Lord, in the power of the Spirit, to worship the Father becomes a place of holy permanence, "a holy temple in the Lord" (Eph. 2:21). This is true even where a mere two or three gather (Matt. 18:20). It is vital for us to grasp this in our time.

Public worship, then, is the very center of the Christian's pilgrim life in this world. The Puritan pastor David Clarkson once preached a sermon titled "Public Worship to be Preferred Before Private," giving twelve reasons for his thesis.[5] When we come together on the Lord's Day, we come out of the world and into God's holy and heavenly presence. We leave "liquidity" behind and find stability. We leave earth for heaven, albeit only an imperfect foretaste.

This truth reveals why we should be concerned to sanctify the Lord's Day week in and week out, attending public worship except by providential hindrance. Wherever the courtyard of the tabernacle was set up became like the ground where Moses knelt (Exodus 3) and the gate of heaven where Jacob slept (Genesis 32). It became a holy place, holy ground, the place of the Lord's very presence. Likewise, when we gather for worship, wherever it might be, that place becomes holy ground. Why? Because the Lord meets with His people there.

Do you long to assemble with your congregation to meet with God? Do you desire to gather with your brothers and sisters for a glimpse of heaven? Are the words of the sons of Korah yours: "For a day in your courts is better than a thousand elsewhere. I would rather be a door-keeper in the house of my God than dwell in the tents of wickedness" (Ps. 84:10)?

This truth is also vital for our individual and family spiritual life. We are called by God to engage in private worship, as well. We are to fill our personal and family lives with reading of the Scriptures, praying, and singing (Deut. 6:4–9). These are what the Canons of Dort describe as "holy exercises of godliness" (5.2) that help us to persevere. When we engage in these holy exercises, both public and private, we find moments of permanence in our impermanent lives.[6] In the words of Isaac Watts, when we worship:

We're marching to Zion,
beautiful, beautiful Zion;
we're marching upward to Zion,
the beautiful city of God.[7]

We come to find permanence in worship because "here we have no lasting city, but we seek the city that is to come" (Heb. 13:14).

ACCESS

Second, the Lord's courtyard provided a place of *access*. The tabernacle did not provide permanence simply by being set up and standing for a time. It had to be used, appropriated, and accessed.

How precious must that screen (Ex. 27:16) have been? The Holy of Holies was inaccessible except to one high priest, who could go past its veil only one day a year (Leviticus 16; Hebrews 9). The Holy Place was inaccessible except to the rest of the Levitical priests, who alone could enter beyond its veil. Then there was a tall screen, which stood like a wall five cubits high (Ex. 27:18), or seven and a half feet, surrounding the entire tabernacle complex. How wonderful it must have been to walk around the outside of the screen and then come to the east side and find a wide screen that was thirty feet long (v. 16), which functioned as "the gate of the court." There was access for all the Israelites at this screen, as they could pass through into the courtyard. In the words of John Calvin, the average Israelites were "forbidden to enter the Temple, whilst at the same time they were reminded that men, although unworthy outcasts, are received by God, if only they seek Him simply, and with due humility, mindful of their own unworthiness."[8] Again, since this screen was to the east (Ex. 27:13, *kedmah mizrahah*), literally, "on the front toward the rising sun," to enter the tabernacle was to go west, as if one were returning to Eden. In the worship of the tabernacle, God provided access to heaven on earth.

Yet, although there was access, we have to remember that it was a limited access. This was still the time of types and shadows. Most Israelites could enter only the courtyard and not the tabernacle itself, and most especially not the Holy of Holies.[9] Further, access was limited among the people on the basis of various factors. Women could not enter after childbirth (Leviticus 12). If a person had a skin disease (Leviticus 13) or a bodily discharge (Leviticus 15), or had touched a dead body (Numbers 19), he was unclean and could not access the court of the Lord for a prescribed period of time. He could not draw near. He could not offer a sacrificial animal for his sins. He could not participate.

Why did the Lord limit access so strictly? God wanted to teach His people that it is a serious thing to come into His presence. This is why Moses was required to remove his sandals before the Lord at the burning bush (Ex. 3:1–6). God wants us to see that He is holy. He wants us to see just how perfect, pure, and spotless we must be. At one time or another, every Israelite likely was excluded. But to be excluded once meant that he deserved to be excluded forever, since he had failed to remain holy his entire life. The lesson was clear: No one deserves to access God's courtyard, His tabernacle, and His presence.

Here is where the stage was set for the coming of our Lord: "The work of Christ has removed the need for this restriction."[10] Jesus touched the diseased. He ate with sinners. He welcomed the outcast, the weak, the sick, and the dying into His presence. He gave access. Jesus even did the unthinkable—He went to the tomb of a dead man, His friend Lazarus (John 11:38–44), and had contact with him, even though this would have made Him unclean. He also touched Jairus' dead daughter in order to raise her up (Mark 5:35–43). Our access to God, then, is through Christ, who "has borne our griefs and carried our sorrows" (Isa. 53:4) so that we might enter God's presence in joy and peace. Because of Him, access is granted to all who call on His name: "There is neither Jew nor Greek, there is neither slave nor free, there is no male and female, for you are all one in Christ Jesus" (Gal. 3:28).

This means that we must make sure we have come to Christ. The Bible says very clearly, "everyone who calls upon the name of the Lord shall be saved" (Joel 2:32; Acts 2:21). We do not need to dress a certain way. We do not need to know secret handshakes. We do not need to be cleaned up and have it all figured out. And we no longer need to bring animal sacrifices, because Jesus is the once-for-all sacrifice (Heb. 7:27; 9:12, 26, 28; 10:10). He takes us, with our infirmities, weaknesses, and especially our sins, and grants us access to the presence of our heavenly Father.

As believers, we must also make sure that we continue to take advantage of our access. The writer to the Hebrews tells us to "come boldly unto the throne of grace" (Heb. 4:16, KJV), because God knows we doubt, get discouraged, and are often fainthearted. Be bold. Go to Him in prayer. You have not because you ask not. Ask, seek, and knock (Matt. 7:7–11).

We live in a liquid society. Our lives are often upside down. We even talk about being "under water" these days in the housing market. But God has provided a place for us to find permanence and to find access to His heavenly throne room, right up to His throne of grace. Come to the Lord in faith; come to Him in worship.

THE PRIESTHOOD
OF THE LORD

Exodus 28:1–2

"Then bring near to you Aaron your brother, and his sons with him, from among the people of Israel, to serve me as priests—Aaron and Aaron's sons, Nadab and Abihu, Eleazar and Ithamar. And you shall make holy garments for Aaron your brother, for glory and for beauty." (Ex. 28:1–2)

We live in a situation that is vastly different from that of our forefathers in the wilderness, with their tabernacle, their priesthood, and their sacrifices. We live mostly in cities; they lived in the desert. We have permanent church buildings; they had a portable tent. We have self-help gurus on television and in the bookstores; they had priests. We have animal rights; they had animal sacrifices. Thus, when we read strange and unfamiliar parts of the Bible, such as the narratives about the clothing of the priests, we can have that strange and uneasy feeling a child has when he first goes to a new place. Yet, we enter this strange place of the Israelites' religious system knowing that this is the

Word of the one true God, whom they believed in and we believe in; therefore, we must read it, exposit it, and apply it.

In this passage, the main concern is the high priest's garments, while the garments of the other priests are described in 28:40 and 42. The high priest had eight articles of clothing: a breastpiece, an ephod, a robe, a coat of checker work, a turban, a sash, a plate of pure gold for his forehead, and linen undergarments (vv. 4, 36, 42). These articles of clothing are described as "holy garments" (v. 2, *bigdei kodesh*). The other, ordinary priests, by contrast, had just four articles of clothing: a coat, a sash, a cap, and an undergarment (vv. 40, 42). These also were called "holy garments" (v. 3).

However, this passage is not just about priestly fashion. It also teaches us significant lessons about *the priesthood of the Lord* itself. This narrative shows us that the Lord's priesthood was both *of the people* and *distinct from the people*. In the words of John Calvin, "The whole body of the people saw a man like themselves, who could not enter the sanctuary trusting in his own innocence, and whose dignity was conferred upon him by adventitious rites, *i.e.*, by anointing and by investiture."[1] These lessons were intended to teach faithful Israelites about the kind of priest God's people, then and now, need, and that this need would be met perfectly in the coming of a final priest, Israel's Messiah, our Lord Jesus Christ.

A PRIESTHOOD OF THE PEOPLE

First, the ancient Israelite priesthood was *of the people*. The Lord commanded Moses to "bring near to you Aaron your brother, and his sons with him, *from among the people of Israel*, to serve me as priests" (v. 1). This teaches us a couple of important theological points.

First, in His infinite wisdom (Isa. 55:8–9), the Lord uses men as the means to accomplish His purposes. The Creator, who is free to work above and beyond any means, chooses to work through His creation. In the beginning, after our first parents, Adam and Eve, sinned, the Lord Himself sacrificed animals and ministered for the sake of His people by covering their nakedness (Gen. 3:21). He did not just tell them they were covered; He used the means of animal skins to signify the covering of their sins. Yet when the unfolding of God's redemptive plan reached the exodus, He pulled out of the congregation a small group of men to be His servants, to act as His hands and mouth to His people. The Lord would no longer do the sacrificing; men would.

Second, the Lord uses men because they know best how to serve their fellow humanity. Let us not think the Lord chose the tribe of Levi to be His servants because they were holier than the other tribes. There is no better illustration of this than Genesis 34. When Dinah, the daughter of Leah, was defiled by Shechem, Simeon and Levi lied about forging a covenant between Jacob's family and Shechem's people, then murdered men throughout the camp. Levi, the father of the priestly line, was described by his father as an angry and violent man (Gen. 49:5–7). Yet God in His grace chose to call His priests from this tribe to illustrate that the Israelites needed ministers who could empathize and sympathize with them.

The same sin that, so to speak, coursed through the veins of Adam in his doubting of the Word of God that led to his giving ear to the Devil; through Abraham in all his lying and doubting; through Jacob in all his cheating and doubting; through Moses in all his doubting of God; and through all the people of Israel in their doubting, complaining, and grumbling against God also ran through Aaron and his sons. We call this, in theological terms, original sin, and all men are infected with it. The priests were no exception.

Yet God chose men to be priests, for they were human and sinners, and therefore they were best suited to minister to their fellow human sinners. God did not choose angels, as they have no acquaintance with our humanity, our weaknesses: "For every high priest chosen from among men is appointed to act on behalf of men in relation to God, to offer gifts and sacrifices for sins. He can deal gently with the ignorant and wayward, since he himself is beset with weakness" (Heb. 5:1–2). The priests of Israel could deal with the ignorant and wayward because they themselves were ignorant and wayward, coming from "among the people" (Ex. 28:1).

125

As a Protestant minister, one of the maxims of my existence is that I am not a priest. If you also are a Protestant pastor, you no doubt think the same of yourself. While this is true, the New Testament does allude to the Old Testament priesthood as an example of the Christian ministry (e.g., Rom. 15:16). While Paul does not say that ministers make sacrifices, the analogy between pastors and priests is that God still uses lowly men for the ministry to accomplish His purposes. Men, not angels, still know best how to serve their people because they, too, are sinners.[2]

THE HIGH PRIEST'S GARMENTS

The illustration depicts the holy garments worn by the high priests (Exodus 28; 39).

The *turban* of fine linen held a plate of pure shining gold, on which were engraved the Hebrew words for "Holy to YHWH."

The *ephod* (a colorful linen torso garment held by a skillfully woven waistband) had two shoulder pieces, each holding an onyx stone. The names of the 12 sons of Israel were engraved on these two stones. The cloth *breastpiece of judgment* had four rows, each with three precious stones. Each of these stones had engraved upon it the name of one of the tribes of Israel. The breastpiece also contained the Urim and the Thummim, and was attached to the ephod by gold chains and rings. The blue *robe* was worn under the ephod (Lev. 8:7–8); colorful imitation pomegranates lined the hem of the robe, alternating with golden bells. The white *coat* or tunic of checkered weave and fine linen was probably held by the embroidered sash under the robe.

What, then, does this mean for Christians who are not ministers in terms of their relationship with God? First, as recipients of the ministry from men, we are called to rejoice in the immense love of God toward His people in this regard. He has not left us alone in our sins to find Him, but has provided us with servants "to act on behalf of men in relation to God" (Heb. 5:1). Your minister is a gift from the ascended Jesus Christ (Eph. 4:11). Praise God for your pastor.

Second, we are to be comforted by the fact that our ministers are able to "deal gently" with us (Heb. 5:2). The great Puritan Thomas Manton said that like Jesus Christ, ministers know what it is to be tempted by Satan, and that God allows them to be tempted so that they might be used "for the recovery of poor souls out of their bondage into the liberty of the children of God."[3] Christ underwent temptation by Satan (Matthew 4) that He might be enabled to help us who are tempted (Heb. 2:18), and the same is true of ministers of the gospel, who are Christ's ambassadors (2 Cor. 5:20). Paul describes ministers as "jars of clay" (2 Cor. 4:7) because they are:

> . . . afflicted in every way, but not crushed; perplexed, but not driven to despair; persecuted, but not forsaken; struck down, but not destroyed; always carrying in the body the death of Jesus, so that the life of Jesus may also be manifested in our bodies. For we who live are always being given over to death for Jesus' sake, so that the life of Jesus also may be manifested in our mortal flesh. So death is at work in us, but life in you." (2 Cor. 4:8–12)

Like the priests in the tabernacle, as a minister I cannot help people who are in bondage to sin unless I know what it is to be a filthy, depraved sinner who constantly feels the Devil's breath on the back of my neck in the midst of a hostile world. This is why Manton said, "Ministers should not only be men of science, but of experience."[4] Your minister knows your weakness. Therefore, pray for him.

A PRIESTHOOD DISTINCT
FROM THE PEOPLE

Second, the priesthood was *distinct from the people*. The Lord commanded Moses to "make holy garments for Aaron your brother, for glory and for beauty" (Ex. 28:2). Despite all their similarity to their fellow Israelites, the priests were set-apart men. "The holy garments were [not only] supposed to conceal his faults [but also] to represent the incomparable adornment of all virtues."[5] These were holy garments, set apart by the Lord, in order to show the glory and beauty of the Lord and to teach the Israelites reverence in their worship.[6]

Here is how the apocryphal book Sirach (also known as Ecclesiasticus) described the high priest Simon in the second century BC:

How was he honoured in the midst of the people in his coming out of the sanctuary! He was as the morning star in the midst of a cloud, and as the moon at the full. As the sun shining upon the temple of the most High, and as the rainbow giving light in the bright clouds. And as the flower of roses in the spring of the year, as lilies by the rivers of waters, and as the branches of the frankincense tree in the time of summer. As fire and incense in the censer, and as a vessel of beaten gold set with all manner of precious stones. And as a fair olive tree budding forth fruit, and as a cypress tree which groweth up to the clouds. When he put on the robe of honour, and was clothed with the perfection of glory, when he went up to the holy altar, he made the garment of holiness honourable. When he took the portions out of the priests' hands, he himself stood by the hearth of the altar, compassed about, as a young cedar in Libanus; and as palm trees compassed they him round about. So were all the sons of Aaron in their glory, and the oblations of the Lord in their hands, before all the congregation of Israel. (Sirach 50:5–13)

128

Notice how this description was derived from all the glory and beauty of the garments described in the rest of Exodus 28. There was gold; there was blue, purple, and scarlet yarn; there was fine twined linen (v. 5); there were beautiful onyx stones (v. 9); there were twelve other precious stones (vv. 17–20); there were pomegranates and golden bells (vv. 33–34); and there were the mysterious Urim and Thummim (v. 30).[7] All these colors and materials in the priestly garments were meant to communicate the glory and the beauty of the Lord that distinguished the priests from the people. In fact, these set-apart clothes were symbolic of the tabernacle itself, with all their glory and beauty, with the different materials that were used in its construction.[8]

What was the purpose of this distinctiveness? It showed the Israelites that they needed someone who was holy, who was utterly dedicated to the Lord night and day, to bring their prayers into the presence of God. The priesthood did just that. The priests were set apart to "serve" the Lord (v. 1) and to "minister in the Holy Place" (v. 43) on behalf of and for the sake of the people.

As I mentioned at the outset of this chapter, no doubt this is very different from the world in which you and I live. However, we learn about our relationship with God from this account. We learn that, just like the Israelites, we, too, need a priesthood and a representative high priest. We, too, need a priest who is of the people, who is human just like us. We also need a priest who is distinct from the people, who is holy and set apart from us and our sins. We need such a priest to stand between God and us because God is holy and we are sinners—and sinners cannot save themselves. As sinners, we cannot just walk into our holy God's presence, as we learn from the example of Isaiah, who, when he entered the presence of the Lord's holiness, cried out: "Woe is me! For I am lost; for I am a man of unclean lips, and I dwell in the midst of a people of unclean lips; for my eyes have seen the King, the LORD of hosts!" (Isa. 6:5). When he entered the heavenly and holy presence of the Lord, he immediately became aware of his sin and guilt. He needed to have his sinful lips cleansed, which the Lord did by touching his lips with a coal from the altar (Isa. 6:6–7).

However, there is one person who can enter the holy presence of God on His own and represent sinners: Jesus Christ. When we read a passage such as Exodus 28, we ultimately learn about our relationship to God through the person and work of Christ. First, the shadows of the Old Testament teach us the reality that we need a priest of the people. Jesus Christ shares in our flesh and blood, that is, our true humanity (Heb. 2:14). He had to be a human like us in every way in order to be a merciful and faithful high priest (v. 17). As the author of Hebrews explains, "because he himself has suffered when tempted, he is able to help those who are being tempted" (v. 18). He can sympathize with our weaknesses because He has been tempted like us in every way, yet without sinning (4:15). Our ancient Christian fathers and brothers summarized this when they described Christ as being "consubstantial with us according to the Manhood" (Definition of Chalcedon). He is of the same substance, the same stuff, as we are, with a body and soul. As we have already noted, priests were drawn from the people so that they would deal gently with the ignorant and wayward (5:1). Jesus Christ is fully human and thus fully able to help us in our sins. He is fully able to hear our cries when we are tempted. He knows what it is to be human and weak. But He is more.

Second, this passage reveals to us that we need a priest who is distinct from the people. We need more than a mere man to be our priest. We need one who is totally distinct from us. The vestments were God's "promise that the Mediator would be far more august than the condition of man could produce."[9] Jesus is this august Mediator. He is distinct because He is of a different priesthood. He is not from the Levitical priesthood, but from the priesthood of Melchizedek (Hebrews 7). But He also is distinct because he is "holy, innocent, unstained, separated from sinners, and exalted above the heavens" (v. 26). Jesus is a sinless, perfect man.

But as amazing as this is, we need still more. We need a priest who is truly God. We need a priest who is a human, in order that He might sympathize with our weaknesses. We need a priest who is God, in order that He might save us from our sins and the results of our sins: death and eternal punishment from God's wrath and justice in hell.

Our historical Protestant Reformation catechisms wonderfully express the truth that Jesus is both God and man, and therefore the perfect remedy for our sins. The Heidelberg Catechism says:

Q. 16. Why must he be a true and righteous man?
A. Because the justice of God requires that the same human nature which has sinned should make satisfaction for sin; but one who is himself a sinner cannot satisfy for others.

Q. 17. Why must he also be true God?
A. That by the power of His Godhead He might bear in His manhood the burden of God's wrath, and so obtain for and restore to us righteousness and life.

The Westminster Larger Catechism expresses this same fundamental truth:

Q. 38. Why was it requisite that the Mediator should be God?
A. It was requisite that the Mediator should be God, that he might sustain and keep the human nature from sinking under the infinite wrath of God, and the power of death; give worth and efficacy to his sufferings, obedience, and intercession; and to satisfy God's justice, procure his favour, purchase a peculiar people, give his Spirit to them, conquer all their enemies, and bring them to everlasting salvation.

Q. 39. Why was it requisite that the Mediator should be man?
A. It was requisite that the Mediator should be man, that he might advance our nature, perform obedience to the law, suffer and make intercession for us in our nature, have a fellow-feeling

of our infirmities; that we might receive the adoption of sons, and have comfort and access with boldness unto the throne of grace.

Because of who He is, Jesus speaks to you who are sinners and invites you to come to Him in your weakness and sin. He invites you who have not trusted in Him before. He invites you who are struggling with your faith. He invites you who cannot break the power of certain sins. He even invites you who are strong in faith to constantly cling to Him and even to be used by Him to serve those who are weak.

All of us have a desperate need of Jesus today—a priest like us, a priest unlike us. Come to Him, for He is willing to deal gently with you. Come to Him, for He is able to act powerfully for you.

THE BENEFITS
OF THE PRIESTHOOD

Exodus 28:3–43; 39:1–43

"And they shall make the ephod of gold. . . . It shall have two shoulder pieces attached to its two edges, so that it may be joined together. . . . You shall take two onyx stones, and engrave on them the names of the sons of Israel, six of their names on the one stone, and the names of the remaining six on the other stone, in the order of their birth. As a jeweler engraves signets, so shall you engrave the two stones with the names of the sons of Israel. . . . And you shall set the two stones on the shoulder pieces of the ephod, as stones of remembrance for the sons of Israel. And Aaron shall bear their names before the LORD on his two shoulders for remembrance. . . . You shall make a breastpiece of judgment, in skilled work. In the style of the ephod you shall make it—of gold, blue and purple and scarlet yarns, and fine twined linen shall you make it. . . . There shall be twelve stones with their names according to the names of the sons of Israel. They shall be like signets, each engraved with its name, for the twelve tribes. . . . So Aaron shall bear the names of the sons of Israel in the breastpiece of judgment on his heart, when he goes into the Holy Place, to bring them to regular remembrance before the LORD. And in the breastpiece of judgment you shall put the Urim and the Thummim, and they shall be on Aaron's heart, when he goes in before the LORD. Thus Aaron shall bear the judgment of the people of Israel on his heart before the LORD regularly. . . . You shall make the robe of the ephod all of blue. . . . And it shall be on Aaron when he ministers, and its sound shall be heard when he goes into the Holy Place before the LORD, and when he comes out, so that he does not die. . . . You shall make a plate of pure gold and engrave on it, like the engraving of a signet, "Holy to the LORD." . . . It shall be on Aaron's forehead, and Aaron shall bear any guilt from the holy things that the people of Israel consecrate as their holy gifts. It shall regularly be on his forehead, that they may be accepted before the LORD. . . . For Aaron's sons you shall make coats and sashes and caps . . . and they shall be on Aaron and on his sons when they go into the tent of meeting or when they come near the altar to minister in the Holy Place, lest they bear guilt and die. This shall be a statute forever for him and for his offspring after him." (Ex. 28:3–43)

"As long as Christ remains outside of us, and we are separated from him, all that he has suffered and done for the salvation of the human race remains useless and of no value for us."[1] This is how the great church Reformer John Calvin described the necessity of benefiting from all that Jesus Christ did by receiving and embracing Him by faith. All who He is as God and man and all that He has done in His birth, life, death, resurrection, ascension, and present intercession, as wonderful as it is in principle, is of no personal benefit unless we receive it by faith and make it our own. A faith like that of the demons is not good enough (James 2:19). But when we apprehend and appropriate Jesus Christ by a true, living faith, that is, by making Him ours, wonderful benefits flow to us. Faith "embraces Jesus Christ, with all his merits, and makes him its own, and no longer looks for anything apart from him" (BC, Art. 22).

The Israelites in the wilderness learned this lesson through the ministry of the priests. We have seen that the Lord chose Aaron as high priest "to serve me" (Ex. 28:1). This chapter goes on to declare that the high priest existed "to serve me" (v. 4) and that he "ministers . . . before the LORD" (v. 35). We also see that Aaron's four sons were to "serve me" and "minister in the holy place" (v. 41) alongside their father as assistant priests. So the priests were in the holy tent of the Lord, serving Him by sacrificing and supplicating day and night.

But what benefit did these priestly ministrations have for the average Israelite? The priests were separated from their fellow Israelites by their calling, as well as by where they lived in the camp, but the Lord did not intend for them to be of no value to His people. By paying close attention to what the Lord said about the array of garments the priests were to wear, we can see how the Israelites were able, by faith, to receive *the benefits of the priesthood*. Three such benefits are revealed in this text: their names were remembered, their sins were removed, and their persons were reconciled. Once again, we learn that these same benefits flow to new-covenant believers through our Great High Priest, the Lord Jesus Christ.

THEIR NAMES WERE REMEMBERED

First, the people benefited from the priesthood in that *their names were remembered*. We read elsewhere in the book of Exodus that the Israelites were to remember the name of the Lord throughout all generations (3:15). They also were commanded not to take this name in vain (20:7). The Lord also said that He would cause His own name to be remembered by them in a location of His choosing when His people entered the Promised Land (20:24). But here in Exodus 28, we learn that by means of the engraved stones in the ephod and breastpiece, the high priest would bring the *Israelites'* names "before the LORD for remembrance" (v. 12). The benefit of the priesthood was not that the Israelites would remember the Lord's name so well or even that the priests would remember every Israelite's name when they prayed, but that the Lord Himself would remember His people, by name.

How exactly are we to understand such language, which seems to suggest that God is like us in needing to remember things? W. H. Gispen writes: "Verse 12 speaks of God in anthropomorphic terms, as happens frequently in the Scriptures; in a sense the entire Bible speaks anthro-pomorphically. The Lord is omniscient, and thus did not need these memorial stones to be reminded of Israel, but it was a consolation for the Israelites, who could see the high priest as a permanent mediator."[2]

The Lord gave His people these stones as visible assurances of His grace and love for them. They were sacramental stones. The language of the Westminster Larger Catechism is helpful here:

Q. 163. What are the parts of the sacrament?
A. The parts of the sacrament are two; the one an outward and sensible sign, used according to Christ's own appointment; the other an inward and spiritual grace thereby signified.

The stones in the breastpiece and ephod were the outward and sensible signs of the inward and spiritual grace of God, in particular, that He knew His people. They were the assurance that the Lord "heard their groaning, and . . . remembered his covenant with Abraham, with Isaac, and with Jacob. God saw the people of Israel—and God knew" (Ex. 2:24–25).

Exodus 28 reveals two aspects of this remembrance. First, it involved *personal knowledge*. We see this with the ephod of gold (v. 6). It was an apparatus with two shoulder pieces (v. 7). On top of the shoulders were two onyx stones, each with the names of six of the tribes of Israel etched into them (vv. 9–11). These were "stones of remembrance for the sons of Israel," and Aaron was to "bear their names before the LORD for remembrance" (v. 12). Likewise, the breastpiece included twelve precious stones, each engraved with the name of one of the tribes (v. 21). Thus, Aaron would "bear the names of the sons of Israel . . . on his heart" (v. 29).

Here we learn that God the Creator, who gives all the millions upon millions of stars their names (Ps. 147:4), is an intimate, personal God who knows each of His people by name. This is a foreshadowing of the very personal work of our Lord Jesus Christ, who, as the Good Shepherd, knows each of His sheep intimately: "I am the good shepherd. I know my own and my own know me. . . . My sheep hear my voice, and I know them, and they follow me" (John 10:14, 27).

Is your name inscribed on the onyx stones? Does the Great High Priest know your name? Of course, Jesus is God and therefore knows us all. But does He know your name as His possession? Does He know your name because you are one of His sheep? Does He know your name because He bore your sins on the cross? You can answer these questions positively when He is no longer outside and useless to you, when you embrace Him by faith, trusting in Him to stand before the presence of God with your name.

Second, this remembrance involved *perpetual knowledge*. As we have seen, the breastpiece that the high priest wore in the presence of God was adorned with twelve precious stones, each engraved with the name of one of the twelve tribes of Israel (Ex. 28:15–21). This was so that "Aaron shall bear the names of the sons of Israel in the breastpiece of judgment on his heart, when he goes into the Holy Place, to bring them to *regular* remembrance before the LORD" (v. 29, emphasis added). As we have seen, in the tabernacle narratives the word translated here as "regular" can also be rendered as "morning and evening." It is a way of saying "perpetually," that is, "at all times."

This is a beautiful picture of what our Lord does for us at the right hand of God. We know Jesus is a priest. We know that a priest makes sacrifice. But a priest also makes supplication. What does this mean? Hebrews 7:25, one of the most profound texts of Scripture regarding our Lord's high priestly work, says, "Consequently, he is able to save to the uttermost those who draw near to God through him, since he always lives to make intercession for them." Why do we believe in the perseverance of the saints, the doctrine that true believers have the assurance that they will ultimately be saved? It is because of our Lord's perpetual prayers on our behalf. We persevere because He preserves. Despite all opposition, Christ leads us through: "Who is to condemn? Christ Jesus is the one who died—more than that, who was raised—who is at the right hand of God, who indeed is interceding for us" (Rom. 8:34). Jesus knows

His people's names personally and prays for them perpetually. Will His prayers go unanswered?

The Canons of Dort speak of the relationship between our weakness and God's power in our perseverance, saying, "So it is not by [our] own merits or strength but by God's undeserved mercy that [we] neither forfeit faith and grace totally nor remain in [our] downfalls to the end and are lost." They go on to say that with respect to us, such falling away "not only easily could happen, but also undoubtedly would happen; but with respect to God it cannot possibly happen." One of the reasons why is that "the merit of Christ as well as his interceding and preserving cannot be nullified" (CD 5.8).

THEIR SINS WERE REMOVED

Second, the people benefited from the priesthood in that *their sins were removed.* Israelites came to the tabernacle every day with sacrifices for their sins. Even when Israelites were not bringing sacrifices, the priests were sacrificing for themselves and for the entire congregation. All of these sacrifices at the tabernacle (and later at the temple) taught the Israelites that they had a serious problem: sin. This was a lesson God their Father earnestly wanted them to learn.

Like the Israelites, we need to learn this lesson, for we can never understand God's grace until we understand our guilt. We can never know what it is to be freed from sin unless we understand that we are in bondage to sin. Knowing "the greatness of my sin and misery" is the first thing we must know to "live and die happily" in the comfort of knowing Jesus Christ (HC, Q&A 2). Do you know your guilt and bondage? Do you know what it is to feel your sins weighing you down, even crushing you? When we perceive how evil our hearts are, we begin to understand how loving the heart of God is toward us. We need to know our sins intimately because this leads us to know our Savior even more intimately. When we learn to plead, "Wretched man that I am! Who will deliver me from this body of death?" we learn to proclaim, "Thanks be to God through Jesus Christ our Lord!" (Rom. 7:24, 25).

Furthermore, we see in this passage the idea that the Israelites' sins were removed. With the Urim ("lights") and Thummim ("perfections") in the breastpiece, Aaron was to "bear the judgment of the people of Israel on his heart before the LORD regularly" (Ex. 28:30). With the golden plate on his forehead, he was to "bear any guilt from the holy things that the people consecrate" (v. 38). The Israelites' sins were symbolically removed from them and borne by Aaron, the high priest.

This is another magnificent foreshadowing of Jesus, who took on Himself all our judgment and guilt. He took the burden of that weight from us. He removed the guilt that had troubled our consciences. He removed the sorrow that our sins had caused. As Paul says, "For our sake he made him to be sin who knew no sin, so that in him we might become the righteousness of God" (2 Cor. 5:21). Amazingly, the Heidelberg Catechism says, "all the time He lived on earth, but especially at the end of His life, He bore, in body and soul, the wrath of God against the sin of the whole human race" (Q&A 37). Jesus lived under the weight of our sins.

There are two practical lessons here for us as Christians. First, since Christ has borne our sins once and for all, we are to continue laying on Him all our burdens from day to day: "[Cast] all your anxieties on him, because he cares for you" (1 Peter 5:7; cf. Ps. 55:22). We need to pray daily for His help in bearing our burdens; and then, when we have done that, we need to continue praying.

Second, since we in the new covenant are all priests of the Lord who can approach Him with boldness and confidence in prayer (Heb. 4:16), we are called by the Lord to bear one another's burdens: "Brothers, if anyone is caught in any transgression, you who are spiritual should restore him in a spirit of gentleness. Keep watch on yourself, lest you too be tempted. Bear one another's burdens, and so fulfill the law of Christ" (Gal. 6:1–2).

How do we bear one another's burdens? There are several ways. First, we do so by praying for each other, taking each other's burdens into the presence of God. Second, we do it by coming alongside our brothers and sisters to help them through trials or difficult seasons in their lives. Third, we do it by stepping into their shoes, taking difficulties away from them, and bearing them in their place.

We see all this in Paul's exhortation to the strong believers in Thessalonica to "help the weak" (1 Thess. 5:14). Whatever the spiritual weakness, Paul's remedy is for the strong to "help" or, literally, "support" them. To support, though, does not connote the idea of beams that hold up a house, but the image of the supporter holding onto one needing support. Do you see the difference? Paul is not saying, "You who are strong should let the weak hold onto you." Rather, he is saying, "You who are strong should hold onto the weak." Those of us who are strong in faith ought to hold the weak in faith, clinging to them and putting our arms around them. They need to know others are with them and will not leave them, picturing the Lord's presence with them.

THEIR PERSONS WERE RECONCILED

Third, the people benefited from the priesthood in that *their persons were reconciled*. What did the priestly bearing of the names of the Israelites and their guilt bring in the end? All these benefits led to one great benefit: acceptance with God.

We see this in the Lord's instructions about the plate of pure gold that Aaron was to wear on his forehead (Ex. 28:36). The reason he was to wear this, again, was that he might symbolically bear the people's guilt (vv. 36–37). Then we read: "It shall regularly be on his forehead, that they may be accepted before the LORD" (v. 38). This was the ultimate purpose and end of this ritual. Calvin described the priestly vestments as signs of acceptance when he wrote, "However vile and abject we may be in ourselves, and so altogether worthless refuse, yet inasmuch as Christ deigned to ingraft us into His body, in Him we are precious stones."[3]

But can sinners be reconciled to a holy God? Can enemies be reconciled to a perfect God? The Apostle Paul certainly taught so:

> For while we were still weak, at the right time Christ died for the ungodly. For one will scarcely die for a righteous person—though perhaps for a good person one would dare even to die—but God shows his love for us in that while we were still sinners, Christ died for us. Since, therefore, we have now been justified by his blood, much more shall we be saved by him from the wrath of God. For if while we were enemies we were reconciled to God by the death of his Son, much more, now that we are reconciled, shall we be saved by his life. More than that, we also rejoice in God through our Lord Jesus Christ, through whom we have now received reconciliation. (Rom. 5:6–11)

Those of us saved later in life no doubt can remember what that initial acceptance by God felt like. We must not forget it. It should kindle a passion in us for our children and for others who are still outside Christ to know that acceptance.

There is a reason Jesus and the Apostles describe this acceptance as being "born again." It gives a new beginning, it gives the assurance that our names are known by the Creator of the universe, it brings the freedom that our sins are taken away, and it gives the blessing of knowing that God accepts us in Jesus Christ as His sons and daughters. It is the benefit of what Paul described in Galatians: "Formerly, when you did not know God, you were enslaved to those that by nature are not gods. But now . . . you have come to know God, or rather to be known by God" (4:8–9). We know God, but more importantly, we are known by God. How? Because of Jesus Christ. What a high priest we have apprehended and appropriated in Jesus.

THE LITURGY
FOR ORDINATION

Exodus 29:1–37; 30:22–33

"Now this is what you shall do to them to consecrate them, that they may serve me as priests. Take one bull of the herd and two rams without blemish, and unleavened bread, unleavened cakes mixed with oil, and unleavened wafers smeared with oil. You shall make them of fine wheat flour. You shall put them in one basket and bring them in the basket, and bring the bull and the two rams. You shall bring Aaron and his sons to the entrance of the tent of meeting and wash them with water. Then you shall take the garments, and put on Aaron the coat and the robe of the ephod, and the ephod, and the breastpiece, and gird him with the skillfully woven band of the ephod. And you shall set the turban on his head and put the holy crown on the turban. You shall take the anointing oil and pour it on his head and anoint him. Then you shall bring his sons and put coats on them, and you shall gird Aaron and his sons with sashes and bind caps on them. And the priesthood shall be theirs by a statute forever. Thus you shall ordain Aaron and his sons. . . . The holy garments of Aaron shall be for his sons after him; they shall be anointed in them and ordained in them. The son who succeeds him as priest, who comes into the tent of meeting to minister in the Holy Place, shall wear them seven days. . . . Through seven days shall you ordain them, and every day you shall offer a bull as a sin offering for atonement. Also you shall purify the altar, when you make atonement for it, and shall anoint it to consecrate it. Seven days you shall make atonement for the altar and consecrate it, and the altar shall be most holy. Whatever touches the altar shall become holy." (Ex. 29:1–37)

Ordination services are wonderful. They are joyful occasions when men are set apart to be used by God to serve His church as gospel ministers. In my ministry, I have participated in four ordination services and celebrated the installation of a minister who was already ordained to serve as a missionary on the island of Kauai in the state of Hawaii. On such occasions, the people are joyful, the pastors are joyful, and those being ordained are joyful. Ultimately, ordination services are joyful because they are celebrations of God's amazing grace.

Exodus 29:1–37 records *the liturgy for ordination* of the priests God had called to minister in the tabernacle. Specifically, this high drama concerned the ordination of Aaron as high priest (vv. 4–7) and his sons as ordinary priests (vv. 8–9). The liturgy included three sacrifices: the bull (vv. 10–14), the first ram (vv. 15–18), and the second ram (vv. 19–34). This ceremony was designed to be repeated over the course of seven days. There was also an anointing ritual (v. 7). The priests, the tabernacle, and all of the tabernacle utensils were to be anointed with oil, setting them aside for sacred service (Ex. 30:22–33). All these commandments here in Exodus 29 and 30 were carried out at the time of the consecration of the tabernacle (Exodus 40) and described in more detail in Leviticus 8–9.[1]

We learn several things about the ministry of the priesthood through reading these verses. Specifically, we learn that this ministry was a gift, that it was frail, that it was temporary, and that it was participatory. These four lessons are highly applicable to us as new-covenant believers, even though we are served by a very different kind of ministry.

THIS MINISTRY WAS A GIFT

First, we learn that *this ministry was a gift*. The priesthood made tangible God's gracious covenant promises to His sinful, undeserving, murmuring, and complaining people. Aaron and his sons were called by the Lord "that they may serve me as priests" (Ex. 29:1). They served Him in sacrifice and supplication, which brought a ministry of grace to sinful people, as verses 38 and following describe. They offered up sacrifices for the sins of the people, showing that the Lord was gracious toward them in their sins. They also received the Word of the Lord, which they were to communicate to the people.

We cannot overlook the fact that while the old covenant with Israel was very legal, it was an administration of the covenant of grace. When Paul spoke to Gentiles in Ephesus who had been converted, he reminded them of their past, saying, "remember that you were at that time separated from Christ, alienated from the commonwealth of Israel and strangers to *the covenants of promise*" (Eph. 2:12, emphasis added). Even the Old Testament saints were recipients of grace in the form of God's wonderful promises. As the Westminster Confession states:

> Man, by his fall, having made himself incapable of life by that covenant [the covenant of works with Adam], the Lord was pleased to make a second, commonly called the covenant of grace; wherein He freely offers unto sinners life and salvation by Jesus Christ; requiring of them faith in Him, that they may be saved, and promising to give unto all those that are ordained unto eternal life His Holy Spirit, to make them willing, and able to believe. (7.3)

This one covenant of grace extends throughout the history of the Lord's dealings with sinful humanity after the fall of Adam. The confession explains the way in which the covenant was administered in the time of the ancient Israelites:

145

This covenant was differently administered in the time of the law, and in the time of the Gospel: under the law it was administered by promises, prophecies, sacrifices, circumcision, the paschal lamb, and other types and ordinances delivered to the people of the Jews, all foresignifying Christ to come; which were, for that time, sufficient and efficacious, through the operation of the Spirit, to instruct and build up the elect in faith in the promised Messiah, by whom they had full remission of sins, and eternal salvation; and is called the Old Testament. (7.5)

The sacrifices, those who offered them, and the place they were offered all were graciously given by the Lord. As a gift to His people, then, the ministry of the priesthood foresignified Christ to come to the Israelites, and finds its fulfillment in Jesus Christ. He was given to us in the Father's vast love and eternal grace. He was given to us to meet our greatest need—reconciliation with God.

THIS MINISTRY WAS FRAIL

Second, *this ministry was frail.* We see this in the fact that the liturgy included the sacrifice of one bull and two rams (Ex. 29:1). The bull was offered as a sin offering (v. 14), the first ram as a burnt offering (v. 18), and the other ram as a food offering (v. 25). These sacrifices were offered every day for seven days (v. 35). This emphasis on sacrifice in the liturgy shows that the priests were fully sinners just as the people were, and therefore just as in need of forgiveness. Hywel Jones writes, "The priesthood itself was not free from sin, and therefore there could be no consecration without atoning blood."[2] The same is true for ministers today. Every minister must be willing to say with the Apostle Paul, "I am the chief of sinners" (1 Tim. 1:15, KJV).

Notice the order of the offerings specified in this liturgy and the later order in the book of Leviticus, which are significant theologically:

Leviticus 1–5	*burnt* (1:3)	⤑	*fellowship* (3:1)	⤑	*sin* (4:2)
Leviticus 6–7	*burnt* (6:9)	⤑	*sin* (6:25)	⤑	*fellowship* (7:11)
Exodus 29	*sin* (v. 14)	⤑	*burnt* (v. 18)	⤑	*fellowship* (v. 24)

What is the significance of this variation? As J. A. Motyer writes, the order prescribed by the Lord in Leviticus 1–5 represents the divine desire for the offerings, beginning with the people consecrating themselves to the Lord in the whole burnt offering, signifying that they wholly belonged to Him, then enjoying fellowship with Him as signified by the food in the fellowship offering; and finally offering another sacrifice for their sins. The order in Leviticus 6–7 is the order the priests actually used in offering sacrifices, again, with the people being consecrated through the burnt offering, but then needing to offer sacrifice for their sins before they could enjoy God's fellowship. So what about the order in our text in Exodus 29? Here we find the order of actual need by the priests: they needed to be cleansed from sin before they could offer themselves in devotion, which led to them enjoying God's fellowship.[3]

Also significant in this liturgy was the fact that the hands of the priests were laid on the animals (vv. 10, 15, 19). Why? As the ancient church commentator Theodoret said, "This was a sign that the victim took the place of the offerer by undergoing death for him."[4] This laying on of hands shows that "the worshipper is intimately involved and represented in what happens to the victim which is his substitute."[5] In a word, "the sacrificial animal became *their* sacrifice, their substitute."[6] Again we learn that the priests were frail and needy sinners (Heb. 5:2–3). Their sins were then symbolically sent outside the camp (29:14), testifying that they were removed from them and from God's sight.

One practical way in which this truth should impact our lives is in our prayers. Let me reiterate that we should be in constant prayer for our frail ministers. Despite what you might be tempted to think, pastors are not sinless. Despite what you might be tempted to believe based on what you observe with your eyes, pastors are not supermen. They need your prayers that they, like you, might resist the onslaught of the Devil's temptation. They need your prayers so "that both by their preaching and living they may set [the Word] forth, and show it accordingly,"[7] and that "they [may] be to all men wholesome examples in faith, word, love, chastity, and fidelity."[8] Satan knows, as John Owen wrote, "If a man teach uprightly and walk crookedly, more will fall down in the night of his life than he built in the day of his doctrine."[9]

We also learn here that we should pray for ourselves as believers. Why? We are called by God to submit to our ministers. Since this is difficult to do, with our sinful hearts knowing our ministers' sinfulness, we need to pray that we will be able to honor and respect them and their ministry to us (1 Thess. 5:12–13; Heb. 13:17).

THIS MINISTRY WAS TEMPORARY

Third, *this ministry was temporary*. It is true that Exodus 29:9 says, "And the priesthood shall be theirs by a statute forever." However, the Hebrew term translated as "forever" can mean forever or an unspecified length of time. Also, we know this statement did not mean Aaron and his sons would be priests forever because their lives would be cut short by death. Their ministry would last only for as long as they lived. Finally, we know that this statement did not mean that the line of Aaron and his sons would have the priesthood forever because of what is written in the book of Hebrews.

In Hebrews 7, we learn that our Lord Jesus' priesthood (in the order of Melchizedek) superseded the Levitical priesthood. Several proofs are given to show that Christ's priesthood is greater than that of Levi. First, Levi paid tithes to Melchizedek (vv. 1–10), since the lesser always pays tribute to the greater. Levi, therefore, confessed his inferiority to Christ typologically. Second, the Levitical priesthood could not bring in perfection because it was limited and weak, but there was a promise in Psalm 110 of a greater priest: "You are a priest forever after the order of Melchizedek" (v. 4). Third, in the greatest contrast of all, the Levitical priests were temporary "because they were prevented by death from continuing in office." In contrast, Jesus "holds his priesthood permanently because he continues forever" (Heb. 7:23–24). The Levites died and were buried; Jesus died and was raised in power.

Why is it so important to bring out this contrast between the Levites and Jesus? First, it means that we have a Savior who is always available to us. Jesus is alive and "always lives to make intercession" for us (Heb. 7:25). This means we can pray to Jesus at any time. We can cry out to him at all hours of the day and night. He is the one of whom the psalmist said: "He will not let your foot be moved; he who keeps you will not slumber. Behold, he who keeps Israel will neither slumber nor sleep" (Ps. 121:3–4).

Second, this means that we have a Savior who is firm and fixed in heaven. This gives us a blessed assurance. Hebrews 6 says God's promises to us are like an anchor that is fixed behind the veil. That is where Jesus is (v. 19). When life seems like the ebb and flow of the sea, we have a deeply entrenched anchor in Jesus Christ.

But there is one interesting way in which the old priesthood continues alongside Jesus': in the priesthood of all believers. The Old Testament prophesied that all God's people would one day be priests (Mal. 3:1–4), and the New Testament proclaims that this prophecy has been fulfilled and all believers in the High Priest are also priests of the Most High God who offer up "spiritual sacrifices acceptable to God through Jesus Christ" (1 Peter 2:5). Further, in Revelation 5, the Lamb is praised because He has made His people a "kingdom and priests to our God and they shall reign on the earth" (vv. 9–10). Last, John says "they are before the throne of God, and serve him day and night in his temple" (7:15).

In the liturgy of the priests' ordination, Moses was commanded to wash the priests with water (Ex. 29:4), to put the holy garments on them (vv. 5–6, 9), and to pour the anointing oil on Aaron's head (v. 7). Then came the threefold sacrifice ritual (vv. 10–25). We, too, have been washed by the blood of the Lamb (1 Cor. 6:11; Heb. 10:22), clothed in His righteousness (Rom. 13:14; Gal. 3:26–27; cf. 2 Cor. 5:21), and anointed with the Holy Spirit (Acts 2:17; 1 Cor. 1:21; 1 John 2:20, 27), and we have received the benefits of Christ's sacrificial offering (Hebrews 10).[10] The Levitical priesthood was temporary, but our Lord, whose priesthood continues, has transformed it so that we might serve and worship God forever and ever. We do so in the anointing of the Holy Spirit, who was typified in the "holy anointing oil" (Ex. 30:31). This anointing of the priests, the tabernacle, and the utensils was so "that the Israelites might learn that all the exercises of piety profited nothing without the secret operation of the Spirit."[11] We now are those who have been anointed by Jesus with the "oil of gladness" (Ps. 45:7). Therefore, we are priests who offer up the spiritual sacrifices of praise and thanksgiving (Heb. 13:15). As the Heidelberg Catechism says:

> Q. 32. But why are you called a Christian?
> A. Because by faith I am a member of Christ and thus a partaker of His anointing, in order that I also may confess His Name, may present myself a living sacrifice of thankfulness to Him, and with a free conscience may fight against sin and the devil in this life, and hereafter in eternity reign with Him over all creatures.

Will you not exercise your participation in Jesus' priestly anointing? Will you not take advantage of your privilege to pray? Will you not enter the Holy Place with boldness to lay before the Lord your burdens, your family's burdens, your church's burdens, and your nation's burdens? We spend so much time texting, Facebooking, "tweeting," surfing the Internet, surfing the waves, practicing music and sports with our kids, watching the NFL, watching college football, and myriad other things, but will we spend time in prayer, today, tomorrow, and all the days of our lives? Jesus said, "Ask, and it will be given to you; seek, and you will find; knock, and it will be opened to you" (Matt. 7:7), but how shall it be given unless we ask; how shall we find unless we seek; how shall the door be opened unless we knock? We will be priests into eternity, but we need to start now.

Owen once asked how we can believe that we will enjoy heaven for eternity if we will not prepare ourselves for it now, praying to the Lord and meditating on His grace and glory? He said: "I cannot understand how any man can walk with God as he ought, or hath that love for Jesus Christ which true faith will produce, or doth place his refreshments and joy in spiritual things, in things above, that doth not on all just occasions so meditate on the glory of Christ in heaven as to long for an admittance into the immediate sight of it."[12]

THIS MINISTRY WAS PARTICIPATORY

Fourth, *this ministry was participatory*. Although the Levites were the only priestly tribe, all the tribes shared and participated in the ministry of the priests. We have already seen this in terms of the offerings given for the building of the tabernacle (Ex. 25:1–9). We see this also in the liturgy for ordination, at the end of the third offering. After the bull for a sin offering (Ex. 29:14) and the first ram for a burnt offering (v. 18), the third ram was offered as a "food offering" (v. 24), which was also known as a peace or fellowship offering. The breast meat was waved before the Lord, then was given to the priests to be eaten. God said, "it shall be your portion" (v. 26) and "it shall be for Aaron and his sons as a perpetual due *from the people of Israel*, for it is a contribution. It shall be a contribution *from the people of Israel* from their peace offerings, their contribution to the LORD" (v. 28, emphasis added).

The Apostle Paul used the priesthood as an example of the ministry of the Word, as we have already seen. Another aspect of that example is set forth in 1 Corinthians 9:13–14, where Paul concludes an argument about the right of ministers to live off their ministry to the church by saying: "Do you not know that those who are employed in the temple service get their food from the temple, and those who serve at the altar share in the sacrificial offerings? In the same way, the Lord commanded that those who proclaim the gospel should get their living by the gospel."

151

We should not think, though, that this is only a one-way street, with the ministers being the only ones benefiting from the offerings of God's people. Paul says that the church at Philippi had a "partnership in the gospel" with him (Phil. 1:5). The term he uses speaks of close, intimate, personal fellowship. He says later that their offerings to support him were "a fragrant offering, a sacrifice acceptable and pleasing to God" (4:18). In the same way, our offerings are a priestly sacrifice to God that He accepts as a pleasing aroma. When we give, we should not do it out of obligation or spite; rather, we should give in gratitude (2 Cor. 9:6–15). My wife and I have taught our sons from as early as they are able to do this. Every time they give the family's offering or one of their own, they say, "Thank you, God."[13] This is a wonderful way to show our thankfulness for what God has given us. We also need to give in the knowledge that we are partnering with our ministers in seeking to see believers transformed and to see more and more unbelievers come to the knowledge of our Lord.

God has given each of us a gift in the ministry that benefits our souls. The ministry is made up of frail men who will serve only temporarily and with whom we participate. Their ministry ultimately is to point not to themselves but to Jesus, God's "inexpressible gift" (2 Cor. 9:15), who must increase while the minister who holds Him forth must decrease (John 3:30).

WHY WORSHIP GOD
AS HE COMMANDS?

Exodus 29:38–46

"Now this is what you shall offer on the altar: two lambs a year old day by day regularly. One lamb you shall offer in the morning, and the other lamb you shall offer at twilight. And with the first lamb a tenth seah of fine flour mingled with a fourth of a hin of beaten oil, and a fourth of a hin of wine for a drink offering. The other lamb you shall offer at twilight, and shall offer with it a grain offering and its drink offering, as in the morning, for a pleasing aroma, a food offering to the LORD. It shall be a regular burnt offering throughout your generations at the entrance of the tent of meeting before the LORD, where I will meet with you, to speak to you there. There I will meet with the people of Israel, and it shall be sanctified by my glory. I will consecrate the tent of meeting and the altar. Aaron also and his sons I will consecrate to serve me as priests. I will dwell among the people of Israel and will be their God. And they shall know that I am the LORD their God, who brought them out of the land of Egypt that I might dwell among them. I am the LORD their God." (Ex. 29:38–46)

In 1667, the English Puritan John Owen wrote that "the right and due observation of instituted worship is of great importance unto the glory of God, and of high concernment unto the souls of men."[1] In other

153

words, to observe all things that our Lord has commanded us, as Jesus spoke in Matthew 28:20, should be of great importance to us as believers, a chief concern of our minds and hearts. Worshiping God according to His Word brings Him glory, honor, and praise because we are submitting to His will and wisdom in giving Him what He requires and desires. Since worship is focused on the glory of God, it should be the highest of priorities for us as His children. This is why John Calvin once described worship alongside the doctrine of justification as the principal parts of true religion:

> If it be inquired, then, by what things chiefly the Christian religion has a standing existence amongst us and maintains its truth, it will be found that the following two not only occupy the principal place, but comprehend under them all the other parts, and consequently the whole substance of Christianity, viz., a knowledge, first, of the mode in which God is duly worshipped; and, secondly of the source from which salvation is to be obtained.[2]

Our souls also should be concerned to do what God says in worship because in doing so we meet with Him face to face and receive amazing spiritual benefits. The end of Exodus 29 shows this to be true. On the heels of chapters 28 and most of chapter 29, in which the Lord spoke of the priesthood's garments and ordination, He gave instructions concerning the daily worship of the priests at the entrance to the tabernacle (Ex. 29:38–42). Then He spoke of the purpose of the morning and evening sacrifices of worship (vv. 43–46). This purpose should be of great importance to us.

In meditating on these words, we find an answer to the question, *Why worship God as He commands?* The answer is that doing so brings four spiritual benefits for our souls: meeting with God, sanctification from God, dwelling by God, and knowledge of God. These four benefits of obedience to the Lord's instituted worship are just as much a part of our relationship with God under the new covenant as they were for our forefathers, the Israelites.

MEETING WITH GOD

First, worshiping God as He commands brings the benefit of *meeting with God.* The Lord said He would meet with His people at the entrance of the tent of meeting (Ex. 29:42). He then reiterated that promise, saying, "There I will meet with the people of Israel" (v. 43). What a benefit this is. In worship, the Lord brings His people into face-to-face fellowship with Himself. In contemporary terms, worship is not about the enthusiasm of the minister or the volume of the praise band, but about meeting with the triune God of grace.

Let me put this amazing benefit into perspective. First, we can see how wonderful this benefit was for the Israelites when we contrast it with the situation that developed between Adam and Eve and the Lord God in the garden. After their sin, the Lord exiled them from Eden and from His immediate presence there (Genesis 3). Ever since that time, human beings have lived "east of Eden" (Gen. 3:23–24), in a wandering existence in the wilderness. Yet the Lord promised Moses that when the priests worshiped Him as He commanded in the daily morning and evening sacrifices at the tabernacle, He would bring them back into His presence and meet with them there. God was showing them a preview that one day He would reverse the curse on Adam and Eve, and once again He would dwell with man.

Second, this was a wonderful benefit because God actually met with men. The holy met with the sinful. The Creator met with the creature. The infinite stooped down and met with the finite. The eternal met with the temporal. God was gracious in drawing His people into a meeting with Him. Remember, the Israelites did not make the tabernacle of their own free will because they were seeking and desiring the Lord. Rather, God in His irresistible grace called a people to Himself and drew them into a meeting with Him.

We, too, enter the heavenly tabernacle to meet with God when we worship as He commands. We come to worship not merely to be passive spectators or to be entertained, but to meet face to face, *coram Deo*, with the living God. In ancient Israel, the meeting happened in the place where sacrifice was offered. Now that our Lord has come—for He is Immanuel, God with us—His once-for-all sacrifice has opened wide the place of meeting with Him. Our Lord says to all who hear His voice that if they will forsake themselves and embrace Him in faith, they not only will be saved from their sins but He will enter into an intimate, personal, and lasting relationship with them: "I will make with you an everlasting covenant, my steadfast, sure love for David" (Isa. 55:3). It is in worship that we come into closest fellowship with Him, meeting with Him face to face as with a friend, as the Scriptures say concerning Moses when he met with God on the mountain (Ex. 3:1–4:17) and in the tent of meeting (33:11).

God's willingness to meet with sinners ultimately reveals to us His nature. Unlike all the so-called gods of the nations and their religions, the one true God is more willing to meet with us than we are to meet with Him. In the words of the Heidelberg Catechism, when it explains the meaning of the word *amen*, "my prayer is much more certainly heard of God than I feel in my heart that I desire these things of Him" (Q&A 129).

SANCTIFICATION FROM GOD

Second, worshiping God as He commands brings the benefit of *sanctification from God*. The word *sanctification* comes from the Latin root word *sanctus*, which means "set apart." Just as a sculptor sets apart a piece of marble and begins chiseling away at it to make his masterpiece, God has set us apart for His work. We are his "workmanship," as Paul says (Eph. 2:10). Sanctification, then, is the process by which God sets apart His people from the rest of the world that they might serve Him and love Him. By it, we become less and less conformed to the pattern of the world (Rom. 12:2) and more and more conformed to the pattern of Jesus Christ, the image of God *par excellence* (Rom. 8:29).

We read in this passage that God said He would sanctify the tabernacle by His glory (Ex. 29:43) and also sanctify the priests for worship in the tabernacle (v. 44). But we need to reflect on the fact that He said nothing about sanctifying the rest of the people. This is because while there were great blessings in old-covenant worship, things were very restricted. We see this as well in the fact that only the high priest could enter the Holy of Holies once a year. This was meant to communicate to the Israelites that something greater, more inclusive, and more intimate was to come in a later age.

The benefit is different now under the new covenant. When we come to worship, we come not only as people who are sanctified all the days of our lives by the Holy Spirit, not only as priests who serve in a tabernacle like the priests of ancient Israel did, but as *high priests*. We are all being made into a spiritual priesthood to offer up spiritual sacrifices acceptable to God (1 Peter 2:4–5, 9). We all come with total access to the Holy of Holies. Because of that, we all receive a special blessing from the Holy Spirit—He works in worship to sanctify us. When we worship, we worship in the Spirit (1 Peter 4:14; Rev. 1:10).

One passage shows this clearly: Hebrews 10:19–25. We have confidence to enter the Holy of Holies because we are all high priests (v. 19). We do so in Christ by means of His once-for-all sacrifice (vv. 19–20) and by means of His high priestly ministry in the heavenly tabernacle (v. 21). Therefore, we are exhorted to draw near "with our hearts sprinkled clean from an evil conscience, and our bodies washed with pure water" (v. 22). Because we have been set apart by the Lord, we draw near, and when we draw near, we are further set apart for the Lord in worship. Although our cleansing is a past event that gives us assurance, the sprinkling and washing mentioned in this passage leads us to live sanctified lives (vv. 23–25). We continue to confess the name of Jesus in the world, stirring each other to love and good works, and assembling together as Christ's return draws near.

We come to worship God and to partake of what we call His means of grace on the Lord's Day—preaching, sacraments (baptism and the

Lord's Supper), and prayer (WLC, Q&A 154). Then we are thrust out into the world as those who love our brothers and sisters, and who confess Jesus in the midst of unbelief, office pressures, family strains, and the world's temptations. Worship is where we receive the empowering of the Holy Spirit to do these things. We need to be asking ourselves what we can do to exhort our fellow members to love their neighbors and to do good works. Instead of being defensive and refusing to hear exhortation, we need to have a desire to be corrected, to want to hear what God will say through others to spur us on. When we come, we should be strengthened in our desire to assemble yet again. Can you imagine what God could do through such a church—a church that comes out of the world to meet face to face with the living God, then to be thrust back into the world? Minds, hearts, lips, wills, and, indeed, entire lives would be transformed.

DWELLING BY GOD

Third, worshiping God as He commands brings the benefit of *dwelling by God.* Lest we think that God planned to meet with His people for just a passing moment or two, He reassured them that He would be *dwelling* among them: "I will dwell among the people of Israel and will be their God . . . that I might dwell among them" (Ex. 29:45–46). The fact that the Lord required a sacrifice every morning and every evening was a reminder that this dwelling of God was still imperfect. The Israelites were constantly reminded of their sins and their need for true propitiation to bring a lasting dwelling with God.[3]

This wonderful promise of lasting fellowship in the presence of God is ours in Christ. In the new covenant, God continues His plan to reverse the curse of separation from fellowship with God, as we see in Ephesians 2:22: "In him [Christ] you also are being built together into a dwelling place for God by the Spirit." When we come together, we taste "the heavenly gift," we "share in the Holy Spirit," and we taste "the goodness of the word of God and the powers of the age to come" (Heb. 6:4, 5). We experience what we also expect: "Behold, the dwelling place of God is with man. He will dwell with them, and they will be his people, and God himself will be with them as their God" (Rev. 21:3).

What does it mean for local congregations as they gather for worship that God dwells in the midst of His people? How should that truth cause us to think, speak, and act when we come together? If you are thinking something like this, "Well, I know that God is holy and I know that I am still an imperfect sinner, so God's dwelling in our midst shows me my sins," you're on the right track. But I hope you're also thinking: "I know that since I now belong to God I should want to be like Him. After all, He is my Father and I am His child."

What is taught here in Exodus will later be expressed in Leviticus with the familiar maxim, "Be holy as the Lord your God is holy" (see Lev. 11:44–45; 19:2; 20:7, 26; 21:8). Liturgy leads to sanctity; access to God leads to holiness for God. That exhortation continues in the church; we see it, for example, in 1 Peter 1:16. Because God is dwelling among us, and we particularly experience His presence in worship, we should desire holiness. Hebrews 12:14 even says that we should "strive . . . for the holiness without which no one will see the Lord."

Are you striving for holiness? Do you want to be holy as the Lord is holy? This is a benefit of coming into the presence of God in worship, because there God meets with us in a special way to forgive us, assure us, and embrace us. Receiving that divine welcome is the power behind desiring holiness.

Evangelical Christians believe in *both* justification and sanctification. Justification is based on the merits of Christ alone, received through faith alone apart from any and all works, and flows out of the eternal, unmerited, free grace of God alone. However, sanctification, holiness, and good works are also necessary. Those two works are not in tension; instead, they are the twin benefits of the new covenant. Justification leads to sanctification, and sanctification is possible because of justification. When we come into God's presence, we should be confirmed in justification that we can be consecrated in sanctification.

KNOWLEDGE OF GOD

Fourth, worshiping God as He commands brings the benefit of *knowledge of God*. God said, "And they shall know that I am the LORD their God who brought them out of the land of Egypt" (Ex. 29:46). As we have already seen, God knows our names personally. The tabernacle teaches us that worship leads God's people to know His name personally. As God dwells among us, we come to know Him as "the LORD," that is, as the faithful, covenant-keeping God who is for His people (Exodus 3).

This "knowledge" is not mere mental knowledge but experiential knowledge. Notice the connection between 29:42 and 46. The Lord said He would speak to the priests (v. 42) at the tent of meeting, and then all the people would "know . . . the LORD their God" (v. 46). The knowledge of God that we receive in worship comes through the means of preaching by the ministers of the Word. This knowledge is not just information. Preaching is not simply communicating facts about the Word of God, but bringing the "living and active" voice of God into the ears of believers (Heb. 4:12), that they might hear Him and obey Him, but especially that they might know Him. I know it's foolish to think that the ordinary words of a man can be the wise words of God, but this is God's wisdom; I know a mere man's words are weak, but they are God's power (1 Cor. 1:25). Through preaching, God has ordained that we might hear His voice and know Him.[4]

So, we have come full circle. Are you desirous and highly concerned to worship God according to His Word? As a child of God, you should be. We should be conscientious to worship God in no other way "than He has commanded in His Word" (HC, Q&A 96). When we do so, there are wonderful blessings in store for our souls. We come together every Lord's Day to meet with our great and gracious God, that He might sanctify us; He sanctifies us that we might dwell with Him, now and forever; and He dwells with us that we might know Him intimately as a child knows his father, crying out, "Abba, Father!" (Gal. 4:6). We truly have an amazing God. It is truly an unspeakable privilege that He invites us—sinful though we are—to approach His throne of grace today and into eternity.

THE ALTAR FOR INCENSE

Exodus 30:1–10, 34–38; 37:25–29

"You shall make an altar on which to burn incense; you shall make it of acacia wood. A cubit shall be its length, and a cubit its breadth. It shall be square, and two cubits shall be its height. Its horns shall be of one piece with it. You shall overlay it with pure gold, its top and around its sides and its horns. And you shall make a molding of gold around it. And you shall make two golden rings for it. Under its molding on two opposite sides of it you shall make them, and they shall be hold-ers for poles with which to carry it. You shall make the poles of acacia wood and overlay them with gold. And you shall put it in front of the veil that is above the ark of the testimony, in front of the mercy seat that is above the testimony, where I will meet with you. And Aaron shall burn fragrant incense on it. Every morning when he dresses the lamps he shall burn it, and when Aaron sets up the lamps at twilight, he shall burn it, a regular incense offering before the LORD throughout your generations. You shall not offer unauthorized incense on it, or a burnt offering, or a grain offering, and you shall not pour a drink offer-ing on it. Aaron shall make atonement on its horns once a year. With the blood of the sin offering of atonement he shall make atonement for it once in the year throughout your generations. It is most holy to the LORD." (Ex. 30:1–10)

The LORD said to Moses, "Take sweet spices, stacte, and onycha, and galbanum, sweet spices with pure frankincense (of each shall there be an equal part), and make an incense blended as by the perfumer, seasoned with salt, pure and holy. You shall beat some of it very small, and put part of it before the testimony in the tent of meeting where I shall meet with you. It shall be most holy for you. And the incense that you shall make according to its composition, you shall not make for yourselves. It shall be for you holy to the LORD. Whoever makes any like it to use as perfume shall be cut off from his people." (Ex. 30:34–38)

"Our thoughts and prayers are with you." How many times have you heard a politician, television commentator, or a friend say that recently? Everyone prays today, although many think and speak of prayer perfunctorily. This should not surprise us in our multicultural world, in which, so it seems, no one can do any wrong when it comes to religion. But Christian prayer is a serious and sacred thing. We learn this lesson from one of the more unusual articles of furniture in the tabernacle.

The opening verses of Exodus 30 speak of prayer by means of *the altar for incense*. It is called "the altar of incense" (*mizbah ha-ketoret*) several times because it was an altar on which incense was burned (Ex. 30:27; 31:8; 35:15; 37:25; Lev. 4:7). It is also called "the altar of gold" (*mizbah ha-zahav*) to distinguish it from the altar of bronze that stood in the tabernacle courtyard (Ex. 39:38; 40:5, 26; Num. 4:11).

This passage speaks of the "what" of the altar: it was made of acacia wood and overlaid with pure gold; it had a gold molding all the way around; it had two gold rings on each side; and there were two acacia poles overlaid with gold to carry it (vv. 1–5). It speaks of the "where" of the altar: it was placed in front of the interior veil, in front of the mercy seat (v. 6). It speaks of the "when" of the altar: fragrant and pleasing incense was to be burned on it every morning and evening (vv. 7–8). The passage also speaks a warning—no "unauthorized incense" (Ex. 30:9, *ketoret zarah*), or, as the King James Version has it, "strange incense," was to be offered on it, as well as no burnt offerings, grain offerings, or drink offerings.

What do all these details teach us? In meditating on these verses, we come to see that this passage is about the theme of prayer. Both the Old and the New Testaments teach us that the incense offered on this altar was symbolic of the prayers of the people of God. In the Psalms we hear David pray: "O LORD, I call upon you; hasten to me! Give ear to my voice when I call to you. Let my prayer be counted as incense before you, and the lifting up of my hands as the evening sacrifice" (Ps. 141:1–2). David was comparing his prayer to the incense that was offered on the altar of gold. Likewise, when the book of Revelation shows us the heavenly scene around the throne of God, we read, "And when he [the Lamb] had taken the scroll, the four living creatures and the twenty-four elders fell down before the Lamb, each holding a harp, and golden bowls full of incense, which are the prayers of the saints" (5:8). Here again, incense serves as a metaphor for prayers. Later in Revelation we read, "And another angel came and stood at the altar with a golden censer, and he was given much incense to offer with the prayers of all the saints on the golden altar before the throne, and the smoke of the incense, with the prayers of the saints, rose before God from the hand of the angel" (8:3–4).[1] The golden altar of incense, then, was a visual symbol to the people of Israel that the priests were offering up their prayers to God in heaven.[2]

What does the Holy Spirit want to say to His new-covenant church about the prayers that were offered at the altar of incense? Exodus 30 teaches us three lessons that help us think and engage in prayer not pedantically but powerfully: God desires our prayers, God accepts our prayers, and God is pleased with our prayers.

GOD DESIRES OUR PRAYERS

First, the altar for incense teaches us that *God desires our prayers*. The Lord commanded Moses to build the altar: "You *shall* make an altar on which to burn incense" (30:1, emphasis added). In offering incense, the priests would be symbolically offering the prayers of the people to God. We must never lose sight of the truth that God commands what

He desires. For example, Paul speaks of the "good pleasure of his [God's] will" (Eph. 1:5, KJV). This means that God desires what He commands. So, when He commanded Moses to build an altar and the priests to offer incense on it, the Lord was revealing that His heart's desire was that His people would offer up prayers to Him.

This is a wonderful truth about our God and our relationship to Him. The altar of incense gives us a glimpse into His thoughts, attitudes, and desires toward us, His people. Put into its greatest context, the God who is eternally self-sufficient and who needs nothing beyond Himself (His attribute of *aseity*) proclaims to us in His Word that He actually desires—indeed, He is eager—to hear us cry out to Him.

In the poetic Song of Songs, there is a beautiful description of the Lord's desire for His people. The beloved one says, "I am my beloved's, and his desire is for me" (7:10). The Lord is like a husband who has taken us, who are like the meanest, nastiest, vilest woman, and bound Himself to us in a marriage covenant. It is as if our Lord has said, "I, Jesus Christ, take thee, Church, to be My wedded wife, to have and to hold from this day forward, for better for worse, for richer for poorer, in sickness and in health, to love and to cherish, till death us do part."[3] That is the kind of desire the Lord has for His people and the kind of desire He has for their prayers. In the words of one song: "He loves us with passion, without regret. He cannot love more and will not love less."[4]

In response to His desire for us and our prayers, we obviously need to desire Him by praying to Him. The Psalms describe this desire with all sorts of verbs. One of my favorites is in Psalm 62:8, which says, "*Pour out* your heart before him" (emphasis added). The Westminster Larger Catechism draws its answer to the question "What is prayer?" from this psalm: "Prayer is an offering up of our desires unto God" (Q&A 178). Our response to the Lord's desire for us should be to open our hearts and pour out our thoughts and affections to Him.

Exodus 30 also shows the Lord's desire for our prayers in His command that Aaron and his sons should burn incense on the altar every day in the morning and at twilight (30:7, 8). This was a way of saying, "Offer

THE ALTAR FOR INCENSE

up prayer to Me constantly, regularly, and perpetually." It was a way for the Lord to show His desire for His people to devote the whole day, every day, to Him in prayer.

We need to desire to offer our prayers to the Lord at all times and in all places. As Paul says, "Pray without ceasing" (1 Thess. 5:17). In Exodus 30, the Lord gives us a structure for doing this. Often, when we learn a major principle of the Christian life, such as the principle that our entire life is to be devoted to prayer, we feel so overwhelmed that we do not actually do it. So, the Lord tells us to begin our days in prayer and to conclude them in prayer. We ought to be developing the holy habit of praying every morning and evening as individuals, as couples, and as families. This is the structure within which we dedicate all that we have and are to the Lord in prayer.

In the Reformed Christian tradition, the authors and composers of our original church songbooks often included example prayers to instruct the people. For instance, when the preacher and churchman Petrus Dathenus (1531–1588) put together the first complete church songbook for Dutch Reformed Christians in 1566, behind all the songs he included sample prayers that Christians could pray every morning and every evening:

Morning Prayer

O merciful Father, we thank Thee that Thou didst keep watch over us this past night, in Thy great faithfulness. We pray that Thou mayest strengthen and guide us henceforth by Thy Holy Spirit, that we may put this day as well as all the days of our life to the service of holiness and righteousness. Grant, we pray Thee, that in all our undertakings we may always have an eye single to Thy glory. May we ever labor in the consciousness of our dependence upon Thy beneficence for the success of our work.

We beseech Thee to forgive all our sins according to Thy promise, for the sake of the passion and blood of our Lord Jesus Christ, for we are truly sorry for all our transgressions. Illumine our hearts, we pray Thee, that we may lay aside all works of darkness and as children of light may lead new lives in all godliness.

May it please Thee to bless us also as we engage in the proclamation of the divine Word. Frustrate all the works of the devil. Endue all the ministers of the Church who are faithful to Thee with strength, and make the magistrates of Thy people strong. Instill comfort in the hearts of all that are distressed, through Jesus Christ, Thy beloved Son. For He has assured us that thou wilt surely grant us all that we ask of Thee in His Name, and has enjoined us to pray after this fashion, saying: Our Father who art in heaven, etc. Amen.

May grace also be given us, we pray Thee, to order our lives according to Thy will which thou didst reveal in Thy law as

166

contained in the Ten Commandments: I am Jehovah thy God, who brought thee out of the land of Egypt, out of the house of bondage. Thou shalt have no other gods before me, etc. Amen.

Evening Prayer

O merciful God, light eternal shining in the darkness, Thou dispellest the night of our sins and the blindness of our hearts. Since Thou didst ordain that man should rest in the night and labor during the day, we pray Thee that our bodies may rest in peace and quiet, in order that they may be enabled to sustain the labors to which we shall again be called. Control our sleep and rule our hearts while we slumber, in order that we may not be defiled in either body or soul, but may glorify Thee even in our nightly rest. Enlighten once more, we beseech Thee, the eyes of our mind, lest we enter upon the sleep of death. Grant that we may ever cherish the expectation of our redemption from the misery of the life that now is. Defend us against all assaults of the devil and take us in Thy holy protection.

We confess that we have not spent this day without grievously sinning against Thee. We pray Thee to cover our sins in Thy mercy, even as Thou dost shroud all the things of earth in the darkness of the night, lest we be cast away from Thy face. Be pleased to bestow comfort and rest upon all that are sick, bowed down with grief, or afflicted with distress of soul, through our Lord Jesus Christ, who would have us pray, saying: Our Father who art in heaven, etc. Amen.[5]

By means of praying such prayers every morning and evening, we pour out our hearts before our Lord in response to His desire for us. In doing this, we grow in our relationship with Him.

GOD ACCEPTS OUR PRAYERS

Second, the altar for incense teaches us that *God accepts our prayers.* While it is true that God does not explicitly say in Exodus 30 that He accepts His people's prayers, the location He specified for the altar for incense shows that He does so. We see this in two ways.

First, it is important to note where the altar of incense was located in relation to the altar of burnt offering. The altar of burnt offering was in the outer courtyard, outside the Holy Place. It was the first thing an Israelite saw upon entering the courtyard. The altar of incense, by contrast, was inside the Holy Place. This arrangement teaches us that we must come to God through a sacrifice for sins before we can come to Him through prayer. Put another way, God must accept us by means of substitution before He will accept what we bring to Him in supplication. God can accept us as sinners along with our sin-stained prayers only if we first come to Him "by the blood of Jesus" (Heb. 10:19). This means that before He will accept us and our prayers, we must accept the reality that we are sinners in need of forgiveness, and that forgiveness of our sins can come only through someone else who is perfect and who has offered Himself in our place. This is what Jesus has done. We must accept His sacrifice.

Second, it is important to note where the altar of incense was located in relation to the rest of the furniture within the tabernacle. The text says that it was located "in front of the veil that is above the ark" (Ex. 30:6a). It was in the Holy Place but outside the Holy of Holies, showing the Israelites "that there was peace between [God] and Israel, a peace in which He wanted to enjoy their incense."[6] The altar for incense was the piece of furniture that was farthest from the entrance to the Holy Place and closest to the entrance to the Holy of Holies.

Yet, the Holy Spirit wanted Moses to record a second phrase about its location. He added that the altar was "in front of the mercy seat" (v. 6b). Although it was in the Holy Place and the mercy seat was in the Holy of Holies, and the two were separated by the great curtain, the Holy Spirit wanted His people to see that the altar was closely associated with the mercy seat of the ark of the covenant. This is why the book of Hebrews says that the altar for incense was actually within the Holy of Holies, "behind the second curtain" (Heb. 9:3; cf. v. 4). Although scholars have debated this and have come up with theories as to why the author of Hebrews "mistakenly" said the altar was in the Holy of Holies, the Holy Spirit was saying that it was at the mercy seat, where the Lord mercifully accepted His people and met with them, that His people's prayers were offered and accepted.

As new-covenant Christians, we need to know why God accepts our prayers. As we read the New Testament, we learn that there are two reasons why the Lord continually accepts our prayers after He has accepted us on the basis of Christ's sacrifice. First, God accepts our prayers because Jesus Christ sanctifies them by His intercession. Jesus intercedes for us at the right hand of God (Rom. 8:34) and "ever liveth to make intercession" for us (Heb. 7:25, KJV). This means no matter how tainted by sin, how clumsy, or how full of doubt our prayers may be, Jesus makes them acceptable to God. Therefore, we ought to pray however we can, in faith, knowing that Jesus will make our prayers His own.

There is no better Mediator and Intercessor than the Lord Jesus Christ. The Belgic Confession wonderfully expresses our confidence in this aspect of His ministry on our behalf:

> But this Mediator, whom the Father has appointed between himself and us, ought not to terrify us by his greatness, so that we have to look for another one, according to our fancy. For neither in heaven nor among the creatures on earth is there anyone who loves us more than Jesus Christ does. Although he was "in the form of God," he nevertheless "emptied himself," taking the form of "a man" and "a servant" for us; and he made himself "completely like his brothers." Suppose we had to find another intercessor. Who would love us more than he who gave his life for us, even though "we were his enemies"? And suppose we had to find one who has prestige and power. Who has as much of these

as he who is seated "at the right hand of the Father," and who has all power "in heaven and on earth"? And who will be heard more readily than God's own dearly beloved Son? . . . What more do we need? For Christ himself declares: "I am the way, the truth, and the life; no one comes to my Father but by me." Why should we seek another intercessor? Since it has pleased God to give us his Son as our Intercessor, let us not leave him for another—or rather seek, without ever finding. For when God gave him to us he knew well that we were sinners. (Art. 26)

Second, God accepts our prayers because the Holy Spirit sanctifies them by His intercession. One of the most powerful verses describing the work of the Holy Spirit in the life of the believer is Romans 8:26: "Likewise the Spirit helps us in our weaknesses. For we do not know what to pray for as we ought, but the Spirit himself intercedes for us with groanings too deep for words." This means that no matter how insufficient or ignorant our prayers are, no matter how badly we miss the mark in praying and interceding for ourselves, our families, our churches, and our world, the Holy Spirit comes alongside of us and makes our prayers as sufficient and efficient as they need to be. Like the "fragrant incense" (Ex. 30:7) that was acceptable to God, the Holy Spirit causes our prayers to be sweet-smelling to our Father in heaven.[7]

As mentioned above, the Westminster Larger Catechism defines prayer as "an offering up of our desires unto God," but it continues, saying, "in the name of Christ, *by the help of his Spirit*" (Q&A 178, emphasis added). Question 182 goes on to expand on the Spirit's work in prayer. In response to the question, "How doth the Spirit help us to pray?" it answers: "We not knowing what to pray for as we ought, the Spirit helpeth our infirmities, by enabling us to understand both for whom, and what, and how prayer is to be made; and by working and quickening in our hearts (although not in all persons, nor at all times, in the same measure) those apprehensions, affections, and graces which are requisite for the right performance of that duty."[8] We should pray, then, knowing that

170

the Spirit will mold our prayers into His own on our behalf.

Simply put, we need the Holy Spirit to pray. The English Presbyterian Thomas Manton told his congregation, "Look, as we breathe out that air which we first suck in, so the prayer is first breathed into us before breathed out by us; first inspired, before uttered."[9] In his exposition of Jude 20, Manton added, "God will own nothing in prayer but what cometh from his Spirit; any other voice is strange and barbarous to him."[10] He went on to say, "we can babble of ourselves, but we cannot pray without the Holy Ghost; we can put words into prayer, but it is the Spirit who puts affections, without which it is but a little cold prattle and spiritless talk."[11]

GOD IS PLEASED WITH OUR PRAYERS

Third, the altar for incense teaches us that *God is pleased with our prayers*. The pleasure of God with the prayers of His people is seen in the description of the incense as "fragrant incense" (Ex. 30:7) or "pure fragrant incense" (37:29). This fragrant incense was an "offering before the Lord" (30:8), and He accepted it as a sweet-smelling aroma, unlike the "strange" or unauthorized incense of Exodus 30:9. As we have already seen in the ordination liturgy of the priests, when God says a sacrifice is "a pleasing aroma" to Him, He is pleased with what has been offered (29:18, 25, 41; cf. Lev. 1:9, 13, 17).

This means that the Lord loves His people's prayers. They "smell" wonderful to Him. He takes pleasure in hearing our prayers as we would take pleasure in smelling freshly bloomed roses or lilies. The psalmist says the Lord takes pleasure in His people (Ps. 149:4), and one of the things that delights Him is our prayers. The book of Proverbs says, "The sacrifice of the wicked is an abomination to the LORD, but the prayer of the upright is acceptable to him" (15:8).

Let me offer two applications of this truth. First, we must always pray in faith, trusting that God our Father is pleased when we pray. When Noah offered up a sacrifice to the Lord after the flood, we read that "the LORD smelled the pleasing aroma," and then "the LORD said in his heart" that He would not curse the earth in the same way again (Gen. 8:21). When we offer up the sacrifice of praise in our prayers, the Lord's heart is moved toward us in love and acceptance. Second, we must not allow the Devil to make us doubt that God accepts our prayers. "Hath God said?" (Gen. 3:1, KJV) is the Devil's question. Our answer from the Word of God must be a resounding yes!

It is good to meditate on this passage in the context of our multicultural world. We have seen that the golden altar of incense teaches us that our Lord desires our prayers, accepts our prayers, and is pleased with our prayers. All of this is true for those who have become children of God by faith in Jesus Christ, covered by the blood of the sinless and righteous Lamb of God "who takes away the sin of the world" (John 1:29). All of this is true because Jesus has torn down the veil (Matt. 27:51) and granted us access into the Holy of Holies so that we can confidently pray, "Our Father" (Matt. 6:9).

THE PRICE
OF REDEMPTION

Exodus 30:11–16

The LORD said to Moses, "When you take the census of the people of Israel, then each shall give a ransom for his life to the LORD when you number them, that there be no plague among them when you number them. Each one who is numbered in the census shall give this: half a shekel according to the shekel of the sanctuary (the shekel is twenty gerahs), half a shekel as an offering to the LORD. Everyone who is numbered in the census, from twenty years old and upward, shall give the LORD's offering. The rich shall not give more, and the poor shall not give less, than the half shekel, when you give the LORD's offering to make atonement for your lives. You shall take the atonement money from the people of Israel and shall give it for the service of the tent of meeting, that it may bring the people of Israel to remembrance before the LORD, so as to make atonement for your lives." (Ex. 30:11–16)

As American children learn in school, the United States of America is the great melting pot of the world. People from all over the world, with different skin colors, languages, and customs, have come here and been melted together as common Americans.

This is a great illustration of life in the church of Jesus Christ. The church is made up of individuals "from every tribe and language, and people and nation" (Rev. 5:9). In any given congregation, there are people who have been brought together from many different ethnicities. There are people who have different political views. Some may have played collegiate or even professional sports, while others may be the best of the best at raising their kids. There may be doctors and there may be students. All have unique personalities and preferences concerning just about everything under the sun. And yet, the Apostle Paul said, we are all melted together in Christ: "There is neither Jew nor Greek, there is neither slave nor free, there is neither male nor female, for you are all one in Christ Jesus" (Gal. 3:28). Only one thing can unify so many diverse people in this way: redemption by Jesus Christ.

Redemption is the theme of Exodus 30:11–16. At first glance, this passage does not seem to fit in the context of the tabernacle narratives. It is preceded by a description of the altar of incense and followed by a description of the bronze basin for washing. It gives a strange account of a census that took place and money that was paid to keep a plague away from the congregation. The census was not the reason for the potential plague, as it was in the days of David (2 Samuel 24), but it was a method the Lord used to teach His children that sin must be paid for by sacrifice. Yet, this census was intimately connected with the work of the ministry and the tabernacle, for the precious metal that was given was "for the service of the tent of meeting" (v. 16). Even more curious, God called the money the Israelites were to give "a ransom" (v. 12) and "atonement money" (v. 16). Why did God command this strange means of averting His wrath?

This question takes us deep into the mysteries of our God and His nature. What, then, does this ransom money—or redemption money— teach us about Him? As we meditate on *the price of redemption*, we are guided to reflect on three of God's amazing attributes: His wrath, His mercy, and His love.

THE WRATH OF GOD

First, we are pointed to *the wrath of God*. Our text speaks three times about a ransom or atonement money "for his life" or "for your lives" (Ex. 30:11, 15, 16). Literally, however, it is speaking of a ransom or atonement "for his *soul*" or "for your *souls*" (*naphshu*). The souls of these people were sinful and God was about to bring a plague on them in His wrath. A price had to be paid in order for them to escape this plague. If this ransom price were paid, God said, there would be no plague; if it was not, a plague would surely come (30:12).

The narratives in Genesis and Exodus up to this point in the Bible are really about two things: man's sin and God's grace. The Bible is a story in which we do the sinning and God does the saving. It's as simple as that. The same is true in this passage. The God who saved the Israelites from Egypt reveals Himself as a holy and just God. Because He is holy, the Scriptures say He is "of purer eyes than to see evil and cannot look at wrong" (Hab. 1:13). Therefore, He must punish sin. As another prophet says, "the soul who sins shall die" (Ezek. 18:4). This punishment of sin is what we call the wrath of God. It is the execution of His perfect justice on sinners. It is necessary because of God's nature. The psalmist spoke of this holy and just wrath when he said, "You hate all evildoers" (Ps. 5:5).

Because the spirit of our age is tolerance, we do not meditate on the wrath of God much these days. Our inherent idolatry latches onto this spirit and causes us to want a tame God we can keep on a leash. We want the kind of God who fits on a dashboard, on a bumper sticker, and on a t-shirt. We want a God who is like a toy we can take off the shelf every Sunday and use for our good, only to put Him back on the shelf Monday through Saturday. We want a God who is not present with us at the office as we join in the crowd's corrupt talk. We want a God who is not with us as we bicker, gossip, and complain with other parents as our kids play at the park. We want a nice God who never confronts our laziness, who never upsets the status quo in our lives, who never tells us that what we are doing is sin. No, it's not God we want by nature, but our desires; it's not God we want to serve, but ourselves.

But the God of the Bible, the God whom we profess to believe, the God whom ministers must never stop preaching, and the God who is in our midst in worship is a God of wrath. The psalmist says, "God is a righteous judge, and a God who feels indignation every day" (Ps. 7:11). Another writes: "But you, you are to be feared! Who can stand before you when once your anger is roused?" (Ps. 76:7) The prophet Nahum says: "The LORD is a jealous and avenging God; the LORD is avenging and wrathful; the LORD takes vengeance on his adversaries and keeps wrath for his enemies. . . . Who can stand before his indignation? Who can endure the heat of his anger? His wrath is poured out like fire, and the rocks are broken into pieces by him" (Nah. 1:2, 6). And do not forget Paul's words: "For the wrath of God is revealed from heaven against all ungodliness and unrighteousness of men, who by their unrighteousness suppress the truth. . . . But because of your hard and impenitent heart you are storing up wrath for yourself on the day of wrath when God's righteous judgment will be revealed" (Rom. 1:18; 2:5).

The Israelites were confronted with this God—their God—in the tabernacle census. Without the payment of a ransom price, they would have faced His wrath in the form of a plague. Before He could dwell in their midst and they could have fellowship with Him in the tabernacle, they had to deal with their sins.

Have you been confronted by this wrathful God? Have you seen His greatness and your smallness? Have you seen His purity and your impurity? Have you seen His wrath and your deserved judgment? According to the Heidelberg Catechism, this is the first thing we must know in this life in order to have true, lasting comfort (Q&A 2). I hope you have come to a knowledge of your sins and the wrath of God against them.

But if you have, what can you do? Thankfully, our passage does not point only to the wrath of God.

THE MERCY OF GOD

Second, we are pointed to *the mercy of God*. God did not leave the Israelites—and He does not leave us—perilously exposed to His wrath. He expressed His infinite mercy by providing a means for His sinful people to escape His infinite wrath. He is the God of whom the psalmist says, "righteousness and peace kiss each other" (Ps. 85:10).

We have seen that God's wrath is the punishment He executes on us for what we deserve. But what is His mercy? God shows His mercy when He does *not* give us what we deserve. God's wrath is like a blazing fire, but His mercy is like a shield. This shield protects us from His own fiery wrath.

This is so important to understand because we often speak of being "saved." We correctly say that God saves us from our sins. We rightly say that God saves us out of the world. We truthfully say that God saves us from the Devil. All this is biblical, but there is another from whom we are saved. We must never forget that, ultimately, God saves us *from* God. As Paul says, it was God Himself who put forward His very own Son "as a propitiation" (Rom. 3:25)—that is, something to turn away His own wrath. That's mercy.

The means of mercy that God gave to the Israelites to avert His wrath was a payment of half a shekel (Ex. 30:13). It was to be given by "everyone who is numbered in the census, from twenty years old and upward" (v. 14). If this payment was made, "ransom for his life" was given (v. 12) and "atonement for your lives" was made (vv. 15, 16), and therefore the Lord's wrath was stayed.

Notice the two words used to describe this mercy of God: *ransom* and *atonement*. First, the depth of God's mercy is seen in the fact that the lives of sinners could be ransomed (*kopher*). The idea was that a person was under someone or something's ownership, and a price could be paid to buy him back or to give him freedom.[1] Second, the depth of God's mercy is seen in the fact that atonement could be made for the sin of sinners. The Hebrew word used here, translated as "the atonement" (v. 16, *kippurim*), is related to the word that we have already seen is translated as "the mercy seat" or "place of atonement" (Ex. 25:17).

This whole scene is strange to us, but the Lord wanted to teach His people about their sins and about His mercy. He also wanted to teach us; we have to remember that the Old Testament was written for us. As Peter says, "It was revealed to [the prophets] that they were not serving themselves but you" (1 Peter 1:12). And Paul says, "For whatever was written in former days was written for our instruction, that through endurance and through the encouragement of the Scriptures we might have hope" (Rom. 15:4).

We learn here about God's plan to redeem us from His wrath. We are sinners and He is holy, just, and wrathful. The only way to escape is through the payment of a price. Paul says, "you were bought with a price" (1 Cor. 6:20), and Peter explains that price, saying, "you were ransomed from the futile ways inherited from your forefathers, not with perishable things such as silver and gold, but with the precious blood of Christ, like that of a lamb without blemish or spot" (1 Peter 1:18–19). Jesus paid a precious price, the price of His own life, for our lives.

In both of these New Testament passages, the Apostles speak of Christ's redeeming work in the context of exhorting us to live as people freed from sin. In 1 Corinthians 6, Paul says that we were bought with a price, and this means we are not our own but belong to the Lord, and we are temples of the Holy Spirit. The Heidelberg Catechism summarizes this Scripture passage; in response to the question, "What is your only comfort in life and in death?" it answers, "That I, with body and soul, both in life and in death, am not my own, but belong to my faithful Savior Jesus Christ" (Q&A 1). Because of this, we are not to engage in the sexual immorality so prevalent in our world. In 1 Peter 1, Peter speaks of our former passions and the ways of our forefathers. He is speaking more generally that we are to be holy in all our conduct at work, at home, and at play, in thoughts, in words, and in deeds, on the Lord's Day and on every other day. In our relationship with God, we are to look back in amazement at the great price our Lord paid for our liberation from those passions and worldly ways, and therefore live lives dedicated to Him.

THE LOVE OF GOD

Third, we are pointed to *the love of God*. Moses speaks of everyone who is counted in the census giving a half a shekel (Ex. 30:14), but notice how the Lord goes on to clarify this: "The rich shall not give more, and the poor shall not give less" (v. 15). He was saying very clearly that the price of redemption was the same for the rich and the poor. God does not love the rich any more than the poor and He does not love the poor any more than the rich.

This illustrates that there is no partiality in the love of God, and He extends His means of mercy to avert wrath equally to all.[2] God loves the world (John 3:16). God loves Jews and Gentiles, rich and poor, free and slave, male and female. God's desire for us to pray for all kinds of people in the world is based on His desire for all kinds of people to be saved (1 Tim. 2:1–5). In the words of W. H. Gispen, the price of redemption teaches us that, "No one was exempted from this offering, but since each individual was equally valuable in the Lord's eyes, no one could give more or less than a half shekel."[3] In John Calvin's words, "He appointed the same sum for all, that every one, of whatever rank, from the least, to the greatest, might know that they were altogether His . . . the same price should be paid for every soul."[4]

What do we learn from this? Like the river that flowed from the temple in Ezekiel's vision (Ezek. 47:1–12), the revelation of God's love gets deeper and wider as we enter the new covenant. Whereas this wilderness census counted only Israelite males, we live in an age in which salvation extends to the ends of the earth: "For God so loved the world, that he gave his only Son, that whoever believes in him should not perish but have eternal life" (John 3:16). Thus, salvation now extends beyond the bounds of Israel and into every Gentile land. The Canons of Dort explain:

In the Old Testament, God revealed this secret of his will to a small number; in the New Testament (now without any distinction between peoples) God discloses it to a large number. The reason for this difference must not be ascribed to the greater worth of one nation over another, or to a better use of the light of nature, but to the free good pleasure and undeserved love of God. Therefore, those who receive so much grace, beyond and in spite of all they deserve, ought to acknowledge it with humble and thankful hearts; on the other hand, with the apostle they ought to adore (but certainly not inquisitively search into) the severity and justice of God's judgments on the others, who do not receive this grace. (3/4.7)

Such humble and thankful adoration has been memorably expressed in the words of the gospel hymn:

O the deep, deep love of Jesus, vast, unmeasured, boundless, free!
Rolling as a mighty ocean in its fullness over me!
Underneath me, all around me, is the current of Thy love
Leading onward, leading homeward to Thy glorious rest above![5]

One of the things we learn from the love of God in the new covenant is that we are to love the world as well. We are not to love the ways of the world but the people who make up our world, so that they might come to know Jesus Christ. According to the teaching of Jesus, we are to indiscriminately spread the seed of the Word of God across the world (Matt. 13:1–9, 18–23). The Canons of Dort also teach us that we are responsible for evangelizing the nations:

Moreover, it is the promise of the gospel that whoever believes in Christ crucified shall not perish but have eternal life. This promise, together with the command to repent and believe, ought to be announced and declared without differentiation or discrimination to all nations and people, to whom God in his good pleasure sends the gospel. (2.5)

In the census of the Israelites in the wilderness, God revealed to His people His attributes of wrath, mercy, and love. These truths about Him have not changed, as He has showed them to us more fully through the ministry of our Lord Jesus Christ. Because of God's wrath against our sins, God sent His Son, whose incarnation, life, death, and resurrection reveal God's protecting mercy and immense love for the world in never-before-seen depth and detail. Under the new covenant, we have been blessed unlike any people in the history of the world in our redemption. Now we must be a blessing to the world. Now we must pray for the world's redemption and declare God's love to all whenever and wherever we can.

THE BASIN FOR WASHING

Exodus 30:17–21; 38:8

The LORD said to Moses, "You shall also make a basin of bronze, with its stand of bronze, for washing. You shall put it between the tent of meeting and the altar, and you shall put water in it, with which Aaron and his sons shall wash their hands and their feet. When they go into the tent of meeting, or when they come near the altar to minister, to burn a food offering to the LORD, they shall wash with water, so that they may not die. They shall wash their hands and their feet, so that they may not die. It shall be a statute forever to them, even to him and to his offspring throughout their generations." (Ex. 30:17–21)

All of us know by experience that water is necessary for life. The human body can last somewhere between two and ten days without water, depending on the outside temperature. Without water, we dehydrate, our organs fail, and we die.

Spiritually speaking, our souls need the grace of the Lord just as our bodies need water. As David prayed, "O God, you are my God; earnestly I seek after you; my soul thirsts for you; my flesh faints for you, as in a dry and weary land where there is no water" (Ps. 63:1). He goes on to quantify his desire for the Lord, saying, "Your steadfast love is better than life" (v. 3). Elsewhere, he expresses the earnestness of his longing for God, saying, "I stretch out my hands to you; my soul thirsts for you like a parched land" (Ps. 143:6).

But water is not just a metaphor for our overall relationship with God. It is also specifically a symbol of cleansing from sin: "Wash me thoroughly from my iniquity, and cleanse me from my sin!" (Ps. 51:2). Exodus 30 speaks about this spiritual cleansing as the Lord gives instructions for *the basin for washing.*

This basin was the final piece of the tabernacle structure and furniture that the Lord revealed to Moses on Mount Sinai. Having received the plans for the courtyard, the bronze altar, the curtains of the tabernacle, the table of bread, the lampstand, the altar of incense, and the ark of the covenant, Moses recorded the Lord's instructions for a little basin of water to be placed in the courtyard between the altar of burnt offering and the tabernacle itself as a "statute forever" (Ex. 30:21).

This basin was made "from the mirrors of the ministering women who ministered in the entrance of the tent of meeting" (Ex. 38:8). Glass was unknown at the time the tabernacle was constructed, so "mirrors" were made from finely polished pieces of metal; such polished bronze mirrors were used to make the tabernacle basin. This laver also had a stand and a large bowl that was filled with water with which the priests were to wash their hands and feet.

But the basin was not merely a container to hold water for washing; it taught the Israelites two significant spiritual lessons about their relationship with the Lord: the need for initial washing and the need for continual washing. These are lessons that are equally important for new-covenant believers.

THE NEED FOR INITIAL WASHING

First, the basin for washing illustrated *the need for initial washing*. Once the tabernacle was erected and all the furniture and utensils were constructed and set up according to the Lord's commands, Aaron and his sons were ready to serve the Lord. But before they could "go into the tent of meeting" or "come near the altar . . . to burn a food offering to the LORD" (Ex. 30:20), their hands and feet had to be cleansed (vv. 19, 21). They had to wash before they could minister. Why was this? What do we learn from this?

First, all the dirt that they got on their hands and feet as they ministered in the wilderness was symbolic of their sin and of how unfit they were to approach the Lord. Their true need was to be washed and cleansed of their sins. They had to be pure.[1] This necessity was graphically impressed on them with the threat of death. Twice Moses records that the priests were to wash "so that they may not die" (vv. 20, 21). Jewish commentator Nahum Sarna writes, "The washing is an indispensable requirement; its neglect renders the priests' service invalid."[2]

Second, the water in the bronze basin was symbolic of the washing away of the priests' sins and the removal of the threat of death that only the Lord could accomplish. There are many examples of such symbolism elsewhere in Scripture. For instance, later in the history of redemption, when the Israelites were in captivity in Babylon because of their sins, the Lord promised to save His people once again. They had "profaned" His name (Ezek. 36:22, 23), but God said He would bring them from the nations back to their own land (v. 24). In that restoration, the Lord promised to cleanse His people: "I will sprinkle clean water on you, and you shall be clean from all your uncleannesses, and from all your idols I will cleanse you" (v. 25). Not only was being washed with water used as a metaphor for cleansing from sin, the Lord Himself was going to do the washing: "I will sprinkle . . . I will cleanse."

In the new covenant, God still uses water to signify cleansing from sins. In the water of baptism, God has given us the visible sign of His washing away of our sins. Peter told the thousands of listeners on the Day of Pentecost, "Repent and be baptized every one of you in the name of Jesus Christ for the forgiveness of your sins" (Acts 2:38). But as 1 Peter 3:21 emphasizes, the water itself does not wash away sins. Instead, the water is the visible sign and seal of what the Lord Himself does internally.

185

In his letter to Titus, Paul describes our life before Christ (3:2–3), then goes on to say, "He saved us, not because of works done by us in righteousness, but according to his own mercy, by the washing of regeneration and renewal of the Holy Spirit, whom he poured out on us so richly through Jesus Christ our Savior" (vv. 5–6).[3] Just as the water in the basin for washing taught the Israelites, so today the water God has provided in baptism points us to the reality that we need an initial washing that we might be acceptable to God and able to serve Him. Only God can accomplish this washing away of our sins through the blood and Spirit of His Son, our Lord Jesus Christ.[4]

This is why the Belgic Confession, a Reformation-era confession of faith, says this about baptism: "So ministers, as far as their work is concerned, give us the sacrament and what is visible, but our Lord gives what the sacrament signifies—namely the invisible gifts and graces; washing, purifying, and cleansing our souls of all filth and unrighteousness; renewing our hearts and filling them with all comfort; giving us true assurance of his fatherly goodness; clothing us with the 'new man' and stripping off the 'old,' with all its works" (Art. 34).

This means that we need to be cleansed in order to approach the Lord. Have you recognized the filth within your head, within your heart, and on your hands? Have you heard the Lord saying to you, "If you do not acknowledge how filthy you are and come to Me for cleansing, you shall surely suffer the agony of death for eternity?" Have you been cleansed? Have your sins been washed away? If not, confess your sins to Jesus Christ and trust in His promise that He will forgive you today. When He forgives you, He removes your sins "as far as the east is from the west" (Ps. 103:12). When He forgives you, you can say with the prophet, "You will cast all our sins into the depths of the sea" (Mic. 7:19b). When He forgives you, you can say with another of the prophets, "you have cast all my sins behind your back" (Isa. 38:17).

But you may be struggling with uncertainty as to whether you have been washed in the blood and Spirit of Christ. You may not have the assurance of the prophets. You know the filthy thoughts that still pervade your mind; you know the filthy desires that still fill your heart; you know the filthy things your hands have done. Let me assure you, if you have confessed your sins and have trusted in Christ, when He washed you of your sins, He also washed away the guilt of your sins. You struggle with the continual corruption that sin brings, but you are no longer under a guilty sentence of eternal death. And the fact that you are struggling and fighting with sinful thoughts, words, and deeds is evidence that you have been washed of the eternal guilt of sin and that you are a new creature in Christ.

THE NEED FOR CONTINUAL WASHING

Second, the basin illustrated *the need for continual washing.* Right after you were born, the blood and vernix on your body was washed off by a nurse or even your mom or dad. Have you taken a bath or shower since the day you were born? Of course you have. Our bodies continually become dirtied, requiring new cleansing. It is the same way with us spiritually. Even after we are born again by the Spirit of God (John 3:1–8), we continue to sin. We have to be washed for the first time by Jesus, but He also continues to wash us of our sins.

The bronze basin filled with water was not placed in the midst of the tabernacle courtyard for a once-for-all initial washing, after which it became a useless relic. It had to be used continually. God required the priests to wash "when they go into the tent of meeting, or when they come near the altar to minister" (Ex. 30:20). How many times was that? It was as many times as they entered the tent, offered a sacrifice, or lifted up a prayer. They had to wash every time with no exceptions, which means they had to do so every day.

This is a great lesson for us today. We live in a time when the gospel of salvation has been divorced from the ordinary and everyday Christian life. With modern methods of crusade evangelism and seeker-sensitive worship services in which the focus is on unbelievers, most Christians today think that the "gospel" is something that we tell unbelievers so that they might be saved. We had to hear it long ago to be saved, and unbelievers now need to hear it to be saved. But we learn something different from this part of Exodus 30. We learn that God's people, who are described in both the Old and New Testaments as "a kingdom of priests" (Ex. 19:6; 1 Peter 2:9), must constantly hear the good news of the gospel and constantly apply its cleansing to their hearts. Just as the priests had to be washed again and again, we need to be washed continually by the good news that Jesus' blood and Spirit have cleansed and continue to cleanse us of our sins. The Apostle John told ancient Christians: "My little children, I am writing these things to you so that you may not sin. But if anyone does sin, we have an advocate with the Father, Jesus Christ the righteous. He is the propitiation for our sins" (1 John 2:1–2a).

Again, the Belgic Confession gives a wonderful expression of this truth, stressing that we need constant cleansing by the blood and Spirit of Christ: "For this reason we believe that anyone who aspires to reach eternal life ought to be baptized only once without ever repeating it—for we cannot be born twice. Yet this baptism is profitable not only when the water is on us and when we receive it but throughout our entire lives" (Art. 34).

The confession is summarizing the Protestant position that baptism benefits us until the day we die; it is a one-time act that benefits us for life. The Puritan preacher Thomas Manton recounted the well-known example of Martin Luther, an example we need to follow: "Luther saith of himself, that when the devil tempted him to despair, or to any doubts and fears about the love of God or his mercy to sinners, he would always answer, *Ecce, ego baptizatus sum, et credo in Christum crucifixum*: 'Behold, I am baptized, and believe in Christ crucified.'"[5] "*Baptizatus sum*," "I am baptized." This is a wonderful way for a believer to embrace the significant benefit of his or her baptism every day. Although we are baptized only once, that baptism testifies to us who believe of our ongoing spiritual cleansing by the blood and Spirit of Christ.

This idea comes directly from the New Testament Apostles. Over and over again in their letters to the early churches, they use the imagery and significance of baptism to bring their readers back to the gospel promises for them. Should we sin that grace may abound? No, because baptism testifies that we have died to sin and been raised to a new life of consecration to God (Romans 6). Should believers bring lawsuits against one another? No, because baptism testifies that we have been washed (1 Corinthians 6). Should we partake of culturally approved idolatrous practices? No, because like our forefathers in the Red Sea, we have been baptized into Christ (1 Corinthians 10). Should we live the Christian life alone? No, because our baptism testifies that we are joined to each other as members of a body (1 Corinthians 12). Should there be division among the people of God, who come from different ethnic and cultural groups? No, because our baptism testifies that human divisions have ceased in Christ (Galatians 3). Do we need to submit to human rules and regulations in order to find wholeness and completeness in this life? No, because our baptism testifies that we are complete in Christ (Colossians 2). Should we be afraid of approaching God? No, because our baptism testifies that we have been made clean to enter God's holy presence (Heb. 10:19–23). Should we show partiality to different people within the church? No, because our baptism testifies that we have all had the same name of God placed upon us in baptism (James 2). Are we to be afraid of suffering as Christians? No, because our baptism testifies to us that our Lord suffered as well (1 Peter 3).

That is a lot of information, but what does all this mean for us as believers in terms of our relationship with God? Let me offer several applications.

First, we must have a deep-rooted desire for a continual cleansing from the Lord so that we might live holy lives. We need to pray and sing with David, "Purge me with hyssop, and I shall be clean; wash me, and I shall be whiter than snow" (Ps. 51:7). We ought to desire the Lord's continual cleansing so that we can go forth to work, to school, and to our neighbors' homes in holiness. One passage of Scripture that should stick in our heads over the course of our Christian lives is Hebrews 12:14: "Strive for peace with everyone, and for the holiness without which no one will see the Lord."

Second, just as the priests cleansed their hands and feet before ministering in the tabernacle, we need to cleanse our hearts and minds in preparation to serve the Lord in worship. We should be in the habit of praying the night before worshiping on the Lord's Day that the Holy Spirit will prepare our hearts to hear the Word. When we wake up on the Lord's Day, it is good to sing and pray as individuals, couples, and families in preparation for public worship. As the Puritan George Swinnock said, "If thou wouldst thus leave thine heart with God on the Saturday night, thou shouldst find it with him in the Lord's Day morning."[6] While we may come to worship and do all the right, pure, and good things that God's Word commands of us, our hearts may still be far from the Lord. Psalm 51 says we need pure hearts in the presence of God.

Third, since the bronze laver speaks of a continual washing, we need to live our lives Monday through Saturday as Christians in a constant state of confession. First John 1:7–9 was not written about public worship on the Lord's Day; it was written for us as we live our daily lives: "But if we walk in the light, as he is in the light, we have fellowship with one another, and the blood of Jesus his Son cleanses us from all sin. If we say we have no sin, we deceive ourselves, and the truth is not in us. If we confess our sins, he is faithful and just to forgive us our sins and to cleanse us from all unrighteousness." We must not be Sunday-only Christians.

Fourth, we need to be spending considerable time in the Word of God. Paul's words to husbands in Ephesians 5 are rooted in the work of Christ, but notice what Christ uses to do His cleansing work: "Husbands, love your wives, as Christ loved the church and gave himself up for her, that he might sanctify her, having cleansed her by the washing of water *with the word*" (5:25–26, emphasis added). The Word is a means of continual cleansing by the Lord and His Spirit. Therefore, it is good to meditate on the passage we hear preached on the Lord's Day all through the following week, to go over our notes, to read through more of the Word during the week, and to come back next Lord's Day to hear the Word again—over, and over, and over again.

What do we learn from the bronze basin for washing? We learn that just as we need water for our earthly life, we need grace for our heavenly life. The Lord has given our souls that spiritual "water" to cleanse us from the guilt of sin initially and from the corruption of sin continually. That water is the grace of God as expressed in the blood of Christ upon the cross and the Spirit of Christ poured out into our hearts. May that water flow in our lives and the lives of all those with whom we come into contact.

16

THE GIFTS GIVEN BY GOD

Exodus 31:1–11; 35:30–36:7

The LORD said to Moses, "See, I have called by name Bezalel the son of Uri, son of Hur, of the tribe of Judah, and I have filled him with the Spirit of God, with ability and intelligence, with knowledge and all craftsmanship, to devise artistic designs, to work in gold, silver, and bronze, in cutting stones for setting, and in carving wood, to work in every craft. And behold, I have appointed with him Oholiab, the son of Ahisamach, of the tribe of Dan. And I have given to all able men ability, that they may make all that I have commanded you: the tent of meeting, and the ark of the testimony, and the mercy seat that is on it, and all the furnishings of the tent, the table and its utensils, and the pure lampstand with all its utensils, and the altar of incense, and the altar of burnt offering with all its utensils, and the basin and its stand, and the finely worked garments, the holy garments for Aaron the priest and the garments of his sons, for their service as priests, and the anointing oil and the fragrant incense for the Holy Place. According to all that I have commanded you, they shall do." (Ex. 31:1–11)

"Every member of a church in order according to the mind of Christ possesseth some place, use, and office in the body, which it cannot fill up unto the benefit and ornament of the whole without some spiritual gift."[1] This is how the great English Puritan John Owen described the work of the Holy Spirit in the lives of believers as members of the body of Christ in one of his last writings, "A Discourse of Spiritual Gifts." As he wrote to English Christians toward the end of his life, he wanted them to know that every believer in Jesus Christ has a place, a use, and an office in the body of Christ, and is equipped by the Holy Spirit for those roles. It was "as if [God] had stretched forth His hand from heaven."[2]

Owen's point is a summary of numerous passages in the New Testament, such as 1 Corinthians 12:4–11 and Ephesians 4:7–16. But what is fascinating to me is that the topic of "spiritual gifts"—so popular in our day and age—is not addressed only in the New Testament. In fact, it is clear as we read the passage before us in this chapter that the Holy Spirit wants us to hear a similar message from the Old Testament. As the heavenly author of spiritual gifts, the Holy Spirit has gifted, equipped, and built up His people from the beginning—even when Israel was in the wilderness. We learn this lesson from the instructions God gave Moses as to how he was to construct the tabernacle.

In Exodus 31:1–11, then, we learn about *the gifts given by God.* There are three things the Holy Spirit wants us to understand about His gifts: God gifts the entire congregation, God gifts diversely, and God gifts for obedience.

GOD GIFTS THE ENTIRE CONGREGATION

First, we learn that *God gifts the entire congregation.* Of course, we know of Moses' many God-given gifts; the book of Hebrews describes him as "faithful in all God's house as a servant" (Heb. 3:5). Despite his protestations to the contrary (Ex. 4:10), we know he "was instructed in all the wisdom of the Egyptians, and he was mighty in his words and deeds" (Acts 7:22). Exodus also speaks of his leadership abilities and wisdom in judging people (chap. 18). We also know that Aaron and his four sons, Nadab, Abihu, Eleazar, and Ithamar, were gifted for service in the tabernacle as priests. All of these men were from the set-apart tribe of Levi.

But what about the rest of the congregation? Were the Holy Spirit's gifts given only to a few special people from one special tribe?

In Exodus 31, we learn that God called by name two particular men out of the congregation to lead the construction of the tabernacle. First, there was Bezalel. His name meant "in the shadow of God." He was not from the tribe of Levi but from the tribe of Judah (v. 2). Then there was Oholiab, whose name meant either "the tent of the father" or "the father is my tent." He also was not from the tribe of Levi but the tribe of Dan (v. 6). These men were spectacularly gifted (vv. 3–6). They had to be, since, as John Calvin said, it was "incredible that any mortals should be able by their art to compass what God commanded."[3]

But the Holy Spirit did not gift merely these two men, but men from throughout the entire congregation, which was the Spirit's way of showing that He gifts entire bodies of believers for His purposes. God said, "And I have given to *all able men* ability, that they may make all that I have commanded you" (v. 6, emphasis added). Later, Moses said, "Bezalel and Oholiab *and every craftsman* in whom the LORD has put skill and intelligence to know how to work in the construction of the sanctuary shall work in accordance with all that the LORD has commanded" (Ex. 36:1, emphasis added). These others—"all able men" and "every craftsman"—were clearly from throughout the congregation, from all the various tribes of Israel. Also, they clearly were especially gifted by the Holy Spirit, for God said, "I have given . . . ability," and Moses affirmed, "the LORD . . . put skill and intelligence" in them.

The Holy Spirit works in the same way under the new covenant. He gives gifts to every believer. This means that each of us needs to find and use his gift or gifts to serve God and to edify everyone else within the congregation. How do we do this?

First, knowing that God gifts His people should cause us to prepare our souls to receive His gifts with humility. They are His gifts, after all, and He gives them to whomever He desires. Like the wind, which "blows where it wishes," the Spirit of God comes to us with His gifts at His time (John 3:8). The various gifts the members of Christ's body have "differ according to the grace given to us" (Rom. 12:6). Recognizing this should make us humble. As Owen said, "The Holy Spirit taketh no delight to impart his especial gifts unto proud, self-conceited men, to men vainly puffed up in their own fleshly minds."[4]

Second, we should pray that the Holy Spirit would make known His gift or gifts to each one of us. One of the means He uses to manifest His gifts in us is a godly desire for gifts that we might serve the body. As we desire gifts in general, and even particular gifts, we come to know how the Spirit will use us. This is what Paul taught when he said to the Corinthians, "But earnestly desire the higher gifts" (1 Cor. 12:31), and, "Pursue love, and earnestly desire the spiritual gifts, especially that you may prophesy" (14:1).

Third, we need to be aware of our natural gifts, abilities, and desires. Those in whom the Lord put skill and intelligence to know how to work in the construction of the tabernacle were already craftsman: "I have given to all able men ability" (Ex. 31:6b). In the words of Calvin, "God had already conferred acuteness and intelligence on the artificers in question; yet their dexterity was only, as it were, the seed; and He now promises that He will give them more than had previously appeared."[5] The Holy Spirit took those with natural gifts, which also came from Him, and used them in a spiritual way to edify the whole congregation. Owen said that we need to be aware of our natural gifts because they may "set off" the spiritual gifts within us.[6] If you are a good listener, this may be the precursor to God using you to show compassion and bring reconciliation in the church. If you are empathetic, be aware of how God can use you to pray and intercede on behalf of others who are struggling greatly. If you are naturally outgoing, God can use you to show hospitality and friendship to strangers and lonely people.

GOD GIFTS DIVERSELY

Second, we learn that *God gifts diversely*. While some throughout the congregation of the Israelites were gifted to construct the tent of meeting, the ark of the covenant, the mercy seat, the table, the lampstand, the two altars, the basin, and their utensils, others were gifted to weave and sew the curtains and the holy garments that the priests wore while ministering on behalf of the people, while still others were gifted to create wonderful perfumes and incense (Ex. 31:7–11; 35:10–19).

At the same time, those who did not assist directly in the construction of the tabernacle or its various pieces were moved by the Holy Spirit with the gift of generosity. We have seen that God called on the congregation to show great generosity in giving gold, silver, and bronze for building the tabernacle; blue, purple, and scarlet yarns for use in tapestry work; animal skins; oils and spices; precious stones; and other items (Ex. 25:1–7). We read that the people did indeed give generously (35:20–29). Likewise, we have seen that the basin for washing was made from the bronze mirrors contributed by the women who ministered before the tent (38:8). Following the command of God, the people had asked the Egyptians to give them these articles on the eve of the exodus, and the Egyptians had done so (11:2; 12:35–36). The Israelites then gave the items to God for use in the tabernacle. In all these ways the Holy Spirit gifted everyone, but He did so diversely.

Again, the Holy Spirit still works in this way. Paul describes the unity and diversity of gifts in the body of Christ by saying: "Now there are varieties of gifts, but the same Spirit; and there are varieties of service, but the same Lord; and there are varieties of activities, but it is the same God who empowers them all in everyone. To each is given the manifestation of the Spirit for the common good" (1 Cor. 12:4–7). All of us are gifted from the same Spirit; all of us are called to serve in the power of the same Lord; all of us are called to be active by the same God; all of us have gifts to serve the common good. As Paul goes on to say to the Corinthians, "all were made to drink of one Spirit" (v. 13).

What is this "common good" of which Paul speaks? It is that God is glorified in the midst of the congregation; for example, in singing. What are you doing to bring that about? The common good is that the lost come to hear the gospel and be saved. What are you doing to serve that glorious purpose, to spread the seed of the Word? The common good is that those in the church who are hurting find healing, the broken find restoration, and the weak find strength. What are you doing to serve others who seem to be hurting, broken, and weak?

Because of cultural influences on the church in America in our time, we tend to treat the church like a drive-through restaurant. We think to ourselves, "It will always be there and it will always have what I want, when I want it." So, some of us attend worship once a week, some twice a month, and, sadly, some of us only occasionally. We come to get something and to leave. If it is not there, we go somewhere else. Others of us treat the church like any ordinary social club, a PTA meeting, a family reunion, or a gathering of friends. We come expecting to talk about work, football, and the latest gossip. We do all of this because we are sinners to be sure, but also because we are products of the world around us.

We need to stop treating the church this way. The church is a body, not a drive-through. It is a group of living people. The church is a spiritual place, not a social club. When we come on the Lord's Day, we need to expect that God is going to meet with us in the power of His Holy Spirit. Further, we need to expect that there will be others there who need our spiritual gifts. The Holy Spirit gives each of us gifts for the common good, so we need to shift our focus from ourselves and use our gifts to serve and edify others. If each of us thinks of ways to serve others—and not how we need to be served—the entire body will function healthily.

GOD GIFTS FOR OBEDIENCE

Third, we learn that *God gifts for obedience.* All the gifts He gave to Bezalel, Oholiab, and the rest of the congregation of Israel were for one great purpose: "And I have given to all able men ability, that they may make all that I have commanded you" (Ex. 36:1).

Do you see what it means that God gifts for obedience? It means that what God commands His people to do, He gives them the spiritual ability to do. Do not misunderstand what I am saying here. I am not speaking here of justification. That is the work of God's grace alone, received through faith alone, on the basis of the work of Jesus Christ alone. That is all of God apart from us. But as those who are justified, we embark on a new life of obedience to God. He does this through the process of sanctification, by which He makes His people more Christlike, and therefore more obedient. God takes men like Bezalel, Oholiab, and the entire congregation, regenerates them, justifies them, and begins to sanctify them. The work of sanctification is, as the Westminster Larger Catechism says, "a work of God's grace"; even more, it is "the powerful operation of his Spirit" (Q&A 75).

At this point, it can be very easy for us to think that sanctification is the work of God in exactly the same way as justification. We think: "Justification is monergistic; therefore, sanctification is monergistic. Justification has nothing to do with me; therefore, sanctification has nothing to do with me." But listen to how the Larger Catechism goes on to explain sanctification in more detail in an often-overlooked question and answer:

> Q. 77. Wherein do justification and sanctification differ?
> A. Although sanctification be inseparably joined with justification, yet they differ, in that God in justification imputeth the righteousness of Christ; in sanctification of his Spirit infuseth grace, and enableth to the exercise thereof; in the former, sin is pardoned; in the other, it is subdued: the one doth equally free all believers from the revenging wrath of God, and that perfectly in this life, that they never fall into condemnation; the other is neither equal in all, nor in this life perfect in any, but growing up to perfection. (Q&A 77)

In justification, God works *in* us, but in sanctification, God works *through* us. In justification, we are *passive*, but in sanctification, we are *active*. In justification, we are *recipients*, but in sanctification, we are *participants*. In sanctification, then, God the Holy Spirit grants us gifts that we might be enabled to serve God. Through our use of those gifts, the Holy Spirit makes us more and more holy—sanctified.

Christians, God not only has delivered you from the guilt of sin by the active and passive obedience of the Lord Jesus Christ (Romans 5), but He more and more is delivering you experientially from the pollution and corruption of sin (Romans 6). As He does so, He gifts you so that you are becoming more and more able and willing to "present yourselves to God as those who have been brought from death to life, and your members to God as instruments for righteousness" (Rom. 6:13). He gifts you so that you are becoming more and more able and willing to "present yourselves . . . as obedient slaves . . . which leads to righteousness" (Rom. 6:16). He gifts you so that you are becoming more and more able and willing to say, "I delight in the law of God, in my inner being" (Rom. 7:21).

As a member of Christ's church, then, you have been gifted by the Holy Spirit to possess a place, a use, and an office in the body. You have been enabled to use the gift or gifts that the Spirit has given you to the glory of God, for the church's edification, and for the world's salvation.

A NEW BEGINNING

Exodus 40

The LORD spoke to Moses, saying, "On the first day of the first month you shall erect the tabernacle of the tent of meeting. And you shall put in it the ark of the testimony, and you shall screen the ark with the veil. And you shall bring in the table and arrange it, and you shall bring in the lampstand and set up its lamps. And you shall put the golden altar for incense before the ark of the testimony, and set up the screen for the door of the tabernacle. You shall set the altar of burnt offering before the door of the tabernacle of the tent of meeting, and place the basin between the tent of meeting and the altar, and put water in it. And you shall set up the court all around, and hang up the screen for the gate of the court. Then you shall take the anointing oil and anoint the tabernacle and all that is in it, and consecrate it and all its furniture, so that it may become holy. You shall also anoint the altar of burnt offering and all its utensils, and consecrate the altar, so that the altar may become most holy. You shall also anoint the basin and its stand, and consecrate it." . . . This Moses did; according to all that the LORD commanded him, so he did. In the first month in the second year, on the first day of the month, the tabernacle was erected. Moses erected the tabernacle. . . . Then the cloud covered the tent of meeting, and the glory of the LORD filled the tabernacle. And Moses was not able to enter the tent of meeting because the cloud settled on it, and the glory of the LORD filled

201

the tabernacle. Throughout all their journeys, whenever the cloud was taken up from over the tabernacle, the people of Israel would set out. But if the cloud was not taken up, then they did not set out till the day that it was taken up. For the cloud of the LORD was on the tabernacle by day, and fire was in it by night, in the sight of all the house of Israel throughout all their journeys. (Ex. 40:1–38)

The book of Exodus presents a sweeping narrative. The story begins in Egypt, moves into the wilderness, and then arrives at Sinai. In it, we hear Israel's prayers and see God's answers. We see Pharaoh's persecution and God's liberation. We read the law and learn how it all points us to the work of Christ and the gospel. We read about the tabernacle, which is "a copy and shadow of the heavenly things" (Heb. 8:5), and learn about the mysteries of our redemption and our relationship to God.

Yet the end of the book of Exodus is really a beginning. From this point in the narrative of God's redemptive plan, Israel begins its journey toward the Promised Land. But this beginning is much more than that. As we read and meditate on the first raising of the tabernacle, it is necessary for us to lift up our hearts and minds to understand its heavenly reality.

This event is nothing less than *a new beginning*, a new creation theologically, a powerful testimony that God is a God of new life, of new beginnings for sinners. The words of Herman Witsius, cited earlier to show that the construction of the tabernacle is analogous to the creation of the world, are worth repeating here: "God created the world in six days, but he used forty to instruct Moses about the tabernacle. Little over one chapter was needed to describe the structure of the world, but six were used for the tabernacle."[1] This new beginning was of such importance that it deserved such space.

We learn that the first assembly of the tabernacle in the wilderness was a new beginning in four details from Exodus 40: the commands, the calendar, the consecration, and the cloud. The lessons communicated here have powerful applications for us as new-covenant believers, for we, like the Israelites, desperately need new beginnings.

THE COMMANDS

First, *the commands* show us that Exodus 40 is a new beginning. This account of the raising of the tabernacle is packed with commands. In the earlier chapters, when the Lord gave Moses instructions on how to make each article for the tabernacle, He listed the curtains, the ark, the veils, and so forth. In this chapter, we see all those aspects brought together piece by piece, according to God's specific commands.

Specifically, there are eighteen commands from the Lord in verses 1–15. After God commands Moses to erect the tabernacle (v. 2), the assembly process works its way out from the Holy of Holies. First, He tells Moses to "put in [the tabernacle] the ark" (v. 3), then to hang the veil before the ark (v. 3), to arrange the table (v. 4), to set up the lampstand (v. 4), to place the altar of incense (v. 5), to set up the screen of the tabernacle (v. 5), to set up the altar of burnt offering (v. 6), to place the bronze basin (v. 7), to hang up the screen around the court (v. 8), to anoint the tabernacle and its furniture (v. 9), to anoint the altar of burnt offering and its utensils (v. 10), to anoint the bronze basin and its stand (v. 11), to wash Aaron and his sons (v. 12), to put Aaron's garments on him (v. 13), to anoint Aaron (v. 13), to put coats on his sons (v. 14), and to anoint them (v. 15).

After these commands, what do we read next? "This Moses did; according to all that the Lord commanded him, so he did" (v. 16). We know it took the giving and work of many of the Israelites to construct what the Lord commanded them through Moses. Many volunteered and some were particularly gifted for the work of building the tabernacle (Exodus 35–36). Likewise, it took many men to set up the tabernacle for the first time. But as we read on, we see Moses named again and again as the one who fulfilled all the commands for the first assembly of the tabernacle (vv. 18–33), until we are told, "So Moses finished the work" (v. 33). All the credit is given to Moses *by* Moses, who is the author of the book of Exodus.

In human terms, this seems like Donald Trump calling himself the builder of the world's greatest buildings. When was the last time Trump picked up a hammer? When was the last time he walked across a steel beam fifty stories high? He calls himself the builder and takes credit because he is in charge of the entire operation. Moses, of course, was the Lord's servant, who mediated between God and His people. For this reason, he is credited with being the one who did the work. He was an obedient servant; as Hebrews 3:5 says, "Now Moses was faithful in all God's house as a servant."

But there is a deeper theological significance to the way in which this chapter is written. The language here should remind us of Genesis 1, where we read repeatedly: "And God said, 'Let there be . . .' And it was so." Just as in creation God commanded and His commands were fulfilled, so it was in the assembly of the tabernacle.[2] The Lord's commands were carried out right away.

We need to pause and reflect on the beauty of the Word of God here. When we do this, we begin to see how themes from earlier parts of Scripture continue throughout the rest of Scripture. In this we see its beauty, which is, of course, a reflection of the beautiful wisdom of God and the beautiful work of the Holy Spirit in inspiring these words. This should cause us to find delight and pleasure in the Word. We should say with the psalmist, "I find my delight in your commandments, which I love" (Ps. 119:47).

THE CALENDAR

Second, *the calendar* shows us that Exodus 40 is a new beginning. God commanded that the tabernacle be set up on the first day in the first month (Ex. 40:2). So, "In the first month in the second year, on the first day of the month, the tabernacle was erected" (v. 17). It was the new year; it was a new beginning, a new creation. In fact, it had been exactly one year since God told Moses that He was restarting the Israelites' calendar. When the Lord spoke of the Passover, He said: "This month shall be for you the beginning of months. It shall be the first month of the year for you" (Ex. 12:2). Then He proceeded to tell Moses all about the Passover celebration and Israel's liberation from Egypt.

God reveals Himself in the Word over and over again as a God of new beginnings. The Bible uses all sorts of terms to describe this in the Psalms and the writings of the prophets: *restoration* (Pss. 23:3; 80:3, 7, 19), *revival* (Ps. 85:6; Isa. 57:15; Hos. 6:2), and *renewal* (Pss. 51:10; 103:5; Isa. 40:31; Lam. 5:21). The author of the epistle to the Hebrews summarizes all the longings of the Old Testament for restoration, revival, and renewal as *reformation* (Heb. 9:10). Call it what you will, the point is that the God of the Bible is the kind of God who brings new beginnings to His languishing people.

Above all, God gives new beginnings to sinners. He says to you today: "If *anyone* is in Christ, he is a new creation. The old has passed away; behold, the new has come" (2 Cor. 5:17, emphasis added). For whom is this "new beginning" intended? *Anyone.* When you turn away from yourself, your selfish lifestyle, and your sinful desires, and turn to Jesus Christ and trust that He lived a perfect life, died on the cross, and rose again all for you, God starts anew with you. He restarts your life clock so that your days are measured not merely by this age but by eternity. But will it last? The Apostle Paul describes being a Christian not only as a once-for-all, immediate new beginning, but as an ongoing metamorphosis: "And we all . . . are being transformed [*metamorphoumetha*] into the same image [of Christ] from one degree of glory to another" (2 Cor. 3:18). God gives new life at the beginning of salvation, He gives new life in the midst of salvation, and He will give new life at the end of salvation, when He will "transform our lowly body to be like his [Christ's] glorious body" (Phil. 3:21).

THE CONSECRATION

Third, *the consecration* of the tabernacle shows us that Exodus 40 is a new beginning. In verses 12–15, we read of God's command that Aaron and his four sons, Nadab, Abihu, Eleazar, and Ithamar, come before Moses to be washed, robed, and anointed to serve as high priest and priests, respectively (cf. Exodus 29; Leviticus 8–9). As we saw in chapter 11, the consecration of the priests was to occur over a period of seven days (Ex. 29:35). They were to be washed, robed, and anointed, then three separate sacrifices were to be offered every day for seven days. Just as God created the heavens and the earth in six days and rested on the seventh, so the assembly of the tabernacle was to occur "on the first day of the first month" (Ex. 40:1), then the seven-day consecration of the priests took place. This would be later paralleled in the building of the temple over seven years (1 Kings 6:38) and its dedicatory feast held over a period of seven days (1 Kings 8:65; 2 Chron. 7:8–9). The implicit reality being taught here is that the seventh day of consecration corresponded with the cloud falling upon the tabernacle (Ex. 40:34–38) as the sign of God's rest and pleasure in what He had made.[3] Just as the six days of creation (Gen. 1:1–31) led to the Sabbath (Gen. 2:1–3), so the "creation" of the tabernacle led to the rest of the Lord within the midst of His people.

Now that Jesus Christ has redeemed us, our lives are oriented forward toward our heavenly rest (Revelation 21–22). In a letter from J. R. R. Tolkien to his son Christopher, he spoke, in part, of this heavenliness of human existence: "We all long for [Eden], and we are constantly glimpsing it."[4] Since our first father, Adam, was made to live with God in the garden, working and then resting in His presence, a vestigial longing for that experience remains in our consciences and souls despite our sin-torn existence. This is what we see in the Old Testament tabernacle. It is a glimpse backward of Eden and a preview forward of heaven.

THE CLOUD

Fourth, *the cloud* shows us that Exodus 40 is a new beginning. Remember Genesis 1:2: "And the Spirit of God was hovering over the face of the waters." Similarly, we read that when the tabernacle was raised, the cloud covered the tent and the glory of the Lord filled it (Ex. 40:34). Just as the Spirit took up residence upon the face of the earth before giving it form and fullness, so He came upon the tabernacle to demonstrate that He was in the midst of His people.

Here is truth that is almost inexpressible. Like the commands, the calendar, and the consecration, the cloud points to God being the giver of new life. The psalmist would later reflect upon the week of creation and say this about the Spirit's relation to everything He made: "When you send forth your Spirit, they are created, and you renew the face of the ground" (Ps. 104:30). It was this life-giving Spirit who fell upon the tabernacle in the midst of God's people.

The cloud filling the tabernacle is also a picture of us, since the New Testament describes Christians as temples of the living God and says that God dwells and walks among us (2 Cor. 6:16–7:1). His Spirit gives us new life and fills us. Similarly, just as the Spirit guided the Israelites during their desert wanderings by means of the cloud (vv. 36–37), so He leads us (Rom. 8:14; Gal. 5:18). We, too, need to learn how to discern when He rises above the tabernacle and moves to another location and when He rests again within the tabernacle. We come to know the Spirit's leading and resting as we know Him through His inspired words (2 Tim. 3:16–17). This is how we "keep in step with the Spirit" (Gal. 5:25, NIV).

Ultimately, the cloud filling the tabernacle is a picture, a type and shadow, of our Lord Jesus Christ. The Apostle John said of Him, "And the Word became flesh and [tabernacled] among us" (John 1:14). The Apostle Paul said of Him, "In him the whole fullness of deity dwells bodily" (Col. 2:9). It is amazing that when we turn to John 1, we find the Apostle reflecting on how our Lord created everything (vv. 1–3). He is not only the Author of the first creation, He is the Author of a new creation, a new beginning. All this occurred by means of the Holy Spirit, who overshadowed the Virgin Mary and conceived in her the Son of God, the Lord Jesus Christ (Luke 1:35).

As we come to the end of Exodus' tabernacle narratives, we come to the beginning of a new phase in Israel's relationship with God. He desired that they embark on a new life of faith and love toward His commands. He desired that their lives begin again. He desired that they enter His holy and consecrated presence. And He desired that they experience

His presence leading them from glory to glory. The same God leads us, even as we sing:

> O sweet and blessed country,
> The home of God's elect!
> O sweet and blessed country
> That eager hearts expect!
> Jesus, in mercy bring us
> To that dear land of rest,
> Who art with God the Father
> And Spirit, ever blest.[5]

CONCLUSION

The tabernacle narratives end in Exodus 40, which begins by calling the tabernacle "the tabernacle of the tent of meeting" (v. 2). These two terms, *tabernacle* and *tent of meeting*, were used earlier in the narratives separately to express what this building was about. It was called a "tabernacle" (25:9) because it was a house for the Lord to dwell in among His people, and it was called a "tent of meeting" (27:21; 28:43; 30:20) because it was the place where He would meet with His people. This was all summarized at the beginning of the tabernacle narratives when the Lord expressed His desire for the tabernacle to be the place where "I may dwell in their midst" (25:8). In short, the tabernacle was a picture of Immanuel, "God with us," in the wilderness.

It also was a picture of heaven. We saw this in the symbolic signs of the tabernacle. Cherubim were woven into the veil of the Holy of Holies (26:31), which reminded the Israelites that access to Eden was forbidden after the fall (Gen. 3:24), but was being opened again in a typological way. The cherubim also were woven into the curtains surrounding the tabernacle (26:1), lifting the minds and hearts of the priests into heaven, where the cherubim surround the Lord (Ezekiel 1). The entranceway into the courtyard, Holy Place, and Holy of Holies was from east to west, that is, in biblical terms, from being outside the presence of the Lord to entering His presence. Also, the curtains surrounding the tabernacle were the color blue, which was the color Moses saw when he was with the Lord on Sinai (24:10).

We also see that the tabernacle was a picture of heaven, the dwelling place of God, by the materials used in its construction. As a person moved closer and closer to the Holy of Holies, the materials were more pure and costly. The courtyard and the things within it were made of linens, bronze, and silver (27:9–19), the tabernacle was made of gold and silver (Exodus 26), and the furnishings were made of gold and pure gold (Exodus 25).

Even the dimensions depict heaven. Again, as a person moved inward, things became more and more perfect. The entire courtyard structure was one hundred cubits long by fifty cubits wide by five cubits high (27:18). The actual tabernacle was divided into two, with the Holy Place being twenty cubits long by ten cubits wide (26:15–30), while the Holy of Holies was ten cubits by ten cubits, based on the fact that the temple was twice the size of the tabernacle (1 Kings 6:2), and the temple's Holy of Holies was twenty cubits by twenty cubits (v. 20).

This heavenly dwelling place of God in the midst of His people came to fulfillment in the incarnation of the Son of God, our Lord Jesus Christ. This is what I ultimately want you to understand as you read the tabernacle story. It is Jesus I ultimately want you to apprehend by faith and appropriate to your spiritual joy. Thus, John says, "And the Word became flesh and dwelt [literally, "tabernacled"] among us" (John 1:14). And just as the glory of God descended on the tabernacle (Ex. 40:34–38), so in Christ "we have seen his glory, glory as of the only Son from the Father, full of grace and truth" (John 1:14).

All the sacrifices and ceremonial rites of the tabernacle foreshadowed the work of our Lord, who is the once-and-for-all final sacrifice (Hebrews 9), who offered Himself in the heavenly tent (Hebrews 8), thus ending the Old Testament sacrificial system (Hebrews 10).

We also have reflected on the truth that in the tabernacle, as the place where God dwelt, we see a type and shadow of the new-covenant church. The New Testament describes the church and its relationship to the triune God in terms of the tabernacle and temple:

> For through him we both have access in one Spirit to the Father. So then you are no longer strangers and aliens, but you are fellow citizens with the saints and members of the household of God, built on the foundation of the apostles and prophets, Christ Jesus himself being the cornerstone, in whom the whole structure, being joined together, grows into a holy temple in the Lord. In him you also are being built together into a dwelling place for God by the Spirit. (Eph. 2:18–22)

In conclusion, as we read the book of Exodus, we see that it begins in the darkness of suffering, but it ends in the light of the gospel. It begins with cries to God that seemed unanswered, but it ends with God's answer in His activity among His people. It begins with the seeming absence of God, but it ends with His precious presence among His people in the tabernacle, even as He is among us today. May God write the story of our ancient family's place of worship in the book of Exodus upon the tablets of our hearts.

APPENDIX:

PREACHING

THE PENTATEUCH

Theology and exegesis are the servants of preaching. If theology is *regina scientiarum*, "the queen of the sciences," as our older theologians used to say, then preaching is her *corona*, her crown.

Therefore, given all that I have said above in terms of exposition and application of the tabernacle narratives, I would like to use this appendix to address pastors and those preparing to enter the gospel ministry on the topic of actually preaching the Pentateuch.[1] I pray my suggestions and comments here are edifying and stimulating to you as you seek to preach the section of the Word in which the tabernacle narratives are found, the Pentateuch.

Preaching from the Pentateuch is a great need of our people, many of whom have never heard sermons from any book of the Old Testament, let alone the Pentateuch. This is also an area of great need for us as preachers, who tend to shy away from the Pentateuch. I will give some evidence of this below, but my experience has confirmed that the Pentateuch is not being preached in Christian churches. As I delivered my sermons on the tabernacle in my series through Exodus, one particular Lord's Day on which a vacationing family worshiped with our congregation stands out. After the service, the grandmother in this family came up to me and said, "I've been a Christian my entire life and just want you to know that I have never heard a sermon on the tabernacle." She was visibly excited, wanted to listen to the sermons she had missed and those that were yet to come on our SermonAudio site,[2] and said she was going to encourage her minister to preach the Old Testament.

A PLEA TO PREACH THE PENTATEUCH

In his book, *Preaching Christ from the Old Testament*, Sidney Greidanus gives a helpful list of "Reasons for the Lack of Preaching from the Old Testament." First, he says the use of lectionaries (books with lists of designated Scripture readings for each day) to guide preaching in some traditions limits Old Testament preaching. The focus in most lectionaries for Lord's Day worship is on the Gospels and Epistles, with only selected parts of the Old Testament. Second, the era of critical Old Testament scholarship has limited preaching from this part of the Bible. This scholarship has cast many doubts on the historicity and veracity of the Old Testament books, leading to the belief that the Old Testament contains nothing more than nice morals clothed in myths. Third, there is an outright rejection of the Old Testament as being for Israel only and not for the new-covenant church; this attitude is especially prevalent in churches with a dispensational (dividing God's dealings with Israel from the church) hermeneutic and theology. Fourth, as I will explain below, there are many difficulties in preaching from the Old Testament.[3]

For conservative, evangelical, and Reformed preachers and future preachers, the first three reasons above are not really problems. It is the fourth reason Greidanus offers that concerns us: *difficulties*. Greidanus lists four difficulties. The first is the historical-cultural difficulty. The Old Testament is very foreign to us and to our people. How many levirate marriages have you performed as a pastor? The second is the theological difficulty. Is the God of Israel really the only God in our pluralistic world? How can we believe that so many cultures and religions are worshiping idols? The third is the ethical difficulty of the Old Testament expressed in the maxim, "an eye for an eye." Given that the Old Testament prescribes capital punishment for witches, does that mean the application for us is to go witch hunting at the local palm-reading center? Seriously, what do we say about God's commands for what we call "ethnic cleansing" in an age that has seen so many atrocities? And these examples from the Pentateuch do not even touch on the issue of the imprecations (from the Latin, *imprecatio*, an invoking of a curse) of the Psalms—those prayers of the godly for the destruction of the ungodly. How is it that those who are commanded to "love your enemies and pray for those who persecute you" (Matt. 5:44) also have these words to sing in the inspired Psalms:

O daughter of Babylon—destined to ruin—
He's blessed who repays as you've done.
How blessed is the one who will seize on your infants
And hurl them to smash on the stone.[4]

I won't answer the question here except to say, as Old Testament scholar Elizabeth Achtemeier writes: "If we have some problem with a passage in the Old Testament, it is not the Bible's problem. It is ours."[5]

The fourth difficulty is the practical problem of the sheer volume of the Old Testament and all the necessary background knowledge that is needed to preach it with any level of intelligence.

Despite these difficulties, I plead with you as a co-laborer in the gospel ministry to "preach the word" (2 Tim. 4:2) in the Old Testament and especially the Pentateuch. I believe we must preach the Pentateuch for four reasons.

Its Need

First, as I mentioned, there is a great need for preaching the Pentateuch in our churches to give our people a well-rounded diet of the "whole counsel of God" (Acts 20:27). No doubt many preachers' experience of their people's lack of Bible knowledge testifies to this. Several recent studies by various denominations have shown that while seventy-five percent of the Scriptures are found within the Old Testament, only twenty percent of sermons come from the Old Testament.[6] Our people need us to do more than merely teach Old Testament Bible stories to our children in Sunday school. They need us to *preach* these stories to *them*.

Its Importance

Second, we must preach the Pentateuch because these books are the foundational books for the rest of Scripture. The doctrines of creation, sin, redemption, covenant, election, and the moral law of God are all revealed here. As the twentieth-century Swiss Reformed theologian Jean-Jacques Von Allmen wrote, "a Church which discards the Old Testament does not achieve a true meeting with Christ."[7] We not only rob our people of vital truth if we do not preach the Old Testament; we rob them of the canvas upon which the Holy Spirit paints Christ in the New Testament.

Its Nature

Third, we need to preach the Pentateuch because the stories within it are exciting, riveting, and heart-pounding. This is the backstory to the drama of Jesus. We preachers need to ask ourselves: are our people clamoring for more application because they are tired of our dry, doctrinal sermons? Or are they tired of us preaching application with nothing to hang it upon? I am convinced one simple remedy is to preach on drama—the drama of God's redemptive story, that is. As we preach from the Pentateuch, God is put at center stage as the chief actor in all these stories.

Its Substance

Fourth, we need to preach the Pentateuch because our Lord taught His disciples that He is the sum and substance of these books (Luke 24:27, 44). He is the eternal Word who created in Genesis 1. He is the reality of circumcision given to Abraham in Genesis 17. He is the Lord of the covenant at Mount Sinai in Exodus 24. He is the rock that gave water to drink in Exodus 17 and the manna that was provided while Israel wandered the wilderness in Exodus 16. As one Dutch homiletician, Wilhelm Vischer, memorably stated, "Jesus Christ provides the vowel-points which give a sense to the consonants of the Hebrew text."[8]

PRINCIPLES FOR PREACHING

So, how can we begin to preach this tough but terrific part of God's holy Word in the Old Testament? Here are some homiletical principles that have guided me in my preaching of the Pentateuch:

Preach Expositionally

First, we should preach expositionally, that is, through entire books of the Pentateuch, chapter by chapter, verse by verse. On this subject, I would highly commend to you the chapter by Derek Thomas in the volume *Feed My Sheep: A Passionate Plea for Preaching*.[9] Too many preachers today lazily "cherry pick" texts, leaving their congregations' spiritual diets to the whims of their feelings week in and week out. Although he was not an expositional preacher in the sense I am advocating, Charles Haddon Spurgeon described what we need to be doing: simply opening our Bibles and letting the Holy Spirit do His work as we would unleash a lion, letting it do what it wishes. Our people need to hear the stories of Genesis, such as the creation, Adam's sin, Noah and the flood, Abram's calling, Jacob's wrestling, and Joseph's preserving of Israel, as well as the seemingly unpreachable genealogy of Esau (Genesis 36) and the sexual deviancy of the Judah and Tamar story (Genesis 38). Our people need to hear the stories of Exodus, such as Moses' preservation in the Nile, his calling at the burning bush, the plagues, the Ten Commandments, and the tabernacle, as well as the seemingly random laws in the so-called "Book of the Covenant" (Exodus 21–23). These are just the tip of the iceberg.

Preach Plainly

Second, we should preach "plainly." The language of the Apostle Paul in 1 Corinthians 2:1–5 and Colossians 4:4 became the rallying cry of the Puritan "plain style" of preaching in the sixteenth and seventeenth centuries. This style emphasized not merely plainness of speech but also plainness of method. In a nutshell, every sermon revolved around two main points: doctrine and use.[10] In our terminology, we should preach with exposition and application.

Here is how the Puritan theologian William Perkins (1558–1602) summed up his vision for preaching:

1. To read the Text distinctly out of the Canonicall Scriptures.
2. To give the sense and understanding of it being read, by the Scripture it selfe.
3. To collect a few and profitable points of doctrine out of the naturall sense.
4. To applie (if he have the gift) the doctrines rightly collected to the life and manners of men, in a simple and plaine speech.[11]

He went on to explain these last two points, doctrine and use, in his classic text *The Arte of Prophecying*.[12]

Perkins' greatest pupil, William Ames (1576–1633), also spoke of these two necessary parts of preaching in these words: "In order that the will of God may be set forth fruitfully for edification two things are necessary. First, the things contained in the text must be stated, second, they must be applied to the consciences of the hearers as their condition seems to require."[13] He went on: "In setting forth the truth in the text the minister should first explain it and then indicate the good which follows from it. The first part is concerned with doctrines and proofs; the latter with application or derivation of profit from the doctrines."[14]

This plain-style method was later codified by the Westminster Assembly in its Directory for the Publick Worship of God under the heading, "Of the Preaching of the Word," which says in part:

[The preacher] is not to rest in general doctrine, although never so much cleared and confirmed, but to bring it home to special use, by application to his hearers: which albeit it prove a work of great difficulty to himself, requiring much prudence, zeal, and meditation, and to the natural and corrupt man will be very unpleasant; yet he is to endeavour to perform it in such a manner, that his auditors may feel the word of God to be quick and powerful, and a discerner of the thoughts and intents of the heart; and that, if any unbeliever or ignorant person be present, he may have the secrets of his heart made manifest, and give glory to God. . . . This method is not prescribed as necessary for every man, or upon every text; but only recommended, as being found by experience to be very much blessed of God, and very helpful for the people's understandings and memories.[15]

To preach the Pentateuch plainly, then, is first to preach *doctrine*. I believe those of us with more of a redemptive-historical mind-set are afraid to preach doctrine because of two pressures. First, we are pressured by the idea that doctrine is not winsome and winning in the twenty-first century. But the Word of God reveals God and our relation to Him, which is doctrinal. Second, we are pressured to think that doctrine is imposed on the text and is not the concern of Christ-centered preaching. But the texts of the Pentateuch are the fertile ground from which the prophets and Apostles reaped their doctrine. Therefore, when you preach on Genesis 1, preach on the doctrine of creation; when you preach on Genesis 2, preach on the Sabbath; when you preach on the flood narrative in Genesis 6–9, preach on divine justice and mercy; when you preach on Abram's call in Genesis 12, preach on election and effectual calling; when you preach on Abram's faith in Genesis 15, preach on justification *sola fide*. The examples of doctrines from the texts of the Pentateuch are too numerous to mention.

To preach the Pentateuch plainly means, second, to preach the *application* and use of the text. The Puritan Thomas Manton once said it like this in a sermon: "Ministers should not only be men of science, but of experience."[16] Let me commend to you Joel Beeke's chapter on

"Experiential Preaching" in the aforementioned volume *Feed My Sheep*[17] for further guidance on application.

This is one area in which we Reformed preachers can be weak, to be honest. The Westminster Directory admits that application will "prove a work of great difficulty to [the preacher], requiring much prudence, zeal, and meditation." To preach, a minister must have a consideration of those to whom he preaches. It takes time to develop this skill because it takes time to get to know yourself, as well as your sheep and their needs, worries, problems, and fears. As John Owen said, "He who hath not the state of his flock continually in his eye, and in his mind, in his work of preaching, fights uncertainly, as a man beating the air." Owen added that preachers are to consider their peoples' temptations and duties, their strengths and weaknesses, their light or darkness of understanding, and the measure of their knowledge.[18]

Yes, applying the text is difficult. Nevertheless, as my pastor in seminary, the Rev. Andrew Cammenga, always told me, "Danny, it's not good enough to tell your people the 'what' of the passage; you need to show them the 'so what?'"

This starts with applying the text to ourselves. Listen, again, to Owen:

No man preaches that sermon well to others that doth not first preach it to his own heart. He who doth not feed on, and digest, and thrive by, what he prepares for his people, he may give them poison, as far as he knows; for, unless he finds the power of it in his own heart, he cannot have any ground of confidence that it will have power in the hearts of others. It is an easier thing to bring our heads to preach than our hearts to preach. To bring our heads to preach, is but to fill our minds and memories with some notions of truth, of our own or other men, and speak them out to give satisfaction to ourselves and others: this is very easy. But to bring our hearts to preach, is to be transformed into the power of these truths; or to find the power of them, both before, in fashioning our minds and hearts, and in delivering of them, that we may have benefit; and to be acted with zeal for God and compassion to the souls of men. A man may preach every day in the week, and not have his heart engaged once.[19]

If the word doth not dwell with power in us, it will not pass with power from us. And no man lives in a more woeful condition than those who really believe not themselves what they persuade others to believe continually. The want of this experience of the power of gospel truth on their own souls is that which gives us so many lifeless, sapless orations, quaint in words, and dead as to power, instead of preaching the gospel in the demonstration of the Spirit.[20]

Why is it so important that your people understand the holiness and justice of God in the plague narrative of Exodus? What do you want your people to do in response to the providence of God in the Joseph narrative? You cannot merely feed your ignorant, helpless, and often-times fearful sheep the meat of the Word; you need to tell them why it is good for them, why they need to eat it, and how they need to eat it. As the Westminster Directory says, in preaching doctrine the preacher must "bring it home to special use, by application to his hearers."

Preach Christologically

At the end of *The Arte of Prophecying*, Perkins gave "The Summe of the Summe" of preaching in these words: "Preach one Christ by Christ to the praise of Christ."[21] Later, the Boston Congregationalist Thomas Foxcroft said that Jesus Christ "must be the substance and bottom of every sermon," and "whatever subject ministers are upon, it must somehow point to Christ."[22] We should proclaim Christ as the eternal wisdom of the Father through whom the universe was made from Genesis 1, proclaim Him as the Savior from judgment in the flood narrative, proclaim Him as the judge of the living and the dead in the plague narratives in Exodus, and proclaim His active and passive obedience in the laws and regulations of the Book of the Covenant and the tabernacle narratives.

In saying this, let me add that you are not merely to preach *about* Christ, but you are to preach Christ as His voice to your congregation. You want people to hear His living voice near them in your voice and not merely as a distant echo. I do this by preaching with passion and urgency, and by speaking often in the first person. This is humbling and frightening. But if Paul says, "who shall believe in him *whom* they have never heard" (Rom. 10:14, emphasis added), and if preaching is not the word of men but the Word of God (1 Thess. 2:13), then your voice is the *viva vox*, the living voice of the Lord.[23] Therefore, preach Christ to unbelievers, calling them to repentance and faith; preach Christ to doubting believers, assuring their hearts of His love; preach Christ to strong believers, calling them to persevere and continue in a living faith; and preach Christ to wayward, lazy, and backsliding members, calling them to grasp the privileges they have and to enter into them through godly sorrow and true, not only historical, faith.

The Pentateuch must be preached, for it is the Word of God. The Pentateuch needs to be preached, for it contains food for our hungry people's souls. Finally, we should desire to preach the Pentateuch, as it leads us and our people by the hand to our Lord and Savior Jesus Christ and our amazing life in Him.

NOTES

Introduction

1   William Brown, *The Tabernacle: Its Priests and Its Services* (1899; repr., Peabody, Mass.: Hendrickson, 1996), 3.

2   See Appendix, "Preaching the Pentateuch."

3   For basic background on the book of Exodus, see the standard introduction in Raymond B. Dillard and Tremper Longman III, *An Introduction to the Old Testament* (Grand Rapids: Zondervan, 1994), 57–71; Albert H. Baylis, *From Creation to the Cross: Understanding the First Half of the Bible* (Grand Rapids: Zondervan, 1996), 99–145. For older introductions, see Edward J. Young, *An Introduction to the Old Testament* (Grand Rapids: Eerdmans, 1949), 67–78; John Howard Raven, *Old Testament Introduction: General and Special* (1906; repr., New York: Fleming H. Revell, 1910), 136–42.

4   Matthew Poole, *A Commentary on the Whole Bible, Vol. 1: Genesis–Job*, 3 vols. (Peabody, Mass.: Hendrickson, 2008), 1:173.

5   Carl Friedrich Keil, *Manual of Biblical Archaeology*, trans. Peter Christie, ed. Frederick Crombie, Clark's Foreign Theological Library, New Series, Vol. XXXII, 2 vols. (Edinburgh, Scotland: T&T Clark, 1887), 1:149.

6   Herman Witsius, *Miscellanea sacra*, 2 vols. (Utrecht, 1692–1700), 1:349ff.; cited in Brevard S. Childs, *The Book of Exodus: A Critical, Theological Commentary* (Philadelphia: The Westminster Press, 1974), 547.

7   For an exposition of this material, you may listen to eight sermons located here: http://www.sermonaudio.com/oceansideurc. See also D. Martyn Lloyd-Jones, *Revival* (Wheaton, Ill.: Crossway, 1987), 148–249.

8   For a brief summary of this issue from a Jewish perspective, see Nahum M. Sarna, *Exploring Exodus: The Origins of Biblical Israel* (1986; repr., New York: Shocken Books, 1996), 196–200. For a Christian perspective, see Childs, *The Book of Exodus*, 529–37. For a classic and substantive critique of the critical scholarship against the Pentateuch, see Oswald T. Allis, *The Five Books of Moses* (1943; repr., Phillipsburg, N.J.: Presbyterian and Reformed, 1949).

9   On the hermeneutics of the Old Testament, see Vern S. Poythress, *The Shadow of Christ in the Law of Moses* (Phillipsburg, N.J.: Presbyterian and Reformed, 1991), 3–8. On

hermeneutics in general, see Louis Berkhof, *Principles of Biblical Interpretation* (1950; repr., Grand Rapids: Baker, 1994); Walter C. Kaiser Jr. and Moisés Silva, *An Introduction to Biblical Hermeneutics: The Search for Meaning* (Grand Rapids: Zondervan, 1994).

10 Hilary of Poitiers, cited in E. P. Meijering and J. C. M. van Winden, *Hilary of Poitiers on the Trinity: De Trinitate 1, 1–19, 2, 3* (Leiden: Brill, 1982), 60.

11 On Philo's allegorical interpretation, see *Philo: Supplement II, Questions and Answers on Exodus*, trans. Ralph Marcus (Cambridge, Mass.: Harvard University Press, 1953), 97–176.

12 Clement of Alexandria, *Stromata* 5.6 in *Ante-Nicene Fathers*, ed. Alexander Roberts and James Donaldson, 10 vols. (1885; repr., Peabody, Mass.: Hendrickson, 2004), 2:452–54.

13 Childs, *The Book of Exodus*, 538.

14 For a brief introduction to the *quadriga*, see R. C. Sproul, *Knowing Scripture* (Downers Grove, Ill.: InterVarsity, 1977), 54–56. For an in-depth historical treatment, see the three-volume series by Henri de Lubac, *Medieval Exegesis: The Four Senses of Scripture* (Grand Rapids: Eerdmans, 1988/2000/2009).

15 For Bede's exposition, see Bede, *On the Tabernacle*, trans. Arthur G. Holder, Translated Texts for Historians 18 (Liverpool, England: Liverpool University Press, 1994). For a survey of medieval exegesis following Bede, see de Lubac, *Medieval Exegesis*, 3:300–311.

16 On Cocceius, see Willem J. van Asselt, *The Federal Theology of Johannes Cocceius (1603–1669)* (Leiden: Brill, 2001); Brian J. Lee, *Johannes Cocceius and the Exegetical Roots of Federal Theology* (Göttingen: Vandenhoeck & Ruprecht, 2008).

17 W. H. Gispen, *Exodus*, trans. Ed van der Maas, Bible Student's Commentary (Grand Rapids: Zondervan, 1982), 14; Childs, *The Book of Exodus*, 538.

18 Herman Witsius, *Sacred Dissertations on What is Commonly Called the Apostles' Creed*, trans. Donald Fraser, 2 vols. (1823; repr., Phillipsburg, N.J.: P&R, 1993), 2:331–32.

19 Witsius, *Sacred Dissertations*, 2:3; Herman Witsius, *The Economy of the Covenants Between God and Man: Comprehending a Complete Body of Divinity*, trans. William Crookshank, 2 vols. (1822; repr., Phillipsburg, N.J.: Presbyterian and Reformed, 1990), 2:208.

20 Brown, *The Tabernacle*, 22.

21 "Preface to the Wittenberg Edition of Luther's German Writings (1539)," in *Martin Luther's Basic Theological Writings*, ed. Timothy F. Lull (Minneapolis: Fortress Press, 1989), 72.

22 See Gerald Bilkes, "Heart-Reading: Recovering a Spiritual Approach to the Bible," *Puritan Reformed Journal* 1:2 (July 2009): 12–22.

23 For a reflection on how Hebrews interprets the tabernacle, see Childs, *The Book of Exodus*, 543–47.

24 Augustine, cited in *Quaestiones in Heptateuchum*, 2.73, in *Patrologia Latina*, ed. Jacques-Paul Migne, 34:623. This volume may be read online at http://www. documentacatholicaomnia.eu/02m/0354-0430,_Augustinus,_Quaestionum_In_Hepta-teuchum_Libri_Septem,_MLT.pdf

25 Gispen, *Exodus*, 251.

26 Robert. B. Strimple, "Amillennialism," in *Three Views on the Millennium and Beyond*, ed. Darrell L. Bock (Grand Rapids: Zondervan, 1999), 85.

27 Witsius, *The Economy of the Covenants*, 2:189.

28 John Owen, "XRISTOLOGIA: Or, a Declaration of the Glorious Mystery of the Person of Christ—God and Man," in *The Works of John Owen*, ed. William H. Goold, 16 vols. (1850–1853; repr., Edinburgh, Scotland: Banner of Truth, sixth printing, 1993), 1:260.

29 See John J. Davis, *Moses and the Gods of Egypt: Studies in Exodus*, 2nd edition (Winona Lake, Ind.: BMH Books, 1986), 257; cf. John J. Davis, *Biblical Numerology* (Grand Rapids: Baker, 1968), 103–49.

30 On a related phrase, *Scripturam ex Scriptura explicandum esse*, see Richard A. Muller, *Dictionary of Latin and Greek Theological Terms: Drawn Principally from Protestant Scholastic Theology* (Grand Rapids: Baker, 1985), 277. For an example of this approach, which John Calvin called a sober approach, see Calvin, *Commentaries on the Last Four Books of Moses Arranged in the Form of a Harmony: Volume Second*, trans. Charles William Bingham, Calvin's Commentaries, 22 vols. (1852–1855; repr., Grand Rapids: Baker, 1996), 2:172–75.

31 On the theological reading of Scripture, see Berkhof, *Principles of Biblical Interpretation*, 133 –66; Kaiser and Silva, *An Introduction to Biblical Hermeneutics*, 193–206.

32 Calvin, *Commentaries on the Last Four Books of Moses*, 2:172–73.

33 For a discussion of biblical typology, see Witsius, *The Economy of the Covenants*, 2:188–231.

34 On ancient Near Eastern portable tent-shrines and sacred places, see Andrew E. Hill, *Enter His Courts with Praise! Old Testament Worship for the New Testament Church* (Grand Rapids: Baker, 1993), 164.

35 G. K. Beale, "The Eschatological Conception of New Testament Theology," in *The Reader Must Understand: Eschatology in Bible and Theology*, ed. Mark Elliott and Kent Brower (Leicester: IVP, 1997), 49.

36 G. R. Beasley-Murray said that this passage was the climax not only of Revelation but of the entire Bible. *The Book of Revelation*, New Century Bible (London: Marshall, Morgan, and Scott, 1974), 305.

37 Robert H. Mounce, *The Book of Revelation*, New International Commentary on the New Testament (Grand Rapids: Eerdmans, 1977), 369.

38 William Hendriksen, *More than Conquerors* (1940; repr., Grand Rapids: Baker, 1990), 198; cf. Herman Bavinck, *Reformed Dogmatics: Holy Spirit, Church, and New Creation, Vol. 4*, ed. John Bolt, trans. John Vriend (Grand Rapids: Baker Academic, 2008), 715–30; Mounce, *The Book of Revelation*, 368; Herman Hoeksema, *Behold, He Cometh!* (Grand Rapids: Reformed Free Publishing, 1969), 675; George Eldon Ladd, *A Theology of the New Testament*, revised edition, ed. Donald A. Hagner (1974; repr., Grand Rapids: Eerdmans, 1998), 682; Irenaeus, *Adversus Haereses* V, 36.

39 For a nuanced view that heaven and earth will be annihilated, see the exegesis of the Lutheran R. C. H. Lenski, *The Interpretation of St. John's Revelation* (Minneapolis: Augsburg, 1963), especially page 614, where he writes, "From Isa. 65:17 we gather that the new heaven and the new earth will involve a creative act of God."

40 For an exposition of this article in the Belgic Confession, see Daniel R. Hyde, *With Heart and Mouth: An Exposition of the Belgic Confession* (Grandville, Mich.: Reformed Fellowship, 2008), 489–98.

41 Hendriksen writes: "This new and holy Jerusalem is very clearly the Church of the Lord Jesus Christ, as is also plainly evident from the fact that it is here and elsewhere (Isa. 54:5; Eph. 5:32). Even in the Old Testament the Church is represented under the symbolism of a city (Isa. 26:1; Ps. 48)." *More than Conquerors*, 199; cf. Hoeksema, *Behold, He Cometh!* 671; Philip Edgcumbe Hughes, *The Book of Revelation* (Grand Rapids: Eerdmans, 1940), 222–23; Anthony A. Hoekema, *The Bible and the Future* (Grand Rapids: Eerdmans, 1979), 284; Strimple, "Amillennialism," 266; Ladd, *A Theology of the New Testament*, 682.

42 Read also the Old Testament background to these descriptions. The engaged spouse of the Lord (Jer. 2:2; Hos. 2:19–20) has become His bride (Isa. 49:18; 54:6; 61:10; 62:4–5; Hos. 2:14–16). The Lord has become the bridegroom (Isa. 54:5; 62:5; Jer. 31:32; Hos. 2:16).

43 Without endorsing any of the respective positions concerning the nature and length of the days of Genesis 1, I recommend the following for help in understanding the beautiful literary structure of the creation narrative: Meredith G. Kline, *Kingdom Prologue: Genesis Foundations for a Covenantal Worldview* (Overland Park, Kan.: Two Age Press, 2000); W. Robert Godfrey, *God's Pattern for Creation: A Covenantal Reading of Genesis 1* (Phillipsburg, N.J.: P&R, 2003).

44 The cubit (*'ammāh*) in Israel was either the "natural" cubit, which was approximately 17.5 inches (Deut. 3:11), or the "royal" cubit, which was 20.4 inches (Ezek. 40:5). Cf. Davis, *Moses and the Gods of Egypt*, 256.

45 Sarna, *Exploring Exodus*, 193; cf. Nahum M. Sarna, *Exodus*, The JPS Torah Commentary (Philadelphia: Jewish Publication Society, 1991), 170–71.

46 Kline, *Kingdom Prologue*, 48–49; Meredith G. Kline, *God, Heaven, and Har Magedon: A Covenantal Tale of Cosmos and Telos* (Eugene, Ore.: Wipf & Stock, 2006), 44–46; Peter J. Leithart, *A House for My Name: A Survey of the Old Testament* (Moscow, Ida.: Canon Press, 2000), 53–54.

47 Meredith G. Kline, *Images of the Spirit* (1980; repr., Meredith G. Kline, 1986), 13–20.

48 Matthew Henry, *Matthew Henry's Commentary on the Whole Bible* (Peabody, Mass.: Hendrickson, eighth printing, 1997), 1565.

49 Leon Morris, *The Gospel According to John*, The New International Commentary on the New Testament (1971; repr., Grand Rapids: Eerdmans, 1989), 102–4.

50 Hilary of Poitiers, *On the Trinity*, in *Nicene and Post-Nicene Fathers: Second Series*, ed. Philip Schaff and Henry Wace, 14 vols. (1899; repr., Peabody, Mass.: Hendrickson, 2004), 9:50.

51 Bard Thompson, ed., *Liturgies of the Western Church* (Philadelphia: Fortress Press, 1961), 170.

52 *Psalter Hymnal* (Grand Rapids: Board of Publications of the Christian Reformed Church, 1976), 185.

53 "The Litany," in *The Book of Common Prayer* (The Standing Liturgical Commission of the Reformed Episcopal Church, 2003), 41.

Chapter One

1   http://www.whitehorseinn.org/

2   Gispen, *Exodus*, 242; Childs, *The Book of Exodus*, 523; Sarna, *Exodus*, 157.

3   "The Collect for Peace," in *The Book of Common Prayer*, 17.

4   Calvin, *Commentaries on the Last Four Books of Moses*, 2:149.

5   Bede, *On the Tabernacle*, 7.

6   This concept is rooted in a misunderstanding of Eph. 4:12. On this, see T. David Gordon, "'Equipping' Ministry in Ephesians 4?" *Journal of the Evangelical Theological Society* 37 (1994): 69–78.

7   Sarna, *Exploring Exodus*, 204.

8   Calvin, *Commentaries on the Last Four Books of Moses*, 2:149.

9   Walter Bauer, *A Greek-English Lexicon of the New Testament and Other Early Christian Literature*, trans. and ed. William F. Arndt and F. Wilbur Gingrich, rev. F. Wilbur Gingrich and Frederick W. Danker (1958; revised, Chicago: The University of Chicago Press, 1979), 438–39.

10 Commentators universally recognize the difficulty of determining what exactly the Hebrew word *tahash* is referring to. Thus, it variously is translated as "goatskins" (ESV), "hides of sea cows" (NIV), "porpoise skins" (NASB), and "badgers' skins" (KJV/NKJV). On this word, see Childs, *The Book of Exodus*, 523; Gispen, *Exodus*, 244; Sarna, *Exodus*, 157–58.

11 Sarna, *Exodus*, 156.

12 Ibid., 157.

13 Theodoret of Cyrus, *The Questions of the Octateuch: Vol. I, On Genesis and Exodus*, trans. Robert C. Hill, The Library of Early Christianity I (Washington, D.C.: The Catholic University of America Press, 2007), 341.

14 Tremper Longman III, *Immanuel in Our Place: Seeing Christ in Israel's Worship*, The Gospel According to the Old Testament (Phillipsburg, N.J.: P&R, 2001), 27–28.

15 Brown, *The Tabernacle*, 20.

Chapter Two

1   For a monumental exegesis of these passages and others, one must consult Geerhardus Vos' chapter, "The Epistle's Philosophy of Revelation and Redemption," in *The Teaching of the Epistle to the Hebrews*, ed. Johannes G. Vos (1956; repr., Eugene, Ore.: Wipf & Stock, 1988), 49–87.

2   Ibid., 58; William L. Lane, *Hebrews 9–13*, Word Biblical Commentary 47b (Dallas: Word, 1991), 248; Philip Edgcumbe Hughes, *A Commentary on the Epistle to the Hebrews* (1977; repr., Grand Rapids: Eerdmans, 1993), 382.

3   Geerhardus Vos, "'True' and 'Truth' in the Johannine Writings," in *Redemptive History and Biblical Interpretation: The Shorter Writings of Geerhardus Vos*, ed. Richard B. Gaffin Jr. (Phillipsburg, N.J.: Presbyterian and Reformed, 1980), 343–51.

4   Longman, *Immanuel in Our Place*, xi.

5   J. A. Motyer, *The Message of Exodus: The Days of Our Pilgrimage*, The Bible Speaks Today (Downers Grove, Ill.: InterVarsity, 2005), 250.

6   Edmund P. Clowney, "The Final Temple," *Westminster Theological Journal* 35 (Winter 1973): 158.

7   To read some of these ancient texts, see Alexander Heidel, *The Gilgamesh Epic and Old Testament Parallels* (Chicago: The University of Chicago Press, second edition, 1949).

8   Sarna, *Exploring Exodus*, 203. On ancient Near Eastern tents, see Davis, *Moses and the Gods of Egypt*, 251–53. On the issue of ancient Near Eastern backgrounds to the Old Testament and the use/abuse of them, see Noel Weeks, *Admonition and Curse: The Ancient Near Eastern Treaty/Covenant Form as a Problem in Inter-Cultural Relationships*, Journal for the Study of the Old Testament Supplement Series 407 (London/New York: T&T Clark International, 2004).

9   Sarna, *Exploring Exodus*, 205.

10 Ibid., 203.

11 Theodoret, *The Questions of the Octateuch, Vol. I*, 315–19.

12 Sarna, *Exploring Exodus*, 205–6.

13 Hill, *Enter His Courts*, 162.

14 On this theme, see Longman, *Immanuel in Our Place*, 3–14.

15 Calvin, *Commentaries on the Last Four Books of Moses*, 2:150.

16 Geerhardus Vos, *Biblical Theology: Old and New Testaments* (1948; repr., Edinburgh, Scotland: Banner of Truth, 1996), 149.

17 Sarna, *Exodus*, 158.

18 For a discussion of this phrase, see Nahum M. Sarna, *Genesis*, The JPS Torah Commentary (Philadelphia: The Jewish Publication Society, 1989), 198n6; Bruce K. Waltke, *Genesis: A Commentary* (Grand Rapids: Zondervan, 2001), 390–91.

19 See Theodoret, *The Questions of the Octateuch: Vol. I*, 315–19.

20 Bede, *On the Tabernacle*, 10.

21 For an excellent exposition of the fulfillment of the tabernacle in Christ, the church, and the kingdom of God, see Keil, *Manual of Biblical Archaeology*, 1:152–58.

22 On the incarnation, see Daniel R. Hyde, *God with Us: Knowing the Mystery of Who Jesus Is* (Grand Rapids: Reformation Heritage Books, 2007).

23 Witsius, *Sacred Dissertations*, 2:1.

Chapter Three

1   Brown, *The Tabernacle*, 73, 75.

2   Sarna, *Exploring Exodus*, 191.

3   Hywel R. Jones, "Exodus," in *The Wycliffe Bible Commentary*, ed. Charles F. Pfeiffer and Everett F. Harrison (Chicago: Moody, 1962), 135.

4   Sarna, *Exodus*, 160–61; cf. Sarna, *Exploring Exodus*, 209–10.

5   On this practice, see Meredith G. Kline, *The Structure of Biblical Authority*, Second Edition (South Hamilton, Mass.: Meredith G. Kline, 1989), 113–30.

6 Keil, *Manual of Biblical Archaeology*, 1:138.

7 Longman, *Immanuel in Our Place*, 50; Sarna, *Exploring Exodus*, 209–11; John Owen, "A Discourse of the Work of the Holy Spirit in Prayer," in *The Works of John Owen*, ed. William H. Goold, 16 vols. (1850–1853; repr., Edinburgh, Scotland: Banner of Truth, sixth printing, 1993), 4:291.

8 On propitiation, see Leon Morris, *The Atonement: Its Meaning and Significance* (Downers Grove, Ill.: InterVarsity, 1983), 151–76.

9 Calvin, *Commentaries on the Last Four Books of Moses*, 2:156.

10 *Psalter Hymnal*, 157.

Chapter Four

1 On the meaning of this title, see Sarna, *Exodus*, 162.

2 *Psalter Hymnal*, 146–47.

3 These utensils are variously translated: dishes, spoons, covers, and bowls (KJV); dishes, pans, pitchers, and bowls (NKJV); plates, dishes, pitchers, and bowls (NIV); dishes, pans, jars, and bowls (NASB); plates, dishes, flagons, and bowls (ESV). On these utensils, see Sarna, *Exodus*, 163.

4 Calvin, *Commentaries on the Last Four Books of Moses*, 2:291–92.

5 Keil, *Manual of Biblical Archaeology*, 1:147–48.

6 Gispen, *Exodus*, 249.

7 Sarna, *Exodus*, 162.

8 Scripture tells us that it fell to the house of Kohath to guard, care for, and transport the table (Num. 3:31; 4:4, 7–8). In fact, they were allotted none of the six carts and twelve oxen for transporting the tabernacle "because they were charged with the service of the holy things that had to be carried on the shoulder" (Num. 7:9).

9 Brown, *The Tabernacle*, 61. On the issue of the frequent celebration of the Lord's Supper, see Michael S. Horton, "At Least Weekly: The Reformed Doctrine of the Lord's Supper and of Its Frequent Celebration," *Mid-America Journal of Theology* 11 (2000): 147–69; Kim Riddlebarger, "The Reformation of the Supper," in *Always Reformed: Essays in Honor of W. Robert Godfrey*, ed. R. Scott Clark and Joel E. Kim (Escondido, Calif.: Westminster Seminary California, 2010), 192–207.

10 J. C. Ryle, *Expository Thoughts on the Gospels: John 10:31–21:25*, 4 vols. (repr., Grand Rapids: Baker, 2007), 4:404–5.

11 "The Order for the Administration of the Lord's Supper or Holy Communion," in *The Book of Common Prayer*, 101.

Chapter Five

1 Sarna, *Exodus*, 165.

2 Longman, *Immanuel in Our Place*, 57.

3 Calvin, *Commentaries on the Last Four Books of Moses*, 2:162.

Chapter Six

1 See note 10 in chapter 1.
2 Davis, *Moses and the Gods of Egypt*, 268.
3 Sarna, *Exodus*, 167, 171.
4 Calvin, *Commentaries on the Last Four Books of Moses*, 2:175.
5 John Dod and Robert Cleaver, *A Plaine and Familiar Exposition of the Ten Commandments* (London: 1628), 143.
6 For the Puritan view of this, see J. I. Packer, *A Quest for Godliness: The Puritan Vision of the Christian Life* (Wheaton, Ill.: Crossway, 1990), 240–41.
7 George Swinnock, *Works* (Edinburgh, Scotland: James Nichol, 1868), 1:239. On the Puritans and the Lord's Day, see Packer, *A Quest for Godliness*, 233–43; James T. Dennison, *The Market Day of the Soul: The Puritan Doctrine of the Sabbath in England, 1532–1700* (1983; repr., Grand Rapids: Reformation Heritage Books, 2008).
8 See Calvin, *Commentaries on the Last Four Books of Moses*, 2:175.
9 On worshiping according to the Word, see Daniel R. Hyde, *What to Expect in Reformed Worship: A Visitor's Guide* (Eugene, Ore.: Wipf & Stock, 2007); Daniel R. Hyde, *Welcome to a Reformed Church: A Guide for Pilgrims* (Orlando, Fla.: Reformation Trust Publishing, 2010), 113–29.
10 Theodoret, *The Questions of the Octateuch: Vol. I*, 321.

Chapter Seven

1 Brown, *The Tabernacle*, 51.
2 On the laying on of hands, see Gordon J. Wenham, *The Book of Leviticus*, The New International Commentary on the Old Testament (Grand Rapids: Eerdmans, 1979), 53, 61–62.
3 Ibid., 61–62.
4 Bauer, *A Greek-English Lexicon of the New Testament*, 511–12.
5 Ibid., 301.
6 "A General Confession," in *The Book of Common Prayer*, 7.

Chapter Eight

1 R. R. Reno, "The Tattoo Fashion," *First Things Online*, August 28, 2008. http://www.firstthings.com/onthesquare/2008/08/the-tattoo-fashion. Accessed December 16, 2011.
2 "Baptism of Infants: Form Number 1," in *Psalter Hymnal*, 124. For the historical background to this prayer, see *Psalter Hymnal Handbook*, ed. Emily R. Brink and Bert Polman (Grand Rapids: CRC Publications, 1998), 831–32; Hughes Oliphant Old, *The Shaping of the Reformed Baptismal Rite in the Sixteenth Century* (Grand Rapids: Eerdmans, 1992).
3 Terence E. Fretheim makes the helpful distinction between the Lord's occasional presence at altars in the days of the patriarchs and His ongoing presence in the tabernacle. *Exodus, Interpretation: A Bible Commentary for Preaching and Teaching* (Louisville, Ky.: John Knox Press, 1991), 264.

4   *First Catechism: Teaching Children Bible Truths* (Suwanee, Ga.: Great Commission Publications, 2003), 6.

5   David Clarkson, *The Works of David Clarkson* (1864; repr., Edinburgh, Scotland: Banner of Truth, 1988), 187–209.

6   On private or family worship, see the following: James W. Alexander, *Thoughts on Family Worship* (1847; repr., Morgan, Pa.: Soli Deo Gloria, 1998); Joel R. Beeke, *The Family at Church: Listening to Sermons and Attending Prayer Meetings* (2004; repr., Grand Rapids: Reformation Heritage Books, 2008); *The Family Worship Book*, ed. Terry L. Johnson (Fearn, Ross-shire, Great Britain: Christian Focus, 1998).

7   From the hymn "Come, We That Love the Lord" by Isaac Watts (1707).

8   Calvin, *Commentaries on the Last Four Books of Moses*, 2:179.

9   Gispen, *Exodus*, 259.

10 Ibid., 260.

Chapter Nine

1   Calvin, *Commentaries on the Last Four Books of Moses*, 2:191.

2   See the proofs offered under the heading "Pastors" by the Westminster Assembly in *The Form of Presbyterial Church-Government*, in *Westminster Confession of Faith* (1646; repr., Glasgow: Free Presbyterian Publications, 2009), 399–400.

3   Thomas Manton, *The Works of Thomas Manton*, 22 vols. (1870–1875; repr., Birmingham, Ala.: Solid Ground Christian Books, 2008), 1:261. For a brief biography of Manton, see Derek Cooper, *Thomas Manton: A Guided Tour of the Life and Thought of a Puritan Pastor* (Phillipsburg, N.J.: P&R, 2012).

4   Manton, *Works*, 1:261.

5   Calvin, *Commentaries on the Last Four Books of Moses*, 2:195.

6   Theodoret, *The Questions of the Octateuch: Vol. I*, 373.

7   Gispen, *Exodus*, 262–70.

8   Kline, *Images of the Spirit*, 42–47. See also Alex T. M. Cheung, "The Priest as the Redeemed Man: A Biblical-Theological Study of the Priesthood," *Journal of the Evangelical Theological Society* 29:3 (September 1986): 265–75.

9   Calvin, *Commentaries on the Last Four Books of Moses*, 2:195. Calvin offers eight distinctions between the Levitical priesthood and Christ's. Ibid., 2:192–93.

Chapter Ten

1   John Calvin, *Institutes of the Christian Religion*, ed. John T. McNeill, trans. Ford Lewis Battles, The Library of Christian Classics, Vols. 20–21 (Philadelphia: The Westminster Press, 1960), 3.1.1.

2   Gispen, *Exodus*, 266.

3   Calvin, *Commentaries on the Last Four Books of Moses*, 2:196.

Chapter Eleven

1   Childs, *The Book of Exodus*, 527–28; Gispen, *Exodus*, 273; Sarna, *Exodus*, 186. On Leviticus 8–9, see Baruch A. Levine, *Leviticus*, The JPS Torah Commentary (Philadelphia: Jewish Publication Society, 1989), 48–58; Wenham, *The Book of Leviticus*, 129–51.
2   Jones, "Exodus," in *The Wycliffe Bible Commentary*, 135.
3   Motyer, *The Message of Exodus*, 275.
4   Theodoret, *The Questions of the Octateuch: Vol. I*, 327.
5   Jones, "Exodus," in *The Wycliffe Bible Commentary*, 136.
6   Gispen, *Exodus*, 275.
7   "The Litany," in *The Book of Common Prayer*, 41.
8   "For Pastors, or Ministers-in-Charge," in ibid., 60.
9   John Owen, "Eschol; A Cluster of the Fruit of Canaan," in *The Works of John Owen*, ed. William H. Goold, 16 vols. (1850–1853; repr., Edinburgh, Scotland: Banner of Truth, sixth printing, 1993), 13:57.
10 Motyer, *The Message of Exodus*, 276–77.
11 Calvin, *Commentaries on the Last Four Books of Moses*, 2:223.
12 John Owen, "Meditations and Discourses on the Glory of Christ," in *The Works of John Owen*, ed. William H. Goold, 16 vols. (1850–1853; repr., Edinburgh, Scotland: Banner of Truth, sixth printing, 1993), 1:388.
13 For more on children in worship, see Robbie Castleman, *Parenting in the Pew: Guiding Your Children into the Joy of Worship* (Downers Grove, Ill.: InterVarsity, 2002).

Chapter Twelve

1   John Owen, "A Brief Instruction in the Worship of God and Discipline of the Churches of the New Testament," in *The Works of John Owen*, ed. William H. Goold, 16 vols. (1850–1853; repr., Edinburgh, Scotland: Banner of Truth, sixth printing 1993), 15:471. On Owen's theology of worship, see Daniel R. Hyde, "Of Great Importance and of High Concernment: The Liturgical Theology of John Owen (1616–1683)." Th.M. thesis, Puritan Reformed Theological Seminary, 2010.
2   John Calvin, "The Necessity of Reforming the Church," in *Selected Works of John Calvin*, ed. and trans. Henry Beveridge, 7 vols. (Grand Rapids: Baker, 1983), 1:126.
3   Cf. Calvin, *Commentaries on the Last Four Books of Moses*, 2:295–96.
4   On preaching in the context of our desire for the visual, see Daniel R. Hyde, *In Living Color: Images of Christ and the Means of Grace* (Grandville, Mich.: Reformed Fellowship, 2009).

Chapter Thirteen

1   Keil, *Manual of Biblical Archaeology*, 1:144–45.
2   Calvin, *Commentaries on the Last Four Books of Moses*, 2:182.
3   "Solemnization of Matrimony," in *The Book of Common Prayer*, 492.

4   From the song "Chorus of Faith" by Michael Card, 1994.

5   *Psalter Hymnal* (Grand Rapids: Board of Publications of the Christian Reformed Church, Inc., 1976), 188–89.

6   Gispen, *Exodus*, 281.

7   Calvin, *Commentaries on the Last Four Books of Moses*, 2:183.

8   John Owen described believers not knowing their own wants in terms of their outward wants, internal wants, and spiritual wants (Owen, *Works*, 9:72–73). Thomas Manton identified four reasons why believers do not pray as they ought: 1) they are blinded by self-love, 2) they are discomposed by trouble, 3) they are struck dumb by guilt, and 4) they are straitened by barrenness and leanness of soul (Manton, *Works*, 12:238–39).

9   Manton, *Works*, 12:232.

10 Ibid., 5:336. Cf. Owen, *Works*, 9:74: "It is the language of faith and love alone, and the like graces of his Spirit, that God hears in his worship. Other voices, cries, and noises he regards not; yea, at least, if not some of them in themselves, yet all of them when these are wanting, are an abomination unto him."

11 Manton, *Works*, 5:337. For more on the Puritans' understanding of the work of the Holy Spirit in our prayers, see Hyde, "Of Great Importance and of High Concernment," 137–55.

Chapter Fourteen

1   On the language of "ransom," see Morris, *The Atonement*, 116–19.

2   Brown, *The Tabernacle*, 9–10; Jones, "Exodus," in *The Wycliffe Bible Commentary*, 136; Matthew Poole, *A Commentary on the Whole Bible, Volume 1: Genesis–Job*, 3 vols. (Peabody, Mass.: Hendrickson, fourth printing 2008), 184.

3   Gispen, *Exodus*, 283.

4   Calvin, *Commentaries on the Last Four Books of Moses*, 1:482–83.

5   From the hymn "O the Deep, Deep Love of Jesus!" by Samuel Trevor Francis.

Chapter Fifteen

1   Calvin, *Commentaries on the Last Four Books of Moses*, 2:185.

2   Sarna, *Exodus*, 197.

3   On this text, see Hywel R. Jones, "Preaching the Doctrine of Regeneration in a Christian Congregation," in *Always Reformed: Essays in Honor of W. Robert Godfrey* (Escondido, Calif.: Westminster Seminary California, 2010), 208–23.

4   Gispen, *Exodus*, 284.

5   Thomas Manton, "How Ought We to Improve Our Baptism," in *Puritan Sermons 1659–1689*, 6 vols. (1845; repr., Wheaton: Richard Owen Roberts, 1981), 2:99.

6   George Swinnock, "The Christian Man's Calling—Part 1," in *The Works of George Swinnock*, 5 vols. (1868; repr., Edinburgh, Scotland: Banner of Truth, 1992), 1:230.

Chapter Sixteen

1 John Owen, "A Discourse of Spiritual Gifts," in *The Works of John Owen*, ed. William H. Goold, 16 vols. (1850–1853; repr., Edinburgh, Scotland: Banner of Truth, sixth printing 1993), 14:517.
2 Calvin, *Commentaries on the Last Four Books of Moses*, 3:296.
3 Ibid., 3:290.
4 Owen, "A Discourse of Spiritual Gifts," in *Works*, 14:519.
5 Calvin, *Commentaries on the Last Four Books of Moses*, 292.
6 Owen, "A Discourse of Spiritual Gifts," in *Works*, 14:520.

Chapter Seventeen

1 Witsius, *Miscellanea sacra*, 1:349ff.
2 Kline, *Images of the Spirit*, 37.
3 For the sabbatical structure, see ibid., 35–47; Sarna, *Exploring Exodus*, 213–15.
4 J. R. R. Tolkien, *The Letters of J. R. R. Tolkien* (Boston: Houghton Mifflin, 1981), 110.
5 From the hymn "Jerusalem the Golden" by Bernard of Cluny (translated by John Mason Neale).

Appendix

1 This appendix is adapted from a lecture I originally gave at Westminster Seminary California to the students from the United Reformed Churches in North America.

For some basic resources on preaching the Old Testament, see Elizabeth Achtemeier, *Preaching from the Old Testament* (Louisville, Ky.: Westminster/John Knox, 1989); Sinclair B. Ferguson, *Preaching Christ From the Old Testament: Developing a Christ Centered Instinct*, PT Media Paper Number 2 (London: The Proclamation Trust, 2002); Sidney Greidanus, *Preaching Christ from the Old Testament: A Contemporary Hermeneutical Method* (Grand Rapids: Eerdmans, 1999); George W. Knight III, "The Scriptures Were Written for Our Instruction," *Journal of the Evangelical Theological Society* 39:1 (March 1996): 3–13; David Murray, "Bright Shadows: Preaching Christ from the Old Testament," *Puritan Reformed Journal* 1:1 (January 2009): 23–33; David Murray, "Bright Shadows (2): Preaching Christ from the Old Testament," *Puritan Reformed Journal* 1:2 (July 2009): 5–11.
2 http://www.sermonaudio.com/oceansideurc
3 Greidanus, *Preaching Christ*, 16–25. Compare David Murray's eight reasons in "Bright Shadows" (January 2009): 23–33.
4 Versification of Psalm 137:8–9 in "By Babylon's Rivers," *The Book of Psalms for Worship* (Pittsburgh: Crown & Covenant Publications, 2009), 137B.
5 Elizabeth Achtemeier, *Preaching Hard Texts of the Old Testament* (Peabody, Mass.: Hendrickson, 1998), xi. As to how Christians can sing these psalms, I have found William Ames' reasons stimulating. In his monumental treatise on Puritan casuistry, *De Conscientia* (1630), he wrote: "Quest. 4. How may we sing those Psalms aright, which contain dire

imprecations in them? 8. A. 1. *We may upon occasion of those imprecations meditate with fear and trembling, on the terrible judgments of God against the sins of impenitent persons. 9. 2. We may thereupon profit in patience and consolation, against the temptations which are wont to [habitually] arise from the prosperity of the wicked, and affliction of the godly. 10. 3. We may also pray to God that he would hasten his revenge (not against our private enemies but) against the wicked and incurable enemies of his Church.*" William Ames, *Conscience with the Power and Cases Thereof* (London, 1639) 4.19.8–10 (English modernized).

6 Greidanus, *Preaching Christ*, 15n35; cf. Michael Duduit, "The Church's Need for Old Testament Preaching," in *Reclaiming the Prophetic Mantle*, ed. George L. Klein (Nashville: Broadman, 1992), 9–16.

7 J.-J. Von Allmen, *Preaching and Congregation*, trans. B. L. Nicholas, Ecumenical Studies in Worship 10 (Richmond, Va: John Knox Press, 1962), 25.

8 Cited in ibid., 25.

9 Derek W. H. Thomas, "Expository Preaching," in *Feed My Sheep: A Passionate Plea for Preaching* (2002; repr., Lake Mary, Fla.: Reformation Trust Publishing, 2008), 35–51; cf. Von Allmen's list of advantages and disadvantages of *lectio continua* and *lectio selecta* preaching in *Preaching and Congregation*, 46–48.

10 On this method of the Puritans, see D. M. Lloyd-Jones, "Preaching," in *The Puritans: Their Origins and Successors*, Addresses Delivered at the Puritan and Westminster Conferences 1959–1978 (1987; repr., Edinburgh, Scotland: Banner of Truth, 1991), 372–89; Peter Lewis, *The Genius of Puritanism* (1977; repr., Morgan, Pa.: Soli Deo Gloria, 1996), 34–52; Packer, "Puritan Preaching," in *A Quest for Godliness*, 277–89.

11 William Perkins, *The Arte of Prophecying: Or A Treatise Concerning the sacred and onely true manner and methode of Preaching* (London: Felix Kyngston, 1607), 148; cf. *The Art of Prophesying* (1606; repr., rev., Edinburgh, Scotland: Banner of Truth, 1996), 79.

12 Perkins, *The Arte of Prophecying*, 90–129; cf. *The Art of Prophesying*, 48–68.

13 William Ames, *The Marrow of Theology*, trans. and ed. John Dykstra Eusden (1968; repr., Grand Rapids: Baker, second printing 1997), 191.

14 Ibid., 191–92.

15 *Westminster Confession of Faith* (Glasgow, Scotland: Free Presbyterian Publications, 2003), 380–81.

16 Manton, *Works* 1:261.

17 Joel Beeke, "Experiential Preaching," in *Feed My Sheep*, 53–70.

18 John Owen, "Sermon V," in *The Works of John Owen*, ed. William H. Goold, 16 vols. (1850–1853; repr., Edinburgh, Scotland: Banner of Truth, sixth printing 1993), 9:456; John Owen, "The True Nature of a Gospel Church and Its Government: The Second Part," in *The Works of John Owen*, ed. William H. Goold, 16 vols. (1850–1853; repr., Edinburgh, Scotland: Banner of Truth, sixth printing 1993), 16:76.

19 Owen, "Sermon V," in *Works*, 9:455.

20 Owen, "The True Nature of a Gospel Church and Its Government: The Second Part," in *Works*, 16:76.

21 Perkins, *The Arte of Prophecying*, 148; cf. *The Art of Prophesying*, 79.

22 Thomas Foxcroft, *The Gospel Ministry*, ed. Don Kistler (1718; repr., Grand Rapids: Soli Deo Gloria, 2008), 5, 9.

23 On this, see the chapter on preaching in Hyde, *In Living Color*, 91–133.

BIBLIOGRAPHY

Achtemeier, Elizabeth. *Preaching from the Old Testament*. Louisville, Ky.: Westminster/ John Knox, 1989.

————. *Preaching Hard Texts of the Old Testament*. Peabody, Mass.: Hendrickson, 1998.

Alexander, James W. *Thoughts on Family Worship*. 1847; repr., Morgan, Pa.: Soli Deo Gloria, 1998.

Allis, Oswald T. *The Five Books of Moses*. 1943; repr., Phillipsburg, N.J.: Presbyterian and Reformed, 1949.

Ames, William. *The Marrow of Theology*. Trans. and ed. John Dykstra Eusden. 1968; repr., Grand Rapids: Baker, 1997.

Augustine. *Quaestiones in Heptateuchum*, in *Patrologia Latina*. Ed. Jacques-Paul Migne. Vol. 34. http://www.documentacatholicaomnia.eu/02m/0354-0430,_Augustinus,_ Quaestionum_In_Heptateuchum_Libri_Septem,_MLT.pdf. Accessed January 24, 2012.

Bauer, Walter. *A Greek-English Lexicon of the New Testament and Other Early Christian Literature*. Trans. and ed. William F. Arndt and F. Wilbur Gingrich. Rev. F. Wilbur Gingrich and Frederick W. Danker. 1958; revised, Chicago: The University of Chicago Press, 1979.

Bavinck, Herman. *Reformed Dogmatics: Holy Spirit, Church, and New Creation, Vol. 4*. Ed. John Bolt. Trans. John Vriend. Grand Rapids: Baker Academic, 2008.

Baylis, Albert H. *From Creation to the Cross: Understanding the First Half of the Bible*. Grand Rapids: Zondervan, 1996.

Beale, G. K. "The Eschatological Conception of New Testament Theology," in *The Reader Must Understand: Eschatology in Bible and Theology*. Ed. Mark Elliott and Kent Brower. Leicester: IVP, 1997.

Beasley-Murray, G. R. *The Book of Revelation*. New Century Bible. London: Marshall, Morgan, and Scott, 1974.

Bede, *On the Tabernacle*. Trans. Arthur G. Holder. Translated Texts for Historians, Vol. 18. Liverpool, England: Liverpool University Press, 1994.

Beeke, Joel. "Experiential Preaching," in *Feed My Sheep: A Passionate Plea for Preaching*. 2002; repr., Lake Mary, Fla.: Reformation Trust Publishing, 2008, 53–70.

———. *The Family at Church: Listening to Sermons and Attending Prayer Meetings*. 2004; repr., Grand Rapids: Reformation Heritage Books, 2008.

Berkhof, Louis. *Principles of Biblical Interpretation*. 1950; repr., Grand Rapids: Baker, 1994.

Bilkes, Gerald. "Heart-Reading: Recovering a Spiritual Approach to the Bible." *Puritan Reformed Journal* 1:2 (July 2009): 12–22.

Book of Common Prayer. The Standing Liturgical Commission of the Reformed Episcopal Church, Third Edition, 2003.

Brink, Emily R., and Bert Polman, eds. *Psalter Hymnal Handbook*. Grand Rapids: CRC Publications, 1998.

Brown, William. *The Tabernacle: Its Priests and Its Services*. 1899; repr., Peabody, Mass.: Hendrickson, 1996.

Calvin, John. *Commentaries on the Last Four Books of Moses Arranged in the Form of a Harmony: Volume Second*. Trans. Charles William Bingham. Calvin's Commentaries, 22 vols. 1852–1855; repr., Grand Rapids: Baker, 1996.

———. *Institutes of the Christian Religion*. Ed. John T. McNeill. Trans. Ford Lewis Battles. The Library of Christian Classics, Vols. 20–21. Philadelphia: The Westminster Press, 1960.

———. "The Necessity of Reforming the Church," in *Selected Works of John Calvin*. Ed. and trans. Henry Beveridge. 7 vols. Grand Rapids: Baker, 1983.

Castleman, Robbie. *Parenting in the Pew: Guiding Your Children into the Joy of Worship*. Downers Grove, Ill.: InterVarsity, 2002.

Cheung, Alex T. M. "The Priest as the Redeemed Man: A Biblical-Theological Study of the Priesthood." *Journal of the Evangelical Theological Society* 29:3 (September 1986): 265–75.

Childs, Brevard S. *The Book of Exodus: A Critical, Theological Commentary*. Philadelphia: The Westminster Press, 1974.

Clarkson, David. *The Works of David Clarkson*. 1864; repr., Edinburgh, Scotland: Banner of Truth, 1988.

Clement of Alexandria. *Stromata*, in *Ante-Nicene Fathers 2*. Ed. Alexander Roberts and James Donaldson. 1885; repr., Peabody, Mass.: Hendrickson, 2004.

Clowney, Edmund P. "The Final Temple." *Westminster Theological Journal* 35 (Winter 1973): 156–91.

Cooper, Derek. *Thomas Manton: A Guided Tour of the Life and Thought of a Puritan Pastor*. Phillipsburg, N.J.: P&R, 2011.

Davis, John J. *Biblical Numerology*. Grand Rapids: Baker, 1968.

————. *Moses and the Gods of Egypt: Studies in Exodus*. 2nd edition. Winona Lake, Ind.: BMH Books, 1986.

De Lubac, Henri. *Medieval Exegesis: The Four Senses of Scripture*. 3 vols. Grand Rapids: Eerdmans, 1988/2000/2009.

Dennett, Edward. *Typical Teachings of Exodus: Being a Simple Exposition*. London: W. H. Broom, 1882.

Dennison, James T. *The Market Day of the Soul: The Puritan Doctrine of the Sabbath in England, 1532–1700*. 1983; repr., Grand Rapids: Reformation Heritage Books, 2008.

Dillard, Raymond B., and Tremper Longman III. *An Introduction to the Old Testament*. Grand Rapids: Zondervan, 1994.

Dod, John, and Robert Cleaver. *A Plaine and Familiar Exposition of the Ten Commandments*. London, 1628.

Duduit, Michael. "The Church's Need for Old Testament Preaching," in *Reclaiming the Prophetic Mantle*. Ed. George L. Klein. Nashville: Broadman, 1992.

Ferguson, Sinclair B. *Preaching Christ From the Old Testament: Developing a Christ Centered Instinct*. PT Media Paper Number 2. London: The Proclamation Trust, 2002.

First Catechism: Teaching Children Bible Truths. Suwanee, Ga.: Great Commission Publications, 2003.

Foxcroft, Thomas. *The Gospel Ministry*. Ed. Don Kistler. 1718; repr., Grand Rapids: Soli Deo Gloria, 2008.

Fretheim, Terence E. *Exodus, Interpretation: A Bible Commentary for Preaching and Teaching*. Louisville, Ky.: John Knox Press, 1991.

Gispen, W. H. *Exodus*. Bible Student's Commentary. Trans. Ed van der Maas. Grand Rapids: Zondervan, 1982.

Godfrey, W. Robert. *God's Pattern for Creation: A Covenantal Reading of Genesis 1*. Phillipsburg, N.J.: P&R, 2003.

Gooding, David. *How to Teach the Tabernacle*. Port Colborne, Ontario: Everyday Publications, 1977.

Gordon, T. David. "'Equipping' Ministry in Ephesians 4?" *Journal of the Evangelical Theological Society* 37 (1994): 69–78.

Greidanus, Sidney. *Preaching Christ from the Old Testament: A Contemporary Hermeneutical Method*. Grand Rapids: Eerdmans, 1999.

Heidel, Alexander. *The Gilgamesh Epic and Old Testament Parallels*. Chicago: The University of Chicago Press, Second Edition, 1949.

Hendriksen, William. *More than Conquerors*. 1940; repr., Grand Rapids: Baker, 1990.

Henry, Matthew. *Commentary on the Whole Bible*. Peabody, Mass.: Hendrickson, eighth printing, 1997.

Hilary of Poitiers. *On the Trinity,* in *Nicene and Post-Nicene Fathers: Second Series* 9. Ed. Philip Schaff and Henry Wace. 1899; repr., Peabody, Mass.: Hendrickson, 2004.

Hill, Andrew E. *Enter His Courts with Praise! Old Testament Worship for the New Testament Church.* Grand Rapids: Baker, 1993.

Hoekema, Anthony A. *The Bible and the Future.* Grand Rapids: Eerdmans, 1979.

Hoeksema, Herman. *Behold, He Cometh!* Grand Rapids: Reformed Free Publishing, 1969.

Horton, Michael S. "At Least Weekly: The Reformed Doctrine of the Lord's Supper and of its Frequent Celebration." *Mid-America Journal of Theology* 11 (2000): 147–69.

Hughes, Philip Edgcumbe. *A Commentary on the Epistle to the Hebrews.* 1977; repr., Grand Rapids: Eerdmans, 1993.

———. *The Book of Revelation.* Grand Rapids: Eerdmans, 1940.

Hyde, Daniel R. *God with Us: Knowing the Mystery of Who Jesus Is.* Grand Rapids: Reformation Heritage Books, 2007.

———. *In Living Color: Images of Christ and the Means of Grace.* Grandville, Mich.: Reformed Fellowship, 2009.

———. "Of Great Importance and of High Concernment: The Liturgical Theology of John Owen (1616–1683)." Th.M. thesis, Puritan Reformed Theological Seminary, 2010.

———. *Welcome to a Reformed Church: A Guide for Pilgrims.* Orlando, Fla.: Reformation Trust Publishing, 2010.

———. *What to Expect in Reformed Worship: A Visitor's Guide.* Eugene, Ore.: Wipf & Stock, 2007.

———. *With Heart and Mouth: An Exposition of the Belgic Confession.* Grandville, Mich.: Reformed Fellowship, 2008.

Johnson, Terry L., ed. *The Family Worship Book.* Fearn, Ross-shire, Great Britain: Christian Focus, 1998.

Jones, Hywel R. "Exodus," in *The Wycliffe Bible Commentary.* Ed. Charles F. Pfeiffer and Everett F. Harrison. Chicago: Moody, 1962.

Kaiser Jr., Walter C., and Moisés Silva. *An Introduction to Biblical Hermeneutics: The Search for Meaning.* Grand Rapids: Zondervan, 1994.

Keil, Carl Friedrich. *Manual of Biblical Archaeology.* Trans. Peter Christie. Ed. Frederick Crombie. Clark's Foreign Theological Library. New Series. Vol. XXXII, 2 vols. Edinburgh, Scotland: T&T Clark, 1887.

Kline, Meredith G. *God, Heaven, and Har Magedon: A Covenantal Tale of Cosmos and Telos.* Eugene, Ore.: Wipf & Stock, 2006.

———. *Images of the Spirit.* 1980; repr., Meredith G. Kline, 1986.

———. *Kingdom Prologue: Genesis Foundations for a Covenantal Worldview.* Overland Park, Kan.: Two Age Press, 2000.

———. *The Structure of Biblical Authority*. Second edition. South Hamilton, Mass.: Meredith G. Kline, 1989.

Knight III, George W. "The Scriptures Were Written for Our Instruction," *Journal of the Evangelical Theological Society* 39:1 (March 1996): 3–13.

Ladd, George Eldon. *A Theology of the New Testament*, revised edition. Ed. Donald A. Hagner. 1974; repr., Grand Rapids: Eerdmans, 1998.

Lane, William L. *Hebrews 9–13*. Word Biblical Commentary 47b. Dallas: Word, 1991.

Lee, Brian J. *Johannes Cocceius and the Exegetical Roots of Federal Theology*. Göttingen: Vandenhoeck & Ruprecht, 2008.

Leithart, Peter J. *A House for My Name: A Survey of the Old Testament*. Moscow, Ida.: Canon Press, 2000.

Lenski, R. C. H. *The Interpretation of St. John's Revelation*. Minneapolis: Augsburg, 1963.

Levine, Baruch A. *Leviticus*. The JPS Torah Commentary. Philadelphia: Jewish Publication Society, 1989.

Lewis, Peter. *The Genius of Puritanism*. 1977; repr. Morgan, Pa.: Soli Deo Gloria, 1996.

Lloyd-Jones, D. M. "Preaching," in *The Puritans: Their Origins and Successors*. Addresses Delivered at the Puritan and Westminster Conferences 1959–1978. 1987; repr., Edinburgh, Scotland: Banner of Truth, 1991: 372–89.

———. *Revival*. Wheaton: Crossway, 1987.

Longman III, Tremper. *Immanuel in Our Place: Seeing Christ in Israel's Worship*. The Gospel According to the Old Testament. Phillipsburg, N.J.: P&R, 2001.

Luther, Martin. "Preface to the Wittenberg Edition of Luther's German Writings (1539)," in *Martin Luther's Basic Theological Writings*. Ed. Timothy F. Lull. Minneapolis: Fortress Press, 1989.

Manton, Thomas. *The Works of Thomas Manton*. 22 vols. 1870–1875; repr., Birmingham, Ala.: Solid Ground Christian Books, 2008.

Meijering, E. P., and J. C. M. van Winden. *Hilary of Poitiers on the Trinity: De Trinitate 1, 1–19, 2, 3*. Leiden: Brill, 1982.

Morris, Leon. *The Gospel According to John*. The New International Commentary on the New Testament. 1971; repr., Grand Rapids: Eerdmans, 1989.

———. *The Atonement: Its Meaning and Significance*. Downers Grove, Ill.: InterVarsity, 1983.

Motyer, J. A. *The Message of Exodus: The Days of Our Pilgrimage*. The Bible Speaks Today. Downers Grove, Ill.: InterVarsity, 2005.

Mounce, Robert H. *The Book of Revelation*. New International Commentary on the New Testament. Grand Rapids: Eerdmans, 1977.

Muller, Richard A. *Dictionary of Latin and Greek Theological Terms: Drawn Principally from Protestant Scholastic Theology*. Grand Rapids: Baker, 1985.

Murray, David. "Bright Shadows: Preaching Christ from the Old Testament," *Puritan Reformed Journal* 1:1 (January 2009): 23–33.

———. "Bright Shadows (2): Preaching Christ from the Old Testament," *Puritan Reformed Journal* 1:2 (July 2009): 5–11.

Old, Hughes Oliphant. *The Shaping of the Reformed Baptismal Rite in the Sixteenth Century*. Grand Rapids: Eerdmans, 1992.

Owen, John. "A Brief Instruction in the Worship of God and Discipline of the Churches of the New Testament," in *The Works of John Owen*. Ed. William H. Goold. 16 vols. 1850–1853; repr., Edinburgh, Scotland: Banner of Truth, 1993.

———. "A Discourse of Spiritual Gifts," in *The Works of John Owen*.

———. "A Discourse of the Work of the Holy Spirit in Prayer," in *The Works of John Owen*.

———. "Eschol; A Cluster of the Fruit of Canaan," in *The Works of John Owen*.

———. "Meditations and Discourses on the Glory of Christ," in *The Works of John Owen*.

———. "Sermon V," in *The Works of John Owen*.

———. "The True Nature of a Gospel Church and Its Government: The Second Part," in *The Works of John Owen*.

———. "XRISTOLOGIA: Or, a Declaration of the Glorious Mystery of the Person of Christ—God and Man," in *The Works of John Owen*.

Packer, J. I. *A Quest for Godliness: The Puritan Vision of the Christian Life*. Wheaton, Ill.: Crossway, 1990.

Perkins, William. *The Art of Prophesying*. 1606; repr., rev., Edinburgh, Scotland: Banner of Truth, 1996.

———. *The Arte of Prophecying: Or A Treatise Concerning the sacred and onely true manner and methode of Preaching*. London: Felix Kyngston, 1607.

Philo. *Philo: Supplement II, Questions and Answers on Exodus*. Trans. Ralph Marcus. Cambridge, Mass.: Harvard University Press, 1953. 97–176.

Poole, Matthew. *A Commentary on the Whole Bible, Vol. 1: Genesis–Job*. 3 vols. Peabody, Mass.: Hendrickson, 2008.

Poythress, Vern S. *The Shadow of Christ in the Law of Moses*. Phillipsburg, N.J.: Presbyterian and Reformed, 1991.

Psalter Hymnal. Grand Rapids: Board of Publications of the Christian Reformed Church, 1976.

Raven, John Howard. *Old Testament Introduction: General and Special*. 1906; repr., New York: Fleming H. Revell, 1910.

Reno, R. R. "The Tattoo Fashion." *First Things Online*, August 28, 2008. http://www.firstthings.com/onthesquare/2008/08/the-tattoo-fashion. Accessed December 16, 2011.

Riddlebarger, Kim. "The Reformation of the Supper," in *Always Reformed: Essays in Honor of W. Robert Godfrey*. Ed. R. Scott Clark and Joel E. Kim. Escondido, Calif.: Westminster Seminary California, 2010.

Ryle, J. C. *Expository Thoughts on the Gospels: John 10:31–21:25*. Repr., Grand Rapids: Baker, 2007.

Sarna, Nahum M. *Exploring Exodus: The Origins of Biblical Israel*. 1986; repr., New York: Shocken Books, 1996.

———. *Exodus*. The JPS Torah Commentary. Philadelphia: The Jewish Publication Society, 1991.

———. *Genesis*. The JPS Torah Commentary. Philadelphia: The Jewish Publication Society, 1989.

Sproul, R. C. *Knowing Scripture*. Downers Grove, Ill.: InterVarsity, 1977.

Strimple, Robert. B. "Amillennialism," in *Three Views on the Millennium and Beyond*. Ed. Darrell L. Bock. Grand Rapids: Zondervan, 1999.

Swinnock, George. *Works*. Edinburgh, Scotland: James Nichol, 1868.

"The Form of Presbyterial Church-Government," in *Westminster Confession of Faith*. 1646; repr., Glasgow: Free Presbyterian Publications, 2009.

Theodoret of Cyrus, *The Questions of the Octateuch: Vol. I, On Genesis and Exodus*. Trans. Robert C. Hill. The Library of Early Christianity I. Washington, D.C.: The Catholic University of America Press, 2007.

Thomas, Derek W. H. "Expository Preaching," in *Feed My Sheep: A Passionate Plea for Preaching*. 2002; repr., Lake Mary, Fla.: Reformation Trust Publishing, 2008.

Thompson, Bard, ed. *Liturgies of the Western Church*. Philadelphia: Fortress Press, 1961.

Van Asselt, Willem J. *The Federal Theology of Johannes Cocceius (1603–1669)*. Leiden: Brill, 2001.

Von Allmen, J.–J. *Preaching and Congregation*. Trans. B. L. Nicholas. Ecumenical Studies in Worship 10. Richmond, Va: John Knox Press, 1962.

Vos, Geerhardus. *Biblical Theology: Old and New Testaments*. 1948; repr., Edinburgh, Scotland: Banner of Truth, 1996.

———. "The Epistle's Philosophy of Revelation and Redemption," in *The Teaching of the Epistle to the Hebrews*. Ed. Johannes G. Vos. 1956; repr., Eugene, Ore.: Wipf & Stock, 1988.

———. "'True' and 'Truth' in the Johannine Writings," in *Redemptive History and Biblical Interpretation: The Shorter Writings of Geerhardus Vos*. Ed. Richard B. Gaffin Jr. Phillipsburg, N.J.: Presbyterian and Reformed, 1980. 343–51.

Waltke, Bruce K. *Genesis: A Commentary*. Grand Rapids: Zondervan, 2001.

Weeks, Noel. *Admonition and Curse: The Ancient Near Eastern Treaty/Covenant Form as a Problem in Inter-Cultural Relationships*. Journal for the Study of the Old Testament

Supplement Series 407. London/New York: T&T Clark International, 2004.

White, Frank H. *Christ in the Tabernacle: With Some Remarks on the Offerings*. Second edition. London: S. W. Partridge, 1873.

Witsius, Herman. *Miscellanea sacra*. 2 vols. Utrecht, 1692–1700.

———. *Sacred Dissertations on What is Commonly Called the Apostles' Creed*. Trans. Donald Fraser. 2 vols. 1823; repr., Phillipsburg, N.J.: P&R, 1993.

———. *The Economy of the Covenants Between God and Man: Comprehending a Complete Body of Divinity*. Trans. William Crookshank. 2 vols. 1822; repr., Phillipsburg, N.J.: Presbyterian and Reformed, 1990.

Young, Edward J. *An Introduction to the Old Testament*. Grand Rapids: Eerdmans, 1949.

SCRIPTURE INDEX

7:25—139
8:1–27—12
8:14—207
8:20–22—114
8:29—156
8:34—137, 169
9:6—77
10:14—222
12:1—38
12:1–2—74
12:2—31, 156
12:6—196
13:14—149
15:4—178
15:16—126

1 Corinthians
1:18–31—93
1:18–2:16—12
1:21—149
1:25—160
2:1–5—217
3:9–17—31
6—178
6:11—149
6:19—31, 65
6:19–20—74
6:20—178
8:6—102
9:13–14—151
10—189
10:1–5—16
10:6–11—16–17
10:16—79
11:26—72
12—189
12:4–7—197
12:4–11—194
12:13—197
12:31—196
14:1—196

2 Corinthians
1:20—1
3–4—12
3:7—7
3:12–18—12–13
3:13—7
3:14–15—7

3:16—33
3:17–18—33
3:18—205
4:3–4—88
4:6—88
4:7—127
4:8–12—127
5:17—205
5:20—127
5:21—139, 149
6:14–18—42
6:16—51
6:16–18—31
6:16–7:1—207
8:9—39
9:6–11—38
9:6–15—152

Galatians
3—189
3:16—6
3:26–27—149
3:28—121, 174
4:6—160
4:8–9—141
5:18—207
5:25—207
6:1–2—139

Ephesians
1:5—164
1:8—38
2:10—156
2:12—145
2:18–22—211
2:19—31
2:20–22—31
2:21—41, 118
2:22—34, 41–42, 158
3:14–19—33–34
4:7–16—194
4:11—127
4:17–19—86–87
4:18—86
5—190
5:25–26—190
5:25–27—19
5:27—74
5:32—226n41

Philippians
1:3–5—40
1:5—152
2:8—61
2:15—90
3:21—205
4:15—40
4:18—152

Colossians
2:9—207
4:4—217

1 Thessalonians
1:9—107
2:13—222
5:12–13—148
5:14—140
5:17—165

1 Timothy
1:15—146
2:1–5—179

2 Timothy
3:15—10
3:16—5, 16
3:16–17—10, 207
4:2—215

Titus
3:2–3—186
3:5–6—186

Hebrews
1:1—12
1:2—12
2:2—74
2:14—130
2:17—130
2:17–18—52
2:18—127, 130
3:1–6—42
3:5—194, 204
4:12—7, 160
4:15—130
4:16—52, 100, 121, 139
5:1—127, 130
5:1–2—125
5:2—127
5:2–3—147

6:4—158
6:5—158
7—130, 148
7:1–10—148
7:23–24—149
7:25—74, 137, 149, 169
7:26—130
7:27—121
8—210
8–9—7
8:5—3, 7, 46, 202
9—120, 210
9:1—47
9:2–5—2
9:3—169
9:4—59, 169
9:10—205
9:11–14—111
9:12—121
9:13–14—66
9:21—3
9:23—46
9:24—14, 46, 53
9:26—121
9:28—121
10—150, 210
10:1–4—110–11
10:10—121
10:19—157, 168
10:19–20—157
10:19–22—92
10:19–23—189
10:19–25—157
10:21—157
10:22—149, 157
10:23–25—157
10:25—79
11:13—115
12:14—50, 159, 189
12:18–24—50
12:23—19
12:28—104
12:28–29—50
13:8—102
13:14—119
13:15—31, 150
13:17—148

SUBJECT INDEX

ABOUT THE AUTHOR

Rev. Daniel R. Hyde is the pastor of the Oceanside United Reformed Church in Carlsbad/Oceanside, California, a congregation of the United Reformed Churches in North America.

A native of Long Beach, California, Hyde was baptized into the Roman Catholic Church. He was converted to Christ at age 17 in a Foursquare Church and encountered the Reformed faith at an Assemblies of God college, where he earned his bachelor's degree in religion.

He earned his master of divinity degree from Westminster Seminary California, where he studied under Drs. W. Robert Godfrey, Michael Horton, and Meredith G. Kline. He earned his master of theology degree in Reformation and post-Reformation theology at Puritan Reformed Theological Seminary, with a thesis on the liturgical theology of John Owen. His thesis readers were Drs. Joel R. Beeke, Mark Jones, and Derek W. H. Thomas.

Hyde has written nine other books, including *Welcome to a Reformed Church* (Reformation Trust) and *Why Believe in God?* (P&R), and coedited another, *Planting, Watering, Growing* (Reformation Heritage Books). He also has written numerous academic and popular articles and chapters for books.

He lives in Oceanside with his wife and college sweetheart, Karajean, and their sons, Cyprian, Caiden, and Daxton.